Susanne Kramarz-Bein,
Birge Hilsmann (Eds.)

Applications of Network Theories

SKANDINAVISTIK

Sprache – Literatur – Kultur

herausgegeben von

Heinrich Anz
(Universität Freiburg)

und

Susanne Kramarz-Bein
(Universität Münster)

in Verbindung mit

Prof. Gustav Korlén
(Universität Stockholm, Ehrensenator der Universität Münster)
Prof. Egil Törnqvist (Universität Amsterdam)

Band 10

LIT

Applications of Network Theories

edited by

Susanne Kramarz-Bein and Birge Hilsmann

LIT

Cover image: Christian Krosing, B. A.

Printed with the financial assistance of
the Rectorate of Münster University; representing the Council of the
Department of Philology at Münster University;
Dr. Heinz-Rudi Spiegel from the E.ON-Ruhrgas scholarship fund;
Norwegian Center for International Cooperation in Education (SIU –
Senter for internasjonalisering av høyere utdanning);
the Royal Norwegian Embassy in Berlin;
the student council at our own Institute for Scandinavian Studies at
Münster University

This book is printed on acid-free paper.

Bibliographic information published by the Deutsche Nationalbibliothek
The Deutsche Nationalbibliothek lists this publication in the Deutsche
Nationalbibliografie; detailed bibliographic data are available in the Internet at
http://dnb.d-nb.de.

ISBN 978-3-643-90586-4

A catalogue record for this book is available from the British Library

©LIT VERLAG GmbH & Co. KG Wien,
Zweigniederlassung Zürich 2014
Klosbachstr. 107
CH-8032 Zürich
Tel. +41 (0) 44-251 75 05
Fax +41 (0) 44-251 75 06
E-Mail: zuerich@lit-verlag.ch
http://www.lit-verlag.ch

LIT VERLAG Dr. W. Hopf
Berlin 2014
Fresnostr. 2
D-48159 Münster
Tel. +49 (0) 2 51-62 03 20
Fax +49 (0) 2 51-23 19 72
E-Mail: lit@lit-verlag.de
http://www.lit-verlag.de

Distribution:
In the UK: Global Book Marketing, e-mail: mo@centralbooks.com
In North America: International Specialized Book Services, e-mail: orders@isbs.com
In Germany: LIT Verlag Fresnostr. 2, D-48159 Münster
Tel. +49 (0) 2 51-620 32 22, Fax +49 (0) 2 51-922 60 99,
E-mail: vertrieb@lit-verlag.de

In Austria: Medienlogistik Pichler-ÖBZ, e-mail: mlo@medien-logistik.at
e-books are available at www.litwebshop.de

Contents

SUSANNNE KRAMARZ-BEIN AND BIRGE HILSMANN   3

Introduction

I: Early Networks: The Middle Ages

RICHARD GASKINS   11

Political Development in Early Iceland: Applying Network Theory to the Sagas

JUDY QUINN   35

Precarious ties. The social critique of dynastic networking in eddic heroic poetry

MATTHIAS EWERING AND CHRISTIAN KROSING   71

Networktheoretical Approaches to Bandamanna saga and Færeyinga saga

MASSIMILIANO BAMPI   89

Network Theory, Polysystem Theory, and Old Swedish Literature: An Experimental Approach

SUSANNE KRAMARZ-BEIN   103

Neuronal Networking in Literary Criticism as exemplified by Medieval Literary Milieus in Scandinavia

WILLIAM LAYHER   123

Network or Net? Filtering the Political Voice in the *Revelaciones* of St. Birgitta of Sweden

II: Modern Networks: 19ᵗʰ and 20ᵗʰ Century

BIRGE HILSMANN — 157

Interlacing Subjects. Networks in Uppsala Romanticism

ELS BIESEMANS AND GODELIEVE LAUREYS — 177

The Reception of Scandinavian Literature in the Netherlands and Flanders 1860-1940. Some preliminary reflections on the role of networks

FELIX K. E. SCHMELZER — 195

The Dynamic Universe of Texts: The Dynamic Web as a Structural Concept of Complexity in both 20th Century Literature and Science

HEIKO UECKER — 209

Some highly tentative considerations on the poetics of Jan Kjærstad – including some critical, though probably irrelevant remarks on the use of the term 'net'

LIST OF AUTHORS — 219

Susanne Kramarz-Bein and Birge Hilsmann
Introduction

The present volume combines proceedings of the conference on "Applications of Network theories", which took place at the Institute of Northern Philology/Scandinavian Studies at Münster University in October 2008, and further essays on the application of network theory in the field of literary studies, with a focus on Scandinavian Studies, which have been inspired by this conference and the work in this particular field since then.

When we talk about Network Theory here, we mainly refer to concepts derived from maths and natural science, as Albert-László Barabási presented them in his book *Linked*, which has been of great influence on most of the conference papers and the essays in this volume. However, delving deeper into the matter, one task of this volume is to venture into the variety of possible applications and the variety of network thought. Therefore, other concepts, for example those developed in Social Studies and Literary Studies themselves, are also taken into consideration.

It has generally been our express purpose to show the wide range of possible applications of network theories, not limiting our scope to Scandinavian literary studies, but inviting other philologies and acknowledging other cultural witnesses besides literary texts – thereby practising academic network studies in a true sense. Such open endeavours will never claim to be complete, without being forced to see this as a downside to the project.

The conference showed a multitude of partly surprising and always inspiring connections between works in various fields of study. We are deeply grateful to all contributors, both to those esteemed colleagues from Scandinavia, continental Europe, and the USA, whose work can be published here, and to those who enriched our exchange of ideas by their reports without contributing to this publication.

Academic conferences and the publication of their proceedings feed not only on the scholars' work but also on the help of sponsors and supporters, to whom we wish to extend our fondest thanks: the Rectorate of Münster University; representing the Council of the Department of Philology at Münster University especially Barbara Eurich for her troubles; the E.ON-Ruhrgas scholarship fund, namely Dr. Heinz-Rudi Spiegel for his support; Norwegian Center for International Cooperation in Education (SIU – Senter for internasjonalisering av høyere utdanning); the Royal Norwegian Embassy in Berlin; the student council at our own Institute for Scandinavian Studies at Münster University.

The contribution of the English Lecturer Dr. Bischoff and of several of our own students and assistants to the edition of a volume in another than our native language must be mentioned in honest gratitude: Catharina Capteyn, Wiebke Denner, Sven Hungenberg, Christian Krosing, Stefanie A. Kunz, Katja Lehmann, Maren Meinert, Tabea Rahma, Amy Steinbach Palm, and Michael Wietholt.

Finally we would like to thank our editor, Martin W. Richter, at the LIT-Publishing House for his advice.

Practising academic network studies invariably means to be caught in several networks, not all of them chosen fields of interest but a number of them unavoidable hindrances to the pursuit of intellectual happiness, so that our volume sees the light of day rather late. We thank all contributors for their patience and trust that our readers will see the relevance of our work.

As mentioned above, this volume gathers most of the papers given at our conference and combines them with essays supplied later in order to widen the scope of network studies.

Just as both at the conference and in this volume, our express motivation has been to show that network studies connect generations of scholars and are relevant to students as well as to young graduates, fellows, professors, and *emeriti*. Therefore all these groups within the academic hierarchy supplied their respective contribution. We decided to present all papers in a purely chronological order without regards to seniority of the authors. Alas, chronology in Scandinavian Medieval Studies always has to compromise regarding the age of manuscripts, texts, motifs and subject matters, meeting a few rather basic philological decisions. Thus our chronology is based on the generally accepted assumptions of literary history as to the time the works in question were created as such.

Still, the first essay in this volume not only reaches back to the oldest texts but also mirrors the beginning of our conference in autumn 2008, when **Richard Gaskins** gave the keynote lecture.

As he did then, he examines here different texts dealing with the stages of *early Icelandic history* (initial land settlement, chieftain system, centralization), both spatial and temporal dimensions of political change. Gaskins not only examines the validity of Barabási's network terminology for cultural analysis; he also shows how narrative features of the sagas reflect network dynamics. Among those features are the prefiguration of constellations of characters within the genealogies and artful combination of static and dynamic periods. The saga texts mirror the insecurity, contingency and ambiguity that have shaped historic Icelandic society.

Judy Quinn's essay deals with nets of kinship in *Eddic poetry*, especially those heroic legends in the *Codex Regius* concerning the Sigurðr matter. These genealogical nets were endangered but also brought dangers to the protagonists, sometimes as a consequence of their own actions, sometimes caused by others. Ambitions, breaches of oaths and comparable moral issues are shown by Quinn to be, via the links of networks, the essential risks. Barabási's terminology proves to be of heuristic value even without focussing on empirical methods, as it does in several of the essays gathered in our volume.

Matthias Ewering and **Christian Krosing** seek to investigate the heuristic potential and benefits of network theory applied to the study of Old Norse literature. The first part of their article discusses several fields of Scandinavian Medieval studies which lend themselves to a network-based approach; the second part analyses *Færeyinga saga* and, more briefly, *Bandamanna saga* in order to demonstrate which kind of networks seem significant in Saga studies.

Massimiliano Bampi compares Barabási's network concepts with the polysystem theory as introduced by Evan-Zohar, analysing the Old Swedish *Eufemiavisor*. Thus Bampi emphasizes four criteria which both theories share: Firstly, both map the architecture of complex systems; secondly, said architecture is hierarchically structured; thirdly, development of these systems depends on the components' competition; fourthly, the systems are characterized by their dynamic.

In this regard, literature can be understood as a system in two ways: as a network of mutually linked texts and as an interconnection between fictional texts and their socio-cultural environment. This second aspect is essential to a comprehension of literature as a semiotic phenomenon.

Susanne Kramarz-Bein's contribution focuses on literary texts of the Old Norwegian literary milieu of origin at Hákon's court and connects them to his cultural and educational politics, especially the *Tristrams saga* and later texts of the literary milieu of the same dynasty, for example *Eufemia visorna*.

In this context, Barabási's network theory is applied as a model of the spread of literary traditions. Additionally, the marriage policies of the Scandinavian dynasties in question can be understood in the context of the mode of action of the network theory, too.

William Layher, in his study on the origins and pre-canonical editions of the *Revelaciones St.ae Birgittae,* focuses on a contrast inherent in the network image itself: networks are built of ties, but existing nets can catch elements as well as sieve them, i.e. either save things or assist in their disposal. Concerning the *Revelaciones,* Layher gives several instances of revision, alleviation and re-interpretation (de-secularization), also done by translators and scribes meaning well on Brigitta's account, as well as by courtiers acting against her. A special focus lies on the relevance of voice and script in dictation, in tradition/transmission, and in the transposition of narrative voices.

This fifth essay on medieval Nordic culture concludes the first section of our volume; the following contributors all concern themselves with modern European literature.

Birge Hilsmann examines the multiple dependency of *Swedish Romanticism* on German ideas and ideals. Autobiographical texts on travels by Atterbom and Silfverstolpe serve as her examples. Thus she can show that certain specific Romantic traits of these texts are unexpectedly inherent in their genre. Several ways of networking prove to be genuinely romantic with respect to the period's poetics.

Godelieve Laureys and Els Biesemans outline a project at the universities of Gent and Groningen, which sets out to explore the late 19th / early 20th century success of Scandinavian literature in Flanders and the Netherlands, along with its ideological causes. It becomes obvious that a variety of networks within the *Flemish movement* intersect each other, even with regard to their use of Scandinavian literature for their own linguistic and political liberation.

Felix Schmelzer's contribution turns to *French Modernists'* lyrics. He points out a connection between literature and physics within these texts, which translate advanced scientific concepts like quantum and relativity to poetry. This is quite surprising, as the late 19th century lyricists in France were explicitly opposed to a scientific worldview. But even in their interpretation of the Romantic idea of an Infinite Book, some hints at maths and network theory can be found, which ultimately derive from a tradition rooting in Ovid's poetics.

Our volume concludes with **Heiko Uecker's** essay, which takes a critical stance on the phenomenon of fashion in literary theory. Uecker's starting point and point of reference is *Jan Kjærstad*'s authorship, as he traces a tradition within

Scandinavian authors' poetics. This tradition combines of explicit links between natural science and literature with varying paradigms. Recently, even these authors' poetics have tended towards nets as their paradigm.

Hopefully, this collection of specialized essays applying network concepts to literary studies can give some insight, inspiration, or orientation to the variety of recent network approaches to literary, mainly Scandinavian, studies. Some stimulations for future works can be derived from it. Further differentiation of network terminology will help its application to the established discourses in literary studies and its acceptance therein. A constant critical look at the heuristic and epistemic value of said application appears to be mandatory. Especially the various dimensions of connections – social ties and intrinsically poetic ties such as intertextuality – are our challenge. The inspiring metaphor of the net (web, cobweb, lace, or sieve) should not be too easily merged with the network dynamics described in mathematical terms, even by critics, but both should be employed and valued in their own right.

Not underestimating these tasks, we have experienced at the conference and, hopefully, have conveyed in this volume the astonishing variety of perspectives, which are opened by way of considering nets and their dynamics.

In conclusion, it can be stated that it is inherent in them that they merge with other concepts or paradigms almost naturally and fruitfully for either side. It is hardly surprising that nets and networks have continued to be dominant concepts within various fields of research since our conference took place, producing a vast number of new titles and projects every year. Meanwhile, their importance as a real-life *dispositif* has continually increased. Expansion of our knowledge and an awareness of the importance of networks to human thought and cultural practice even long before the invention of telecommunication, let alone the World Wide Web, might help to understand the dynamics of our contemporary digitally connected global society.

I: Early Networks: The Middle Ages

RICHARD GASKINS

Political Development in Early Iceland: Applying Network Theory to the Sagas

> "...history, the spatio-temporal evolution of civilization, cannot be regarded independently of the particular fictions of coherence produced by those civilizations."[1]

Historians face major challenges in trying to integrate the spatial and temporal dimensions of political change in early Iceland (870-1264 CE). The historical record is sufficient to show that social ties among early settlers moved through a series of discrete spatial patterns over four centuries, ending in bitter political competition and collapse. But it is not clear in dynamic terms how and why these relationships traveled along specific paths. Historians have tended to focus attention on one or more structural paradigms, but they have been unable to specify the mechanisms driving the evolution of forms. In a stateless settler society, the successive emergence of political roles, regional competition, and centralization are dynamic events that overwhelm the spare historical data, as found in the surviving annals, historical fragments, and legal documents.[2]

This paper proposes new methods for expanding that historical record by mobilizing two essential resources: 1) the saga texts produced in Iceland near the end of, and just after, the historical period under discussion, and 2) a body of 21st-century interpretive tools based on the dynamic logic of networks. Saga scholars have long pondered whether and how to apply the rich cultural contents of these vernacular prose tales and epics to the historical conditions they purport to describe.[3] Building on those approaches, this paper suggests new ways to link saga narratives to the flow of historical patterns in the Icelandic case. These methods are adapted from recent experiments with network analysis—a rela-

---

[1] ASSMANN: The Mind of Egypt, p. 6.
[2] For a critical and comprehensive overview of sources and relevant research, see KARLSSON: Goðamenning. An important shift toward dynamic analysis can be found in SIGURÐSSON: Chieftains and Power.
[3] The applications of saga scholarship are discussed in ÓLASON: Dialogues with the Viking Age.

tively new approach developed for the age of information networks, with increasing applications to social, physical, economic, and cultural fields.[4]
Combining these two disparate sources may produce mutual benefits. The scope of saga scholarship is expanded if texts can thus be used to specify dynamic elements in early Icelandic culture and society. But network theory can likewise extend its reach, if the cultural contents of saga narratives are able to weave their way into the web-like graphs currently being studied by physicists, sociologists, and economists. There is both risk and reward in juxtaposing elements from such different disciplines. Take, for example, the intriguing parallel between political development in early Iceland and the global spread of financial capital in the early 21st century, as regional financial centers compete for dominance.[5] Despite the obvious gulf in historical time and economic complexity, there is a topographic similarity in the global dispersal of financial power, followed by competition and concentration (not to mention collapse), which recalls the rise of the Icelandic chieftain system, followed by a struggle for dominance among a diminishing group of powerful coalitions. There is no need here to dissolve real historical differences into a set of abstract models. Each episode has its own distinct qualities, and of special importance in the Icelandic case is the unique saga commentary—"particular fictions of coherence"—which embed these evolving patterns in everyday human projects.

I. Historical dynamics

This paper opens up a broad research question, exploring how network analysis might be applied to the dynamics of social change in the early history of Iceland. The goal is to suggest a research program for mapping the mechanisms of political development, using sagas on several levels of analysis. A network approach may be powerful enough to deepen our understanding of prevailing social and cultural forces during the period of the Icelandic commonwealth, lasting for some four centuries from 870 to 1264.
Political development during this period must have been driven by subtle forces that resist capture in historical snapshots or static legal structures. The turn to dynamics calls for a new research design using more complex analytical tools. Historians have provided a solid data base on which to build, but further ques-

---

[4] For basic references see WATTS: Six Degrees; and WHITE: Identity and Control. There is a long prior history of static analysis of social networks, summarized and updated in both works. A more accessible introduction to this field is BARABÁSI: Linked.
[5] See SASSEN: The Locational and Institutional Embeddedness of Electronic Markets.

tions remain about the sources and direction of change across the four centuries. Those dynamics are largely overlooked by interpretations focused on individual Icelanders as agents of change (whether real or fictional agents).⁶ Although individual actors play important roles, their impact depends on the structural pivots that transform local actions into wider social effects. Similarly, it is necessary to move beyond theoretical axioms that approach historical change through well-worn scholarly formulas, ranging from class struggle to rational choice.⁷ And it is likewise insufficient, in my view, to attribute historical change to broad mechanical causes acting through ideologies, conceptual schemes, ecological determinism, or the diffusion of cultural world-views. To be sure, all of these approaches may find some role within network analysis. But we need more fluid connections: actors whose behavior takes on contextual meaning; and structures that expand along a distinct evolutionary path.⁸ Most of all, we need to anchor this research more concretely in the rich narratives of the sagas.

The core problem is to explain how a settler society from the late 9th century, in the remarkable absence of centralized political authority, passes through discrete phases of political development, culminating in the destructive conflicts of the 13th century. Given the lack of formal state institutions, the customary default explanation for political change is missing from the Icelandic context, thereby opening the field for new kinds of explanation. The flow of early Icelandic self-governance must be found in highly distributed social forces, evidence for which appears in the extensive self-commentary offered by sagas compiled or written near the end of this period. Within this body of writing, modern network analysis may find distinctive elements of self-organization, expressed in both thematic contents and narrative structures. To the extent sagas

---

⁶ In recent years historians have been eager to restore individual "agency" to their analysis, seeking to personalize the older causal abstractions of ideology and material determinism. For Icelandic history, plausible historical figures are easiest to identify from the final decades of the commonwealth, drawing on vivid portraits of rivalries and ambitions contained in the samtíðarsögur. Among historical writers who emphasize personalities from saga sources (while not ignoring social relations) see BYOCK: Viking Age Iceland; MILLER: Bloodtaking and Peacemaking; NORDAL: Ethics and Action in Thirteenth-Century Iceland.

⁷ Sverre Bagge has usefully discussed the application of such standard formulas to historical development in early Iceland. BAGGE: Society and Politics in Snorri Sturluson's Heimskringla.

⁸ On various modes of historical explanation (dispositional, systemic, and transactional), stressing the advantages of transactional networks, see TILLY: Identities, Boundaries, and Social Ties.

themselves analyze these shifting human ties in social and cultural relations, they signal the key transition phases in the very society that created and valued these retrospective works. While the present goal is to clarify development in the Icelandic case, network analysis of the sagas may also suggest fundamental dynamic patterns applicable to other historical settings, including other settler societies spread cross a wide swath of time and place.[9]

II. Phases of Icelandic development: historical stages and literary sources

Nearly 400 years of Icelandic history separate the arrival of Norse seafarers, around the year 870, from the demise of the Icelandic commonwealth (*þjóðveldi*), which fell under the rule of Norway in 1262-64. The political development of a stateless settler society takes place on many levels, in response to a range of environmental constraints and emerging social and cultural identities. Change is continuous but punctuated by phases that provide the general framework for analysis. While historians have speculated about dynamic forces operating during these four centuries, the bulk of their research can be summarized in terms of static models or snapshots, presenting three distinct structural patterns:

1) The pattern of initial land settlements (landnám), 870-930
2) The pattern of a chieftain system (goðar), 930-1080
3) The pattern of regional coalitions or "domains" (ríki), 1080-1264[10]

The time periods noted here are obviously quite rough, especially when seen from a dynamic perspective. For the sake of completeness, two additional time periods need to be mentioned:

4) The pre-settlement period (before 870), as a source of social and cultural energy,[11] and
5) The post-1264 period as a retrospective era, building on cumulative, concurrent political and cultural ties to Norway and other points in Western Europe.[12]

---

[9] The most likely arena for comparative study is the settlement of New Zealand in approximately the 13th century CE, at the spatial and temporal end of the chain of Polynesian voyages of discovery and settlement. For an overview of research and controversies, see HOWE: The Quest for Origins.

[10] See references in note 2 above. These patterns follow the basic outlines of Jón Viðar SIGURÐSSON's analysis.

[11] The model here is Part III of Sigurður NORDAL's Íslenzk menning.

[12] TULINIUS: The Matter of the North.

Although this paper remains focused on the first three patterns, the flow of development could be further graphed in relation to cultural data from all five time periods, for all of which independent historical documentation exists. Supplementing the scant historical records, distinct groups of indigenous saga literature can be assigned to each of these periods, according to the narrative time periods and places typically portrayed in each group.

1) Settlements: *Íslendingabók* and *Landnámabók* (historical surveys)
2) Chieftains: *Íslendingasögur* (family sagas)
3) Domains: *samtíðarsögur* (contemporary sagas)
4) Pre-settlement: *fornaldarsögur* (legendary sagas)
5) Post-1264 and European settings: *riddarasögur* (chivalric sagas)[13]

As saga scholars have long emphasized, the time periods portrayed in each group of sagas is distinct from their dates of composition.[14] Nearly all were composed closer to the end of these four centuries, and mainly in the 13th century, despite learned controversies over fragments, verse elements, and *þættir*, which may stem from earlier periods by way of oral memory.[15] The two works covering settlements are indeed older, and are currently assigned to the early 12th century.[16] Only the "contemporary sagas" from the 13th-century describe the same general period in which they were written. Many experts find a connection between the cultural stimulus that produced these diverse saga types and the intensifying conflicts during the final half-century of the commonwealth. I have not mentioned here the important sagas about the history of Norwegian kings, which are relatively early works, nor the sagas of bishops—although both genres might well provide useful material for network analysis. And then there is always the poetry to fit into this whole mosaic.[17] For this preliminary discussion, it will be sufficient to define a network-analytic approach to the first three historical patterns and saga categories.

Given their literary form and retrospective vision, the sagas may be seen as supplying contemporaries with a usable past, or with what historian Jan Ass-

---

[13] For an overview of saga groups see KRISTJÁNSSON: Eddas and Sagas.
[14] This point was emphasized by the generation of critics that included Sigurður NORDAL. In addition to the work cited below in note 15, see ANDERSSON: The Growth of the Icelandic Sagas (1180-1280).
[15] See SIGURÐSSON: The Medieval Icelandic Saga and Oral Tradition.
[16] On the dating and authorship of Íslendingabók and Landnámabók, see the preface by Jakob Benediktsson in BENEDIKTSSON: Íslenzk fornrit 1.
[17] See CLOVER and LINDOW (eds.): Old Norse-Icelandic Literature.

mann describes as "cultural memory."[18] Unlike conventional history, according to Assmann, cultural memory allows societies under stress to assert normative continuity by adapting past traditions (including oral or customary memory) to changing circumstances. The fictions of coherence in written texts are more nuanced and malleable than the rituals and doctrines of coherence found in more tradition-bound societies. In a dynamic environment, the written text reshapes past norms, reconstructing the past to prepare for future challenges. Linear history thus finds a vertical anchor in cultural reflection, achieving systemic depth alongside the diachronic flow of events. In the Icelandic case, indeed, saga writing anticipates the structural concerns of modern network analysis by charting evolving patterns of behavior in the everyday lives of Icelanders, going back to the period of original settlement. Assmann believes that a people will turn to retrospective writing for normative footing at precisely those moments when contact has been lost with living models from the past[19]—a situation found in the turbulent age of saga writing near the end of the commonwealth era. The implications of this functional theory of cultural memory are developed more fully below.

III. Modeling historical dynamics

The first step in tracking historical development is to focus on transitions between these sequential patterns, moving across the four centuries. Network theory does not see these transitions as the work of vast supra-historical forces, but rather as unintended effects of mundane conflicts generated by human actors at each stage along the punctuated evolutionary path. The actions of ordinary people continually bump up against the limits of social possibility, framed by the topology of social relations. Pent-up conflicts eventually reach a tipping point; and as underlying topologies change, so are these limits suddenly expanded. In this careful balancing of micro-actions and emergent macro-effects, network theory positions itself to discover useful data in the sagas.

As one pattern of social relations yields to its successor, network analysis provides general models for mapping the emergent properties of each new phase. These dynamic models—still very much under review by contemporary net-

---

[18] See the essays collected in ASSMANN: Religion and Cultural Memory.
[19] ASSMANN: Religion and Cultural Memory, p. 69.

work specialists[20] —are designed to highlight possibilities and constraints embedded in contrasting relational patterns. As the discussion below will illustrate, structural transitions alter the rules of the social game, creating new frameworks of stability and conflict. When conflicts compound and reach a critical state, new phase transitions reconstitute the operating rules to accommodate new patterns of social ties. These changes may include broader geographic links, more diversified types of social alliances, as well as new topologies of political relations.

To illustrate these points we may consider three critical transition phases in the Icelandic case:

1) From settlement to chieftains. A highly dispersed group of settlers around the periphery of Iceland, in the course of everyday interactions, gives rise to an emerging pattern of localized chieftains, who seek to cooperate in regional and national assemblies.[21] By 930 the island crosses a certain population threshold, and qualitatively new social connections appear that shift the highly clustered geographical settlements into the "small-world" pattern, thus enabling the brokerage functions of chieftains (*goðar*) within loosely defined local territories (*goðorð*). As Norse seamen first regarded the new land from various circum-navigational routes, they settled along the peripheral coastlines and fjords, in addition to a few notable inland valleys.[22] Names and boundaries for original settlements derive mainly from the two historical works identified earlier, along with other sources—all of which are by no means consistent. Nor is this information everywhere consistent with land settlements described in the family sagas. Beyond dispute, however, is the foundational geographic pattern of highly distributed, clustered settlements.[23]

The central dynamic in this first transitional phase is the shift in relations from highly localized ties to more distant and complex alliances. Network theorists analyze this movement as the emergence of a "small-world" pattern, which opens qualitatively new opportunities for actors prepared to break out of their

---

[20] The theory of "evolving networks" (little more than a decade old,) shifted the analytical focus from static systems to network growth. BARABÁSI's book (note 4 above) explains this breakthrough in accessible terms, especially pp. 90-92.
[21] See SIGURÐSSON (note 2 above), pp. 39-62.
[22] For Norse exploration routes and for settlement pattern in Northwest Iceland, including a typical map of clustered coastal settlements, showing the area of the northwest fjords, see JÚLÍUSSON: *Íslenskur Sögu Atlas I.*
[23] For a literary and functionalist view of settlement narratives, see WHALEY: A Useful Past.

local webs.[24] Despite the name, the "small-world" concept refers here to more diverse personal relationships played out on a larger geographic scale. Initially, within relatively closed coastal communities, existing "strong ties" are based on attributes of kinship, migration, and prior geographic proximity. As time passes, new generations reach across social distances, bringing new dimensions to personal relations throughout the entire system. More nuanced social ties create complex identities, promoting more varied cooperative alliances and the early functions of political representation, including the emergence of chieftains as geographically distributed power brokers.[25] The emerging multiplicity of identities beyond blood kinship sets the stage for the sharpening of role conflicts and cultural tensions—precisely the concerns of the masterful family sagas, as well as the more numerous and briefer *þættir*. The "small-world" transition captures dynamic features of a society that are opaque to actors operating within its parameters. It presumes no forms of central planning or sweeping historical forces. What impel actors in this phase are conflicts arising within an older structure of relations built on close kinship and proximity of settlement. To resolve the conflicts typical for this foundational pattern, as rivalries emerge within second and third generations, a broader web of social alliances provides some stabilizing weight, but also allows more complex conflicts among cross-cutting ties with distant clans and localities. New social and political identities are forged at the crossroads of these multiple connections, opening up new opportunities, while exposing the structural gaps present in the social and cultural norms of more insular communities. Network theorists have coined the term "structural holes" to designate the spaces in emerging social relations that open up for social, political, and cultural entrepreneurs.[26] As we shall explore later on, the sagas seem to be mapping these same contours of novelty and conflict, in retelling the stories of enterprising and contentious Icelanders during the post-settlement period.

2) From chieftains to domains. The second transition for analysis is the movement to more concentrated forms of power, beginning toward the end of the 11th

---

[24] On "small-world" dynamics, see (in addition to works cited above in note 4) the early popular article by WATTS and STROGATZ: Collective Dynamics of 'Small-world' Networks; For the schematic diagrams, see BUCHANAN: Small Worlds.

[25] For the distribution of goðorð held by chieftains in the 10th century, see JÚLÍUSSON: *Íslenskur Sögu Atlas I*.

[26] This theory comes out of the older static forms of network theory, but anticipates the turn to network dynamics. See BURT: Structural Holes.

century.[27] From this point forward, actions taken by individuals are increasingly caught up in a thickening web of regional alliances and quasi-political relations, dominated by prominent families with ambitious (if erratic) offspring.

In network analytic terms, this historical phase can be identified with the evolution of small-world systems into hub-and-spoke structures,[28] with increasing centralization of governing functions within some seven family-dominated groups. We can look specifically to scale-free networks[29] to model the transition from initially distributed power nodes of chieftains[30] to regimes in which a few central families come to predominate.[31]

There is something of a gap in saga events dating from these decades of transition, but we can turn to stock elements in 13th-century saga narratives to imply these transitional movements. Such stock elements, which are familiar to all saga readers, perform various functions of self-commentary.[32] Repeated elements in the plot capture the standard bases of personal conflict and competition, while the narrative structure conveys a deeper background level of collective vulnerability and transition. Both conflict and continuity are played out in a cultural landscape framed by economic and environmental constraints, by contests over positional status as kinship systems erode, and by tensions emerging in the realms of culture, religion, and morality. These constraints, contests, and tensions provide the narrative energy that drives the more complex

---

[27] See Jón Viðar SIGURÐSSON (note 2 above), pp. 62-70.

[28] For Constrasting network structures: distributed power nodes versus the hub-and-spoke organization, see BUCHANAN: Small Worlds.

[29] The concept of scale-free networks was central to the dynamic turn in recent network theory. The distributed network of the goðar advances to the hub-and-spoke model through the preferential affiliations of social clients with a shrinking subset of chieftains. A scale-free evolution allows the terms of affiliation and political brokerage to change as associations become more dense. New patterns are self-organizing and thus vary from the older-scale relationships of prior patterns. In addition to the works cited in note 4, for an overview of scale-free models across disciplines, see CALDARELLI: Scale-Free Networks.

[30] For the distribution of goðorð held by chieftains in the 10th century, see JÚLÍUSSON: Íslenskur Sögu Atlas I. It represents the fully elaborated small-world structure.

[31] For Regional domains at the height of power of the Sturlungar (1230-35), marking the intense rivalries within hub-and-spoke power networks, see JÚLÍUSSON: Íslenskur Sögu Atlas I.

[32] According to Jan Assmann, building cultural memory depends on identifying "typical" actions, conflicts, and responses, thus elevating ephemeral events into "timeless simultaneity." It is these "systemic networks of synchronicity" that provide meaning, orientation, and coherence in the retrospective search for cultural memory. See ASSMANN: Religion and Cultural Memory (note 18 above), p. 171.

Íslendingasögur and the samtíðarsögur. 3) Increasing conflict among domains and the collapse of the commonwealth. Bringing this sequence to a close, we can ask why the domain system lacked the stability that might have allowed a lasting federation of regional entities. The seven domains passed through their respective consolidation phases at different times after the late 11th century; but after 1220, with the rise of the Sturlungar,[33] a new and more destructive form of power struggle entered the picture.[34] We have the riveting testimony of the samtíðarsögur, and especially Sturla Þórðarson's masterwork, Íslendinga saga, as a contemporary portrayal of these dramatic events.[35] Here the localized conflicts of prior eras gave way to multi-dimensional alliances, climactic battles, and geopolitical maneuvering, amid strategic triumphs and reversals, all within the compressed span of four decades. The lines between the provisional winners and losers were continually redrawn in the tumultuous run-up toward the demise of the commonwealth.[36]

In network analytic terms, this final transition can be compared to the diffusion of social gossip, the spread of human viruses and computer viruses, cascading bank failures, and events governed by tipping points, critical mass, and threshold effects.[37] Where much applied network analysis (especially in economics) focuses on positive network effects, we may steel ourselves—in solidarity with the implied saga audience—to ponder the darker side of negative impacts and failures.[38] From an analytic point of view, to be sure, any ultimate judgment about transitions remains mathematically neutral, in the sense that there will always be winners and losers as evolving systems pass through phase transitions. And indeed, one senses this calm neutrality in the narrative voice toward the end of Íslendinga saga, as events reach the critical endpoint of 1262 and suddenly fade away—as though the events themselves might just continue to evolve indefinitely.

---

[33] For Regional domains at the height of power oft he Sturlungar (1230-35), marking the intense rivalries within hub-and-spoke power networks, see JÚLÍUSSON: *Íslenskur Sögu Atlas I*.

[34] See Jón Viðar SIGURÐSSON (note 2 above), pp. 71-83.

[35] The major compilation of these sagas is published as JÓHANNESSON, FINNBOGASON, and ELDJÁRN: Sturlunga Saga.

[36] For Consolidating domains in the intense power struggles nearing the end of the commonwealth period, see JÚLÍUSSON: *Íslenskur Sögu Atlas I*.

[37] For network theoretical concepts of threshold effects and critical states, see BUCHANAN: Ubiquity.

[38] See chapters 9 and 10 of Barabási (note 4 above). An important sociological treatment can be found in VAUGHAN: The Dark Side of Organizations.

The retrospective focus on the years 1262-64 as a time of collapse may reflect a romanticized view of the commonwealth as an experiment in stateless self-government. Such a view resonates with the anxieties of modern political thinkers, not to mention the practical aims of later Icelandic nationalists. But saga narratives do not shy away from such tumultuous transitions at all levels, however calmly they advance the surface story.[39] We can assume that saga writing carried its audience into more complex realms of cultural meaning, where governance systems were judged by humanistic standards, including ethical verdicts delivered by the passage of time. This is not precisely Hegel's "cunning of reason," but perhaps an equally elusive kind of cosmic judgment, notwithstanding the balanced tone and striking impersonality of the narrative voice heard in these sagas. This wider aspect of saga meanings lies at the far end of the research program outlined here.

IV. Changing topographies of social ties: dynamic patterns in the sagas

A new research program is needed to map the contours of political development in the Icelandic commonwealth period, reaching across four centuries, passing through the phases just outlined. Saga texts can support this effort by providing evidence for complex transitions, showing us how variable micro-motives of individual actors connect to macro-effects at the level of society, politics, and culture. This way of interrogating the sagas reflects 21st-century concepts and may at first seem reductive. But the analysis itself requires immersion in standard elements of saga narrative—stock situations and repeated patterns, interrupted by unpredictable shifts, when the cultural rules of the game suddenly seem to change. By positing relational patterns and emerging variations, the sagas appear to conduct their own structural commentary on earlier social dynamics.

The remaining sections of this paper review saga elements familiar to modern readers, suggesting their topographic relevance to emergent social relations: the opening of small-world connections; distributed political brokerage; hub-and-spoke consolidations; regional competition; and efforts to centralize power, ending with the collapse of the commonwealth. This section presents textual examples applicable to the initial phases of this evolutionary process; while the next section completes the circuit with a different set of examples. It goes with-

---

[39] Vésteinn Ólason (note 3 above) explores the deeper waters surrounding that "laconic coolness" of the narrative voice.

out saying that these examples are but a small sample of countless episodes to be found in the sagas.

The most fundamental network elements in the sagas are the familiar tales of alliance building, often described in typical small-scale, incremental story lines, but conveyed also in more expansive dimensions of human numbers, geographic reach, and qualitative shifts in the meaning of social ties. These simple alliances represent discrete methods by which the closed structures of kinship are expanded, stretched thin, and ultimately surpassed in new relations of power and culture.[40] Examples include stock episodes of forming strategic alliances through marriage, initiating fostering relationships, providing surety for legal settlements, and enlisting neighbors for armed encounters, both offensive and defensive. The sagas contain hundreds of specific instances, inviting us to consider a range of roles and reasons for the expansion of social connections. Overlapping the strong ties of kinship, new identities arise that cut across clustered patterns rooted in the period of settlements. Much drama in the sagas arises from conflicting loyalties resulting from these mixed alliances. *Njáls saga*, in particular, explores new modes of outreach with clinical precision and cumulative impact, portraying the standard mechanisms by which the highly clustered population of the settlement period was transformed into the selectively cosmopolitan pattern of the "small-world."

Elsewhere I have described in detail a coordinated chain of actions taken by Njáll to neutralize tensions arising between two extended families, tensions based on a sequence of killings that carry the major plot lines.[41] The strategic use of cross-cutting identities to counter traditional revenge norms is a major theme in *Njáls saga*, going to the core of Njál's reputation as a powerful "lawyer," a "wise man," but also a figure who becomes entangled in the expanding webs that he himself has enabled. The geographic scope of saga action is unusually large in *Njáls saga*, which was likely written around 1280, among the later Íslendingasögur. Njál's stratagems link powerful families from the western and eastern extremes to his own kin structure in south Iceland, and the ensuing conflicts expand still farther to transmit tension through inchoate networks into far-flung regions. The leader of the expedition that eventually destroys Njáll and his notorious sons, Flosi Þórðarson Freysgoða from southeastern Iceland,

---

[40] The relentless dynamic pressures on Icelandic kin relations were already in place at the time of settlements. See the important study by PHILPOTTS: Kindred and Clan. Chapter 1.
[41] GASKINS: Network Dynamics in Saga and Society, pp. 201-16.

has no choice for his subsequent defense but to scour the far reaches of the commonwealth, seeking support from influential men with whom he had no prior connection.[42] These incidents fit comfortably into one of the best-known theorems in recent network analysis, Mark Granovetter's notion of "the strength of weak ties."[43]

There are, of course, simpler examples of alliance-building, brokerage, and conflicting ties that cut across kinship relations, spread throughout the family sagas and þættir. One could construct a basic inventory of brokerage connections presented within this cultural laboratory of the sagas, all of which shortened the social distance between diverse kinship clusters in the transition away from early settlement patterns.[44] In this context it makes no difference whether these familiar saga tales correspond to actual historical events. It is enough for sagas to offer a selection of paradigms or types, so long as it seems plausible that comparable events occurred sometime during the period portrayed in these retrospective tales. The tendency of sagas to stereotype events, characters, and stories fits well with modern network analysis, which likewise seeks to group data on individual actions and identities into types, facilitating a powerful form of analysis known as "block-modeling."[45] Of course, the dense webs of conflict and violence found in the sagas tell us nothing about the true incidence of violence in Icelandic communities, whether in the 10th or 13th centuries. Such behavior need not be ubiquitous, but merely typical of events through which social identities were being transformed.

Saga narrators often refer to stretches of time when "nothing happened," reserving their narrative craft for those events where new social or cultural identities were forming and old patterns were being challenged. Saga episodes concentrate on stock incidents where personal decisions and actions conform to prior modes of social connection; but they also highlight exceptional cases where qualitatively new connections emerge, where discrete actions open out into new

---

[42] The relevant chapters are in Einar Ólafur SVEINSSON: Brennu-Njáls saga, chapters 93-97, p. 134.
[43] GRANOVETTER: Strength of Weak Ties, pp. 1360-80.
[44] A recent analysis of brokerage functions relating to the theory of structural holes is BURT: Brokerage and Closure, especially chapter 1.
[45] In addition to Jan Assmann's perspective on the importance of "typical" events for cultivating cultural memory (note 32 above), the field of network analysis emphasizes the usefulness of "stereotyped stories" to bridge the gap between narrative evidence and network modeling. See Harrison C. White (note 4 above), pp. 27-40. See generally TILLY: Stories, Identities, and Political Change.

social spaces. The prominence of these transitional moments in the sagas tells us several things about the interests of saga narrators: precisely where they expected changes to emerge, how changes came about, and how they were to be judged under shifting cultural norms.

The decline of kinship as the dominant social link occurred as successive generations moved beyond the age of settlements, operating in an environment where scarcity of new land and other resources made competition inevitable. The positional attributes of honor and fame allowed for status to shift away from families tied to pre-settlement heroic deeds and mythic ancestors. The cultural landscape laid out in these sagas expands into a larger playing field, where the rules of older games were fading, and new games proliferated.

I mention examples from *Njáls saga* as a practical matter, given the popularity and richness of that work. For reasons that can be put to the test, I believe the best place to find network-analytic elements for the first phase of political development is in the family sagas and the þættir. This is not because these sagas portray events within the narrative timeframe of the post-settlement era. And it is not because we ascribe some of these stories and threads to an oral tradition formed during that earlier period—or to some hypothetical 10th-century mentality. Rather it seems plausible that the 13th century's aim in compiling and crafting these family sagas was to project a retrospective view on basic, elemental forces, answering 13th-century questions about how the Icelandic commonwealth got to where it was. In many respects the saga writers have anticipated our present concerns as network analysts, albeit with a far more poetic touch. I once incautiously ascribed to Njáll himself an understanding of Granovetter's theory of weak ties, for which I received some deserved skepticism. (Njáll was, of course, described in the saga as a wise fellow with an ability to see into the future, so anything is possible.) My point, nonetheless, is to highlight reflexive, structural elements in the family sagas that let us interpret them as experiments in historical self-commentary.

It would be conceivable to sort saga texts in the same genre by year of composition, to the extent we can assign reliable dates to major texts. Theodore Andersson has recently argued that *Njáls saga* is one of the most fully articulated works in this genre, compared especially to what he sees as a simpler structure in Egils saga, which was probably written 60 years earlier.[46] It makes sense to search for paradigms and typical elements in more than one place, so that alli-

---

[46] ANDERSSON: Growth of the Icelandic Saga (note 14 above).

ance patterns found in *Njáls saga* could be distinguished from those found in *Egils saga* or perhaps the þættir. I raise this as a possibility in moving to still another unfounded assertion, that the contemporary sagas should be a preferred source of more complex dynamic elements, more suitable for graphing the remaining historical phases that encompass the growth of domains as well as the collapse of the multiple-domain system. The contemporary sagas compiled in the Sturlunga collection were themselves written at different times and describe events attributed to the period from 1118 to 1264. Until we can say more precisely what we hope to find in any of these sagas, however, about all we can do is to clarify some initial research assumptions. My intuition is that the contemporary sagas, and especially Sturla Þórðarson's *Íslendinga* saga, will yield the richest material for mapping the expanding forces operating in the later phases of Icelandic political development.

Let me provide one further example of contrasting rule systems, also taken from Njál's saga, showing how saga narrative pivots away from older norms into a new prefigured cultural space. The example comes from a feud episode occurring early in the saga, one that has been commented on frequently in the critical literature.[47] Within the space of ten short chapters, the saga describes a sequence of revenge killings (or "feud chain" in Jesse Byock's terms[48]) instigated by the wives of the two central figures: Hallgerðr, the wife of Gunnarr, and Bergþóra, wife of Njáll. Like most feud chains this one begins with trivial slights: bruised feelings over seating order at a feast; verbal insults directed to unsightly fingernails. The proud spirits of both women betray more subtle tensions that they are unable to control—in contrast to the spectacular restraint displayed by their husbands. Under pressure from escalating violence stoked by both women, the feud chain leads to the point where Gunnarr himself must either strike the next blow, or end the process by conspicuously doing nothing. Demonstrating the kind of restraint counseled by Njáll, the two men step away from the old pattern of revenge duties, and in so doing they open up a new social field of cooperation, organized under entirely different rules.

---

[47] For example, see LÖNNROTH: Njáls Saga: A Critical Introduction, p. 26, p. 76.
[48] BYOCK: Feud in the Icelandic Saga. Despite his extensive structural analysis of this episode, Byock does not detect its function of introducing emergent norms (180-90). Nor does Theodore M. Andersson, who dismisses it as "a bit of unattached prefatory matter. The fact that it is so elaborately worked out actually misleads the reader into seeking some function for it which it does not possess" (ANDERSSON: Icelandic Family Saga, p. 46. [quoted in BYOCK]).

To give a blow-by-blow description: Hallgerðr avenges the social slights she suffered at the feast by enlisting her overseer, the slave Kolr, to kill Bergþóra's slave Svartr. Bergþóra then enlists a stranger, the freed slave Atli, to kill Kolr. Atli is killed in turn by a distant relative of Hallgerðr, Brynjólfr, who wanders into the saga at just the right moment. Bergþóra initiates the next killing, enlisting a man named Þórdr, who was the foster father of her famous sons. In this classic exchange of killings the social status of each perpetrator is shifting upwards, and the proximity of relationship draws ever-closer to the husbands themselves. Hallgerðr persuades a kin relation of Gunnarr (his mother's cousin Sigmundr Lambason) to kill Þórd. She thus draws into the matrix the whole Sigfúss clan from the West, who will figure heavily in later events. For Bergþóra's response, her choice of agent is her own son, the colorful and erratic Skarpheðinn Njálsson. According to the rules of the precise game being described, Gunnarr faces the prospect of personally slaying the son of his best friend Njáll. But he is also in a unique position to bring this feud chain to an abrupt and surprising end, by simply doing nothing. And that is precisely how this narrator ends the episode, describing a long hiatus, after which Njáll and Gunnarr settle up the financial details and profess lifelong friendship, thus activating an emerging ethical norm. Even so, the seeds of later conflict have also been planted.[49]

V. Fictions of cohesion and fragmentation: mapping links across multiple levels

For a dynamic society, classic network graphs of social ties may seem to place too much emphasis on the static qualities of associations—like a single snapshot taken on a busy urban street. It is not enough to string several snapshots together, when a more fluid analysis allows networks to evolve through multiple forms. A dynamic analysis of social relations is a better match for the art of saga literature, which integrates multiple fields of action, casting the immediate conflicts among individuals against a shifting background of identities and values.[50] Sagas provide cultural and ethical webs in which saga characters move

---

[49] SVEINSSON: Brennu-Njáls saga, chapters 35-45.
[50] Contemporary network analysis is still in the process of shedding its static orientation, and is actively searching for applications that integrate temporal and spatial dimensions. In this respect, the layering of temporal and systemic elements in saga narrative may be seen as a poetic advantage over the current taste for mathematical network modeling. Network analysis as the interplay of multiple identities lies at the heart of Harrison C. White's recent updated volume (note 4 above). Some years back, Peter S. Bearman

about like spiders, constantly reweaving their own connections into new configurations.

Within these sagas a prominent story line focuses on deeds of high-profile actors, while other narrative elements supply various frameworks for action. These background frameworks should be understood as fractured, rather than monolithic, and are rife with critical gaps or "structural holes." They provide baseline terms within which actors calculate the competing merits and demerits of acting on customary expectations. At critical moments these calculations are finely balanced, and the outcomes may suddenly tip the other way, as actors shift between such identities as kinsmen, strategic allies in property disputes, or affiliates within new trust networks.

Essential to this background are cultural and ethical frameworks, in which chosen actions acquire meaning and value.[51] These frameworks too are fragmented and fuzzy at the margins. Longer and more complex sagas exploit this indeterminacy in posing conflicts that are internalized by protagonists. Such conflicts allow for central actors to exercise choices at the margins of custom, which may suddenly propel them into entirely new social or ethical spaces. Whether powerful individuals earn success or defeat depends on the horizon of possibilities available to them, defined by the subtle framing qualities of saga narrative. Even the strongest individuals must take their chances in situations where limits are never fully specified in advance, where outcomes are contingent, and where cultural and ethical ironies abound. In using the sagas for network analysis, we must consider both the actors and the shifting webs in which their actions are embedded—and judged.

Sagas famously employ genealogies to compress and consolidate various modes of relation, using them as a preface to narrative action. In recent decades, social network theory has shown its own fondness for genealogical data, true to its original snapshot approach to social diagrams. More recent theory has developed ways of merging actor-networks with group identities, constituting "bipar-

---

noted that social network methodology should be extended "to contexts in which time could be integrated more fully as a continuous variable, rather than relying on cross-sectional snapshots of social structure" (BEARMAN: Relations into Rhetorics, p. 180).

[51] On ethical frames as variable elements of saga narrative, see ÁRNASON: Ethos in Transformation. For an earlier treatment see ÁRNASON: Morality and Social Structure, pp. 157-74.

tite" networks or networks with multiple "modes."[52] Before turning to this analytic device, it may be useful to show how sagas generate narrative action out of compact tableaux of family connections. While modern readers often declare them tedious, genealogical preambles forecast the diachronic unfolding of saga events. The action later plotted in the stories gives concrete life to the multiple identities embedded in family structures, which span several generations of cross-cutting ties.

Elsewhere I have described the beginning of one of the shorter contemporary sagas, which tells the story of two neighboring chieftains competing for the loyalties of farmers within their adjacent districts.[53] As a prelude to this story, the saga recounts the genealogical ties surrounding the two main figures, Hvamm-Sturla and Þorgils Oddason.[54] The genealogies foretell the actions yet to come, as for example in listing the nine children of Þorgils, each one constituting a link to other families whose allegiance and support will prove relevant to events set to unfold in the saga. Two of these sons, Oddi and Einarr, move quickly to the center of saga action, where they will extend the web of the Þorgils clan into new relationships with distant families. It is Einarr, son of Þorgils, who enters into direct competition with Hvamm-Sturla, scion of the rival clan, in a prototype of how, after the 1220's, the Sturlungar would come to amass their regional power. This shift in power relations is prefigured in the strategic marriage that links the two families—the marriage between Sturla and Ingibjörg, the daughter of Þorgils' cousin. The broader implications of this strategic link would have been plain to the 13th-century Icelander from the very outset; and they are duly played out as the saga plot unfolds. There is more to be said about this saga and its mode of development. For our purposes here, it is enough to show how saga narrative strikes its own artful balance between static and dynamic modes of presentation.

This brief synopsis alerts us to the dynamic possibilities found in the overlapping layers of saga narrative. At a formal level, modern network analysis integrates multiple attributes in a variety of ways, including, as mentioned, bipartite networks. In such networks, ties between individuals are supplemented by concurrent ties to various groups, which in turn form their own distinctive ties at

---

[52] In addition to Harrison C. White (note 4 above), see the applications developed by DE NOOY: Exploratory Social Network Analysis with Pajek. Chapter 11 of this work deals with genealogies.
[53] See GASKINS (note 41 above).
[54] JÓHANNESSON: Sturlunga saga, chapter 1 (note 35 above).

the group level.⁵⁵ Group ties may include relations among families, clans, or the clustered constituencies of rival chieftains or domains. They may also include groups united by common cultural or ethical commitments. At every moment in the plot, individual actors must bear the full weight of these concurrent identities. The narrative compels them to compute their relational choices through more than one mode, acting both as individuals and as members of disparate groups. Conflicts arising on the individual level may be transformed when actors are forced to confront the burdens of cross-cutting group identities.

Sagas from the contemporary group are especially open to these bipartite complications, which pile constraints on individual actors, as they also build tension into the dramatic flow. From the perspective of modern network analysis, the pressure from balancing multiple identities can push a given system into the distinctive hub-and-spoke structure, replacing the more evenly distributed pattern.⁵⁶ The same pressures may lead to still further imbalances and strife among the prominent hubs. Such formal dynamics are currently being studied in a host of modern settings, from the structure of global financial centers to the deregulation of the airline industry.⁵⁷

This view of interlocking network structures requires us to distinguish the spiders from their continually shifting web formations. It permits us to look beyond the foreground of prominent actors toward the action-frameworks, which serve as repositories of meaning and value. As identities shift beyond the surface attributes of individuals to the level of groups and cultural collectivities, the saga narrative can itself be seen as constituting cultural meanings through its own categories and conventions. Indeed, group identities on the level of ethics and culture may be defined best through parsing narrative formulas.

Despite the steady, calm narrative voice, the rich texture of the contemporary sagas supports the complexity of the events being portrayed, opening up competing sources of virtue and legitimacy. This skillful interweaving of stories makes it possible to trace the evolution of ethics and culture in the midst of political fragmentation and collapse. Identities formed on these collective and conceptual levels are endemic to the art of saga narration. It has been said that "narratives organize elements into interpretable patterns/sequences to reveal a

---

[55] For Cross-cutting ties: models of „bipartite" or „bimodal" networks, see WATTS: Six Degrees.
[56] For Contrasting network structures: distributed power nodes versus the hub-and-spoke organization, see BUCHANAN: Small Worlds.
[57] See RAUCH and CASELLA: Networks and Markets.

process."[58] These artful fictions of coherence are indispensable for explaining both why and how complex events unfold on multiple levels.

Network analysis of the sagas may aspire to chart overlapping identities on five levels of narrative structure.[59] These levels include 1) saga description of key players, which assigns individuals to relevant social identities; 2) saga action, in which players forge new affiliational identities in inchoate civic relations, 3) saga conflict, in which the actors' selection of normative paths leads to the construction of ethical identities; 4) saga narrative voice, which offers restrained guidance on the cultural meaning of variable ethical identities; and 5) saga impact or reader-response, in which the contemporary audience for saga writing formed contestable judgments about the cultural, ethical, political, and social identities woven into the fabric of saga narrative.[60] As Jan Assmann points out, our word "text" derives from the Latin verb "I weave," and it is this web-like texture of Icelandic sagas that resonates with modern network analysis.[61]

VI. Conclusion: networks of trust and conflict

Across all levels of human activity and across all historical periods, networks represent the importance of being connected—replacing the atomistic model of rugged individualism.[62] For self-evolving social networks, in the absence of any master planner, the driving humanistic force is trust. Trust in oneself is good, as far as it goes, but is no substitute for trust in one's chosen allies. No one can be self-sufficient; and no one has enough wisdom to see where history will end up, or enough power to impose some grand design. In sagas, the fluidity of culture is tied to the emergence of conflict, while the promise of trust is found in tentative resolutions. At deeper narrative levels, balancing this flow of relationships requires a sense of contingency, underscored by the famous lack of intrusiveness in the narrative voice, and the acknowledgment of fate.

---

[58] BEARMAN and STOVAL: Becoming a Nazi, p. 76. I am grateful to my colleague David Cunningham for drawing my attention to this essay.
[59] These five layers corollate with Harrison C. White's "Five Senses of Identity." See WHITE: Identity and Control, pp. 17-18 (note 4 above).
[60] Vésteinn ÓLASON (note 3 above) has explored each of these narrative layers in the sagas, using different terminology while speaking to similar cultural functions.
[61] ASSMANN (note 18 above), p. 101.
[62] Charles Tilly makes the fundamental point that trust should be seen as "a property of interpersonal relations in which people took risks of each other's failure or betrayal," rather than an individual attitude or personal orientation. See TILLY: Trust and Rule, xii.

The notion that trust evolves as a property of networks is entirely consistent with the value system on display throughout the sagas, which grants highest priority to honor even at the cost of an individual's own life.[63] The fact that trust is constantly being tested in the sagas by personal ambition, by sheer evil, and even by bad luck only adds to its premier value for maintaining alliances. The importance of trust is communicated also in the special qualities of saga narrative: the detached tone, never entirely overcome by even the most appealing actors; the conspicuous sense of balance, anchored somewhere beyond the personal interests of saga characters; the realization that survival properly belongs to the aggregate, not the heroic individual. The saga world seems quite distant in many ways, but it may also seem strikingly familiar to modern network analysis in its respect for uncertainty, contingency, and ambiguity, all of which hold the keys to understanding a dynamic society.

Bibliography

ANDERSSON, Theodore M.: *The Growth of the Icelandic Sagas (1180-1280)*, Ithaca: Cornell University Press, 2006.

ANDERSSON, Theodore M.: *The Icelandic Family Saga: An Analytic Reading*, Cambridge: Cambridge University Press, 1967.

ÁRNASON, Vilhjalmur: „An Ethos in Transformation: Conflicting Values in the Sagas", in: *Gripla* Vol. 20 (2009), pp. 217-240.

ÁRNASON, Vilhjalmur: „Morality and Social Structure in the Icelandic Sagas", in: *Journal of English and Germanic Philology* Vol. 90 (1991), pp. 157-74.

ASSMANN, Jan: *Religion and Cultural Memory*, Stanford: Stanford University Press, 2006.

ASSMANN, Jan: *The mind of Egypt: history and meaning in the time of the Pharaohs*, Cambridge: Harvard University Press, 2003.

BAGGE, Sverre: *Society and Politics in Snorri Sturluson's Heimskringla*, Berkeley: University of California Press, 1991.

BARABÁSI, Albert-László: *Linked: The New Science of Networks*, Cambridge MA: Perseus Publishing, 2002.

---

[63] While much has been written on this aspect of the sagas, of particular interest are the brief essays by Helgi ÞORLÁKSSON in the volume edited by ÞORLÁKSSON: Sæmdarmenn.

BEARMAN, Peter S. and Katherine STOVAL: „Becoming a Nazi: Models for Narrative Networks", in: *Poetics* Vol. 27 (2000), pp. 69-90.

BEARMAN, Peter S.: *Relations into rhetorics: local elite social structure in Norfolk, England, 1540-1640*, New Brunswick: Rutgers University Press, 1993.

BENEDIKTSSON, Jakob: *Islenzk fornrit 1: Islendingabók, Landnámabók*, Reykjavík: Hið íslenzka fornritafélag, 1986.

BUCHANAN, Mark: *Small Worlds and the Groundbreaking Theory of Networks*, New York: Norton, 2002.

BUCHANAN, Mark: *Ubiquity: Why Catastrophes Happen*, New York: Random House, 2000.

BURT, Ronald S.: *Brokerage and closure: an introduction to social capital*, Oxford: Oxford University Press, 2005.

BURT, Ronald S.: *Structural Holes: The Social Structure of Competition*, Cambridge MA: Harvard University Press, 1992.

BYOCK, Jesse: *Feud in the Icelandic Saga*, Berkeley: University of California Press, 1982.

BYOCK, Jesse: *Viking Age Iceland*, London: Penguin Books, 2001.

CALDARELLI, Guido: *Scale-Free Networks: Complex Webs in Nature and Technology*, Oxford: Oxford University Press, 2007.

CLOVER, Carol J. and John LINDOW (eds.): *Old Norse—Icelandic Literature: A Critical Guide*, Ithaca: Cornell University Press, 1985.

GASKINS, Richard: „Network Dynamics in Saga and Society", in: *Scandinavian Studies* Vol. 77.2 (2005), pp. 201-16.

GRANOVETTER, Mark S.: „The Strength of Weak Ties", in: *American Journal of Sociology* Vol. 78 (1973), pp. 1360-80.

HOWE, K. R.: *The Quest for Origins: Who Discovered and Settled the Pacific Islands?*, Honolulu: University of Hawai'i Press, 2003.

JÓHANNESSON, Jón, Magnús FINNBOGASON and Kristján ELDJÁRN (eds.): *Sturlunga Saga*, Reykjavík: Sturlunguútgáfan, 1946.

JÚLÍUSSON, Árni Daniel, Jón Ólafur ÍSBERG, and Helgi Skúli KJARTANSSON (eds.): *Íslenskur Sögu Atlas I.*, Rekyjavík: Almenna Bókafélagið, 1989.

KARLSSON, Gunnar: *Goðamenning: Staða og áhrif goðorðsmanna í þjópveldi Íslendinga*, Reykjavík: Heimskringla, 2004.

KRISTJÁNSSON, Jónas: *Eddas and Sagas: Iceland's Medieval Literature*, Reykjavík: Hið íslenzka bókmenntafélag, 1992.

LÖNNROTH, Lars: *Njáls Saga: A Critical Introduction*, Berkeley: University of California Press, 1976.

MILLER, William Ian: *Bloodtaking and Peacemaking: Feud, Law, and Society in Saga Iceland*, Chicago: University of Chicago Press, 1990.

NOOY, Wouter de; Andrej Mrvar and Vladimir Batagelj: *Exploratory Social Network Analysis with Pajek*, Cambridge: Cambridge University Press, 2005.

NORDAL, Guðrún: *Ethics and Action in Thirteenth-Century Iceland*, Odense: Odense University Press, 1998.

NORDAL, Sigurður: *Íslenzk menning*, Reykjavík: Mál og menning, 1942.

ÓLASON, Vésteinn: *Dialogues with the Viking Age: Narration and Representation in the Sagas of the Icelanders*, Reykjavík: Heimskringla, 1998.

PHILPOTTS, Bertha S.: *Kindred and Clan in the Middle Ages and After*, Cambridge: Cambridge University Press, 1913.

RAUCH, James E. and Alessandra CASELLA (eds.): *Networks and Markets*, New York: Russell Sage, 2001.

SASSEN, Saskia: „The Locational and Institutional Embeddedness of Electronic Markets: The Case of the Global Capital Markets", in: M. BEVIR and F. TRENTMANN (eds.): *Markets in Historical Context*, Cambridge: Cambridge University Press, 2004, pp. 224-46.

SIGURÐSSON, Gísli: *The Medieval Icelandic Saga and Oral Tradition*, Cambridge MA: Harvard University Press, 2004.

SIGURÐSSON, Jón Viðar: *Chieftains and Power in the Icelandic Commonwealth*, Odense: Odense University Press, 1999.

SVEINSSON, Einar Ólafur (ed.): *Brennu-Njáls saga. Íslenzk fornrit 12*, Reykjavík: Hið íslenzka fornritafélag, 1954.

ÞORLÁKSSON, Helgi: *Sæmdarmenn: um heiður á þjóðveldisöld*, Reykjavík: Háskoli Íslands, 2001.

TILLY, Charles: *Identities, Boundaries, and Social Ties*, Boulder CO: Paradigm Publishers, 2005, pp. 13-21.

TILLY, Charles: *Stories, Identities, and Political Change*, Lanham MD: Rowman and Littlefield, 2002.

TILLY, Charles: *Trust and rule*, Cambridge: Cambridge University Press, 2005.

TULINIUS, Torfi: The Matter of the North: The Rise of Literary Fiction in Thirteenth- Century Iceland, Odense: Odense University Press, 2002.

VAUGHAN, Diane: „The Dark Side of Organizations", in: *Annual Review of Sociology* Vol. 25 (1999), pp. 271-305.

WATTS, Duncan J. and S.H. STROGATZ: „Collective Dynamics of 'Small-world' Networks", in: *Nature* Vol. 393 (1998), pp. 440-42.

WATTS, Duncan J.: *Six Degrees: The Science of a Connected Age*, New York: Norton, 2003.

WHALEY, Diana: „A Useful Past: Historical Writing in Medieval Iceland", in: Margaret Clunies Ross (ed.): *Old Icelandic Literature and Society*, Cambridge: Cambridge University Press, 2000, pp. 161-202.

WHITE, Harrison C.: *Identity and Control: How Social Formations Emerge, 2nd ed.*, Princeton: Princeton University Press, 2008.

JUDY QUINN

Precarious ties. The social critique of dynastic networking in eddic heroic poetry

Though set in the ancient past, and in lands far away from the island in the north-west Atlantic where they were committed to vellum in the late thirteenth century, many eddic heroic poems demonstrate a profound concern with social networks, in particular with the bonds of loyalty and trust forged by marriages between the powerful dynastic families around whom the stories revolve. Some eighteen poems survive in the second part of the Codex Regius anthology of eddic poems, GkS 2365 4to (Reykjavík, Stofnun Árna Magnússonar í íslenskum fræðum), a collection which was originally more substantial,[1] but which nonetheless forms the core of the eddic heroic corpus.[2] The heroic poems of the Codex Regius collection are copied in a sequence which is broadly chronological, though it is the style of many of the poems, which feature a great deal of dialogue, to range backwards and forwards across events in movements of foreboding and regret, of scheming and recrimination. While the desirability of stable networks forged through marriage and blood-brotherhood can be read as a given in the social world the poems depict, the story-lines of many of them involve broken expectations on the part of those forging network bonds, thereby exposing the risks involved in the process and the precarious nature of the ties once forged.

Estimating the date of composition of any of the eddic heroic poems – and therefore the historical period out of which such expressions of fraught social

---

[1] The manuscript now consists of forty-five leaves, written in a single hand in Iceland around 1270 (LINDBLAD: Studier i Codex regius, p. 233). The forty-five leaves are arranged in six gatherings, the first five of eight leaves each, and the last of only five leaves. There is a substantial lacuna in the manuscript between the fourth and fifth gatherings (HEUSLER: Introduction, p. 15) If, as seems probable, the gathering contained eight leaves, a substantial body of verses has been lost; given the variable length of eddic heroic poems (from eleven to 105 stanzas), it is not possible to know the precise number of poems once contained in the gathering,

[2] Additional single poems are preserved in heterogeneous contexts in other manuscripts from the medieval period and later. One poem in this category treated in this essay is *Rigsþula*, which is preserved in Codex Wormianus, AM 242 fol. (Copenhagen, Den Arnamagnæanske Samling). Poetry of a similar style dealing with ancient heroes is also preserved as quotations within *fornaldarsögur* and edited by Heusler and Ranisch as *Eddica Minora*. For a general account of the extent and preservation of the eddic corpus see HARRIS: Eddic Poetry.

negotiation might have arisen – is a difficult matter since our only material record of most of them is the manuscript text of GkS 2365 4to. The accounts of social relations recorded in some of the poems are paralleled to some degree by the prose account and occasional verse quotation preserved in the single manuscript of *Völsunga saga*, produced around the turn of the fourteenth century (NkS 1824 b 4to, Copenhagen, Det kongelige bibliotek), but comparison of these sources does little to illuminate the long life of many of the poems before they came to be copied into compilations and preserved for posterity.[3] The subject matter of the heroic poems includes mention of historical figures from late antiquity, such as the fifth-century King of the Huns, Attila, and much of the story material has parallels in contemporary continental literature (in particular the *Nibelungenlied*), indicating that a common Germanic tradition extending back centuries and stretching across many lands is likely. Moreover, the poems in the first part of the Codex Regius manuscript are set in the pre-Christian world of heathen gods and giants, a setting which points to a tradition reaching back centuries before the written tradition of eddic poetry began (in the late twelfth century at the earliest). Palaeographical analysis of the Codex Regius by Gustav Lindblad has revealed patterns of orthographic affiliation between groups of poems, indicating that the compilation had probably been built up out of earlier pamphlets produced in the middle decades of the thirteenth century.[4]

To account for the preservation of such ancient traditions we must therefore reckon on a considerable period of oral transmission for most if not all of the poems in the Codex Regius (some, it is conceivable, may have been composed at the time of the compilation or shortly beforehand), and in some cases the period of oral transmission may have stretched back centuries. Attempts to date the poems relative to one another have resulted in groupings of poems that are considered 'early' and 'late', although a robust methodology of dating, and the possibility of a finer calibration of dates, remain elusive given the textual evi-

---

[3] For a detailed comparison of sources, see von SEE: Kommentar Edda, 4: pp. 4-6.
[4] The most striking palaeographic boundary Lindblad observed was between the collection of mythological poems (ending with *Alvíssmál*) and the heroic cycle beginning halfway down folio 20a (LINDBLAD: Studier i Codex regius, pp. 266-7). Beyond the two main blocks of text, Lindblad also perceived fine-grained divisions between other poems. These patterns suggest that the Regius scribe, or possibly someone before him, interleaved poems or pairs of poems from different sources, and perhaps their organisation can be attributed in part to the groupings in which they made their way to him, or even the sequence in which they were received.

dence.⁵ While the process of aural memorization, recollection and recitation may have resulted in poems of more or less fixed form and content over time, it is possible that changes in wording, dramatization and even the configuration of the plot occurred as different minds rehearsed the poems and different communities responded to performances of them.⁶ Isolating the historical period during which each poem may have been composed and first recited is therefore of less importance than the vitality of the tradition across the generations, the earliest renderings of the heroic feats of the past apparently being memorised and performed again and again to new audiences, giving rise to new versions of events by new poets in succeeding generations, as well as the conservation of older poems through re-performance, probably within the same milieu. The overlap of subject matter between the heroic poems of the Codex Regius reveals that by the second half of the thirteenth century, multiple poems describing essentially the same events were in circulation, and whoever the audience of the collection might have been, they clearly had a taste for such variety. While modern editors have needed the specification of titles to distinguish poems now known in the critical literature as *Helgakviða Hundingsbana I* and *Helgakviða Hundingsbana II*, or *Guðrunarkviða I*, *Guðrunarkviða II* and *Guðrunarkviða III*, the compiler made sense of the works with simpler and more generic names or rubrics identifying the protagonists of each work: *Völsungakviða*, 'Frá Völsungum', *Guðrunarkviða, Guðrunarkviða* and *Kviða Guðrunar*.⁷

In oral performance, we might assume, different poems about the same legendary events also had currency, the taste for varied representations of encounters between famous figures of the past whetting the audience's appetite for the recitation of newer poems alongside older ones. In this regard, it is interesting that some poems attracted the epithet *inn förni* ('the ancient'), indicating that, to the compiler at least, a distinction was observed between poems of more recent

---

⁵ Bjarne Fidjestøl has undertaken a detailed study of the methodology used by scholars to date eddic poems, a body of poems he regards as 'lacking all certain chronology' (FIDJESTØL: Dating of Eddic Poetry, p. 195). Tables 1 and 3 (pp. 106-7 and pp. 183-4) nonetheless usefully set out Finnur Jónsson's and Jan de Vries' postulated chronology of the eddic poems.
⁶ The most distinctive example of textual variation that appears to have arisen during oral transmission is the poem *Völuspá*, which is preserved within the Codex Regius and in an independent text in the compilation manuscript, Hauksbók. For a discussion of the versions, see QUINN: Völuspá and Composition.
⁷ See QUINN: Naming of Eddic Poems.

provenance and those from the distant past.[8] Poems on similar subjects also occur within the same broad palaeographic grouping (the Guðrún poems, for instance), making it unlikely that the coincidence of subject matter was a product of the final compilation. Identifying the provenance of the manuscript as a whole is difficult on account of insufficient palaeographic comparanda,[9] and this renders the closer identification of the sources for its constituent precursors recedingly likely. In one case, however, there are distinctive orthographic and palaeographic features that separate one poem from those around it[10], and that poem, *Atlamál*, is introduced in the preceding prose by: 'Enn segir gløggra í Atlamálum inum grœnlenzkum'.[11] Coincidence of subject matter might be explained by differing geographic provenance for other poems as well – where isolated poetic traditions might have developed and been transcribed together in the manuscript – but no strong marks of such origins have been preserved in other cases.

Taken together, the extant heroic poems of the Codex Regius collection traverse the complex plot lines of several families' interactions with each other in a manner which suggests a deep and abiding interest on the part of poets composing in the eddic tradition in the probity with which social ties are formed and maintained. That there are often differences in the interpretation of the ancient events that make up the eddic heroic tradition is probably a consequence of the engaged deliberation by eddic poets over the ethical behaviour of cultural paragons, rather than the result of misguided composition or faulty transmission, as it is often assumed to be. While the social world presented in the poems is set in the distant past, at a considerable distance from the world of their audience, the continued engagement of generations of audiences with their subject matter indicates that the issues raised by relations between and within powerful fami-

---

[8] The last poem in the manuscript is designated *Hamðismál* by the rubric, and *Hamðismál in fornu* in the closing phrase at the end of the text. There is also a reference to a poem called *Guðrunarkviða in forna* in the prose between *Brot af Sigurðarkviðu* and *Guðrunarkviða I* which seems to refer to *Guðrunarkviða II*.

[9] See KARLSSON: Localisation and Dating.

[10] See LINDBLAD: Studier i Codex regius, pp. 268-9.

[11] 'And it is told more clearly in the Greenlandic *Atlamál*'. For a discussion of the provenance of the poem see DRONKE: Poetic Edda, p. 45 and pp. 107-112. All quotations of eddic poems are in normalised orthography and based on the fourth edition of Gustav Neckel and Hans Kuhn. Translations are my own, though Carolyne Larrington's translations (see LARRINGTON: Poetic Edda) inform them at many points. So too her perceptive comments on an earlier draft of this essay have sharpened my thinking on a number of points, for which I record my gratitude.

lies were by no means removed from the preoccupations of successive generations of listeners. The convention of drawing attention to the ancient times in which the action is set might even be regarded as a topos which works to signal the continuing relevance of the issues raised by the behaviour of figures who are of foundational cultural significance:

> Ár var alda, þat er arar gullu,
> hnigu heilug vötn af Himinfjöllum;
> þá hafði Helga, inn hugumstóra,
> Borghildr borit í Brálundi.[12]
>
> Ár var, þatz Sigurðr sótti Gjúka,
> Völsungr ungi er vegit hafði . . .[13]
>
> Ár var, þatz Guðrún gørðiz at deyja
> er hon sat sorgfull yfir Sigurði . . .[14]

In addition to establishing the ancient setting, some poets also validate the narrator's sources in the opening stanza of the poem by mentioning the traditional accounts on which the story line is based –

> Ár kváðu ganga grœnar brautir
> öflgan ok aldinn, ás kunnigan,
> ramman ok röskvan, Ríg stíganda.[15]

– while others draw attention to the communal nature of the tradition detailing ancient dynastic feuds:

> Frétt hefir öld ófu, þá er endr um gørðu
> seggir samkundu . . .[16]

---

[12] *Helgakviða Hundingsbana I*, 1 'It was in ancient times that the eagles shrieked, the sacred waters flowed down from Himin Mountains; then Borghildr in Brálund gave birth to Helgi, the stout-hearted.'
[13] *Sigurðarkviða in skamma* 1 'It was long ago that Sigurðr, the young Völsung who had killed, visited Gjúki . . .'.
[14] *Guðrúnarkviða I*, 1 'It was long ago that Guðrún prepared to die, when she sat, sorrowful, over Sigurðr . . .'.
[15] *Rígsþula* 1 'It was long ago, they said, that a clever god, powerful and in his prime, walked along the green paths, strong and brave Rígr, striding.'.

The opening of the poem *Oddrúnargrátr* brings to the fore the narrator's own first-hand access to ancient traditions despite the antiquity of the material, rendering each recitation of Oddrún's lament a fresh appraisal of age-old events:

> Heyrða ek segja í sögum fornum,
> hvé mær um kom til Mornalanz . . .[17]

In a similar vein the closing stanzas of poems provide narrators with an opportunity to reflect on the relevance of the subject matter for contemporary audiences. There is no doubt that the poet of *Atlamál* regarded the resilient children of Gjúki as exemplary social figures for the listening community, however removed they may have been in space and time from the setting of the action:

> Sæll er hverr síðan, er slíkt getr fœða,
> jóð at afreki, sems ól Gjúki;
> lifa mun þat eptir á land hverju,
> þeira þrámæli, hvargi er þjóð heyrir.[18]

Similarly, the narrator of *Atlakviða* clearly endorsed the heroic behaviour of a sister who took up a sword to avenge her brothers:

> Fullrœtt er um þetta; ferr engi svá síðan
> brúðr í brynju brœðra at hefna . . .[19]

Even if the behaviour of ancient heroes and heroines is not explicitly presented as exemplary, the accounts of their fortitude and uncompromising defiance are offered as solace to audiences whose own family misfortunes and personal grief are tacitly acknowledged:

---

[16] *Atlamál in grœnlenzku* 1 'People have heard of the hatred, when long ago men held a meeting . . .'.
[17] *Oddrúnargrátr* 1 'I heard it said in ancient sagas, how a girl came to Mornaland . . .'.
[18] *Atlamál in grœnlenzku* 105 'Blessed is the man who since then manages to father children of such outstanding achievements as Gjúki did; their words of defiance will live on in every land wherever people hear them.'.
[19] *Atlakviða* 43 'This has now been told in full; never since has a bride in a mail-coat avenged her brothers in such a way . . .'.

> Munu við ofstríð allz til lengi
> konur ok karlar kvikvir fœðaz . . .[20]
>
> Jörlum öllum, óðal batni,
> snótum öllum sorg at minni,
> at þetta tregróf um talið væri.[21]

That the recitation of ancient familial disputes might alleviate present sorrow for the audience reveals a perceived link between the contemplation of familiar heroic stories and a form of social catharsis, which is somehow enabling for those facing anguish born of similar social forces. While an audience of some social distinction is implied by the poet of *Guðrúnarhvöt*, the design of other poets is to affect any individual (*hverr maðr*) who must negotiate familial duties and face compromises in the fulfillment of their own personal desire:

> Saztu ok hlýddir meðan ek sagðak þér
> mörg ill um sköp mín ok þeira;
> maðr hverr lifir at munum sínum.
> nú er um genginn grátr Oddrúnar.[22]

There are many aspects of the subject matter of eddic heroic poetry that repay consideration in terms of network analysis:[23] dissent within a family over arranged marriages, in particular the choice of a husband for a daughter; entangled loyalties resulting from ties between blood kin and ties between married kin; and complications arising from alliances formed by spoken pledges are some of the most striking. Presented within these plots are what might be regarded as 'small-scale' interactions within wider social networks, the reduced focus, as we shall see, producing an intensification of consequence for each point of failure as alliances are made and remade. In order to examine these interactions in more detail, it is first necessary to provide a brief (and very much simplified) account of the dynastic networks that the eddic heroic poems depict.

---

[20] *Helreið Brynhildar* 14 'All too long in suffering must women and men – those who are living – spend their lives . . .'.
[21] *Guðrúnarhvöt* 21 'To all high-born men, may your fortune improve, to all ladies, may your sorrow be assuaged, now this chain of anguish has been recounted.'.
[22] *Oddrúnargrátr* 34 'You sat and listened while I told you the great evils in my fate and theirs; each person lives according to their desires – now Oddrún's lament is finished.'.
[23] For an outline of network theory, see BARABÁSI: Linked.

The circumstances leading to the doomed marriage of Helgi Hundingsbani Sigmundarson is the focus of the first and third poems in the cycle, *Helgakviða Hundingsbana I* and *Helgakviða Hundingsbana II*, the hero seduced into marriage by the valkyrie-princess, Sigrún Högnadóttir, thus foiling the princess's male kin who had made arrangements for her to marry Höðbroddr Granmarsson. In opposition to the judgement of her father, who must have seen political advantage in an alliance with Höðbroddr's family, Sigrún disparaged the king as an unsuitable husband for her, describing him as 'konung óneisan sem kattar son'.[24] In the second poem, which takes the plot beyond the initial romance between the hero and the valkyrie, Helgi is killed by his bride-to-be's brother, Dagr Högnason, after Helgi had killed Sigrún's father and the rest of her brothers in battle. The spurning of arranged husbands is highlighted in both poems, the second poem depicting Sigrún seeking out the dying Höðbroddr on the battle-field to taunt him with the news that the bride he sought will never fall into his arms, and that instead the grey herd of the giantess (that is, wolves) will get his corpse ('Muna þér Sigrún frá Sefafjöllum, Höðbroddr konungr, hníga at armi; . . . opt náir hrævi gránstóð gríðar. . .'; *HHII* 25/1-7). In these poems, a sister's bid for self-determination in choosing a husband puts her at odds with her brothers and father, the discrepancy between siblings' differing assessments of familial advantage played out as duel or feud between the prospective husband selected by male kin and the one chosen by the prospective wife. While the poems do not present the discussions between father and daughter that precede dissent, some parallels are found in the situation depicted in chapters 3-8 of *Völsunga saga* when King Völsungr betroths his daughter Signý to King Siggeirr. She herself is reluctant – although her brothers are keen and support her father's decision – and she pleads with her father not to make her leave her natal home after the marriage. Her pleas are ignored and her father and most of her brothers are soon betrayed and murdered by King Siggeirr. The early generations of the Völsung dynasty, as they are described in *Völsunga saga*, in fact constitute a study in the risks posed to the fledgling dynasty by marriage outside the kin group, necessitating a number of inventive stratagems (including incest and conception by means of an apple delivered by a valkyrie in the form of a crow) to create offspring without having to face the compromises in-laws bring with them.[25] It is noteworthy that the first poem of Helgi Hundingsbani ends at

---

[24] *Helgakviða Hundingsbana I*, 18/7-8 '. . . as bold a king as a kitten'.
[25] See further QUINN: Realisation of Mythological Design.

a promising point in the young lovers' lives, with the valkyrie-princess declaring the success of their alliance (*HHI* 56). The second poem, however, follows the marriage made contrary to family arrangements to its ruinous conclusion as Helgi's death in battle leads quickly to Sigrún's death through grief. The plots invite speculation on alternatives to marriages arranged against a daughter's will although the plot line of the second poem ultimately underscores the potentially destructive force of a daughter's defiant action in unilaterally choosing her own husband. In this case, interfamilial violence and the death of promising sons is the price paid for the fulfillment of a daughter's personal desire. The inclusion of both poems in the collection demonstrates the capacity of the eddic tradition to pursue different emphases in the extrapolation of social consequences from a single network link, that of Sigrún's marriage to Helgi. In the first poem the story line stops at their marriage while in the second the entailment of Helgi's action is pursued with a scene between bereaved brother and aggrieved sister followed by another scene between doomed husband and death-defying wife, both scenes playing out a range of attitudes and reactions to the conflicted situation each family member finds themselves in.

The first poems in the eddic heroic cycle display and scrutinize the crucial initial stage in the forging of strategic relationships through marriage alliances for the Völsungar: without the compliance of the prospective bride, the alliance seems doomed to fail even if the match is otherwise judged by the males of the family to be advantageous in terms of developing the family's systems of support and extending its power. The conception of the plot, however, plumbs a deeper level of social dynamics than the straightforward willingness of a daughter or sister to accede to the imperatives in forming political alliances devised by her father and brothers. By underwriting the identity of the daughter/sister as a valkyrie – a mythological figure who is an arbiter of valour on the battlefield and who chooses the very best warriors to join Óðinn in Valhöll in preparation for the ultimate campaign against the giants and other forces at *ragna rök* – the poets are exploring the serious contestation of judgement within families about marriage alliances. Sigrún's low estimation of Höðbroddr is as a king, as much as a husband, though she has apparently been unable to convince her family to pursue her high standards in trying to augment their power and prestige by profiting from the qualities embodied by Helgi Sigmundarson through marriage with him. Dagr, for his part, is disconcerted by the force of his sister's fury and her vehement cursing of him when he tells her he has killed Helgi. He unsuccessfully offers her compensation for her loss – red-gold rings, half of the family's land ('þér býðr bróðir bauga rauða . . . hafðu hálfan heim harms at gjöldum . . .' *HHII* 35/1-7) – in a bid to turn her loyalty back to her blood kin.

The choosing of a husband by a valkyrie-princess is also at the heart of the plot of *Helgakviða Hjörvarðssonar* (a poem positioned in the cycle between the two poems of Helgi Hundingsbani). In this instance, Sváva Eylimadóttir provides Helgi Hjörvarðzson with his name – her choice of name might be understood to confer a blessing on the new alliance[26] – and protects him in battle as well as from the malevolent desires of a giantess, Hrímgerðr Hatadóttir, who wants to destroy him in retaliation for him having killed her father. Although Sváva's male kin do not figure in the poem, her marriage to Helgi is apparently doomed because his own brother swears an oath to marry Sváva himself and Helgi subsequently dies in battle at the hands of Álfr Hróðmarsson. Contestation for the same bride by two brothers might well lead to acrimony and fratricide were these poems simply about family dynamics rather than dynastic politics. In this and other poems in the first movement of the heroic cycle, the ideological undercurrent of the plot is the pre-eminence of the family line selected by the valkyrie, singled out by her for protection and promotion. So it is that with Heðinn's remorse for his reckless oath to marry his brother's wife and Helgi's persuasion that his widow should afterwards love his brother that Sváva declares such an arrangement acceptable. From the outset, she says, she had been determined not to embrace willingly a man of no reputation: 'Mælt hafða ek þat . . . myndiga ek lostig . . . jöfur ókunnan armi verja' (*HHz* 42). What matters to her is not so much the individual, but her estimation of the reputation of the prospective husband in terms of his family and the heroic traits they are known for. These are immediately confirmed, as Heðinn invites Sváva to kiss him and promises at once to hunt down and dispatch Helgi's killer (*HHz* 43). The theme of vexed familial relations brought about by marriage aspirations continues in the prose passage following the three Helgi poems, *Frá dauða Sinfjötli*, in which the murder of Helgi Sigmundarson's step-brother, Sinfjötli Sigmundarson, is described: having killed his rival for an unnamed bride, Sinfjötli is poisoned by the slain man's sister, Borghildr, who is also married to Sig-

---

[26] For an account of the etymological interpretation of the name Helgi, see von SEE: Kommentar Edda, 4: p. 107 and pp. 167-8.

mundr and is therefore Sinfjötli's step-mother.[27] Her vengeful act is directed against her step-kin once the dynastic engineering she was conducting on behalf of her own kin was thwarted by Sinfjötli's murder of her brother. Having by this point also lost his second son, Helgi, Sigmundr is devastated by the death of his oldest son, Sinfjötli; in time, according to the account of *Frá dauða Sinfjötli*, he marries another woman, Hjördís Eylimadóttir, with whom he has another son, Sigurðr Sigmundarson, who is the catalyst for the events of the remaining poems in the heroic cycle.[28]

The next cluster of poems in the manuscript, from *Grípisspá* to *Guðrunarkviða II*, is principally concerned with the fraught marriage alliances between two powerful dynasties, the Gjúkungar and the Buðlungar, both families linked through betrothal, oath or marriage vow to the youngest of Sigmundr's sons, Sigurðr Fáfnisbani. Although the landscape of eddic heroic poetry is too sparsely populated to be amenable to full-blown sociological analysis, Sigurðr nonetheless figures very much as the 'consequential stranger' in the transformation of both family groups,[29] entering their lives and forming strong friendship ties with Gunnarr and Högni Gjúkason, a marriage bond with their sister Guðrún Gjúkadóttir, and – in tension with these – an ambiguous relationship through mutual vows with Brynhildr Buðladóttir. The binding nature of interpersonal pledges – both of betrothal and of blood-brotherhood – is a flash-point in the life stories of Sigurðr Sigmundarson, Gunnarr Gjúkason, Högni Gjúkason and Brynhildr Buðladóttir, yet it is the innocent party in the series of intrigues, Guðrún Gjúkadóttir (the wife of Sigurðr), who carries the poetic sequence forward into the last cluster of poems in the Codex Regius. The poems which deal with the aftermath of the Gjúkung brothers' murder of Sigurðr, their sister's husband, and the subsequent suicide of Gunnarr's wife, Brynhildr, involve a wider network of players, including Guðrún's mother, Grímhildr, her aunt Gjaflaug, her sister Gullrönd, her next two husbands, Atli Buðlason and King Jónakr, and various of Guðrún's children including her daughter with Sigurðr, Svanhildr, who marries the powerful King Jörmunrekkr. In some poems, members of Atli's family and court are drawn from the periphery into the centre of

---

[27] This event is also described in *Völsunga saga*; see von SEE: Kommentar Edda, 5: pp. 116-17.
[28] The prose account of *Frá dauða Sinfjötli* mentions another son named Hámundr between Helgi and Sigurðr, though no extant poems describe his life.
[29] On the use of this designation in network theory, see FINGERMAN: Consequential Strangers.

the action; these include his sister, Oddrún, his mistress, Herkja, and a visiting king, Þjóðrekr. Nonetheless the cast list is much shorter than the extensive range of characters who populate works such as the *Nibelungenlied* and *Þiðreks saga* with its more detailed depiction of the politics of court life and its broader focus on court entourage as well as dynastic family. Eddic poets clearly preferred an intimate cast to play out the intense dramas of betrayals of trust and revenge and they preferred a more starkly designed stage for them to play on. Though their interest is trained on so few players, the magnitude of the discord among them that arises from competing bonds has profound implications for all members of wider networks, with eddic audiences invited by poets to reflect on the fragility of the ties that are meant to bind.

While more than a few players are rarely present in the scenes depicted in eddic heroic poems, those taking part may include figures from beyond the human world, such as the giantess who accosts Brynhildr on her journey to the world of the dead, the dragon Fáfnir and the dwarf Reginn (both of whom Sigurðr kills after having extracted advice and wealth from them), and the god Óðinn and the valkyrie Sigrdrífa (both of whom provide Sigurðr with practical learning). The supernatural dimension is important in demonstrating the significance of the Völsungar to the establishment of heroic society: the sons of Völsungr, especially Helgi and Sigurðr, are marked out as valiant warriors as well as excellent sires for the next generation of heroes. Chosen by valkyries, and favoured by Óðinn, they are exemplary leaders, and yet in their own home lives they face dilemmas and conflicts of loyalty which test their mettle. More importantly, they face challenges which are not so different from those faced by successive audiences of the heroic poems: the forging of political alliances through oaths of loyalty, the furthering of the interests of the family through marriage alliances, and the maintenance of family honour in the wake of murder of siblings, parents or children. Even a cursory reading of *Sturlunga saga*, which recounts the interactions between powerful families in thirteenth-century Iceland, reveals that these issues were no less important in the social politics of the thirteenth century than they had been in earlier centuries. But whereas the *realpolitik* of the eddic audience's own community (whether of the thirteenth century or earlier) would have involved very complex social networks and only some of the jostling for strategic advantage that was going on behind the scenes would have been public, in the recreated world of ancient heroic society the number of players is limited with the result that the challenges and dilemmas facing them can be displayed in their full intensity. So, for instance, both Brynhildr and Sigurðr emerge onto the eddic scene as loners, Brynhildr as a particularly wilful valkyrie who has defied Óðinn and been condemned by him to sleep in an isolated shield-hut until a particular hero, who knows no fear, can wake her,[30] and Sigurðr, a prince of the Völsung dynasty who arrives on the set as a kind of lone ranger. In the prose passage introducing the poems about Sigurðr, *Frá dauða Sinfjötla*, the others Völsung brothers – all of whom were 'langt um fram alla menn aðra um afl ok vöxt ok hug ok alla atgervi'[31] – fall away from the narrative which focuses solely on Sigurðr: 'Sigurðr reið einn saman ok kom til hallar . . . Sigurðr var auðkennr.'[32]

But the treatment of the hero Sigurðr by eddic poets, particularly in relation to his culpability as an oath-breaker, varies considerably from poem to poem in the Codex Regius collection, with varying perspectives exposed as characters hammer out their differences in the fraught conversations which constitute most of the verse.[33] For instance, in *Grípisspá* (a poem I will return to later in this essay), Sigurðr expresses his undisguised alarm at the implications of the oath-breaking that lies ahead of him, whereas in other poems prominence is given to his keeping of his pact with the Gjúkung brothers instead. While the seriousness of oaths is never in doubt among poets, there seems to be casuistic ingenuity on the part of some poets in lightening the burden of Sigurðr's guilt in pledging his troth to Brynhildr through various ploys of double identity: his as Gunnarr, and hers as Sigrdrífa. Other media, such as wood-carvings and rune-stones, concentrate on Sigurðr as a dragon-slayer,[34] an event that is almost side-lined by eddic poets who focus instead on his probity as a leader of men and husband. Eddic poets' flexing of the plot-line (post-Fáfnir) and their interrogation of the values Sigurðr stands for indicate a profound interest in him as a cultural model, tested in complex familial and social situations to assess the quality of his judgement.

---

[30] The complicated relations between the story of the sleeping valkyrie and the eddic portrayal of Brynhildr and Sigrdrífa are set out in von SEE: Kommentar Edda, 5: pp. 507-516.
[31] '. . . far surpassed all other men in strength and stature and courage and all abilities'.
[32] 'Sigurðr rode by himself and came to a hall . . . Sigurðr was easy to recognise'.
[33] The variegated treatment of Sigurðr in eddic heroic poetry was the subject of a paper I presented at the Fourteenth International Saga Conference in Uppsala in August 2009, QUINN: Betrothal and betrayal, where my focus was on the capacity of the eddic tradition to generate a multiplicity of perspectives on heroic behaviour through the composition of different genres out of the same plot material.
[34] See ROWE: Quid Sigvardus cum Christo.

The circumstances of the oath-making and breaking are set out in more or less chronological order in *Sigurðarqviða in skamma*, a poem reckoned among the younger compositions preserved in the Codex Regius collection, and as such, one that is to some extent in dialogue with older poems. Like *Völsunga saga*, the poem follows the sweep of narrative the encounter between the Völsungar and the Gjúkungar engenders, drawing multiple perspectives together through a sequence of short dramatic scenes: the days of drinking and debate between the young Völsung and the Gjúkung boys before they set off to woo Brynhildr; the laying of the exposed sword by Sigurðr between his body and Brynhildr's; the intense soliloquy Brynhildr begins outdoors on a glacier at dusk as she acknowledges her desire to have Sigurðr and no-one else – a speech she continues inside, as heated incitement, to the husband she was not meant to marry; and Gunnarr's anguished reflection on what, in the circumstances, he should do once she announces she will leave him to return to her natal kin unless Sigurðr is killed. And all that in just the first thirteen stanzas of the 71-stanza poem. Like *Völsunga saga*, the poem aims to present a chronological narrative, linking events through reported dialogue in which characters' motivations are sometimes articulated but more often only obliquely revealed.

According to *Sigurðarqviða in skamma*, in return for marriage to Guðrún Gjukadóttir, Sigurðr agrees to betrothe himself to Brynhildr while impersonating Guðrún's brother Gunnarr. The narrative obscures the detail of the deal –

> . . . tók við trygðum tveggja brœðra;
> selduz eiða eljunfrœknir.[35]

– but it does register the exchange that takes place: a bride for a favour.

> Mey buðu honum ok meiðma fjölð,
> Guðrúnu ungu, Gjúka dóttur;
> drukku ok dœmðu dœgr mart saman,
> Sigurðr ungi ok synir Gjúka.[36]

---

[35] *Sigurðarkviða in skamma* 1 '. . . he [Sigurðr] accepted pledges from both brothers; the energetic warriors made oaths'.

[36] *Sigurðarkviða in skamma* 2 'They offered him a bride, and a lot of wealth, they offered him young Guðrún, Gjúki's daughter; they drank and talked for many days together, young Sigurðr and the sons of Gjúki'.

The Gjúkungar understandably wish to make favourable marriage alliances and to augment their political network with promising in-laws. The challenge for them, as they cultivate new connections and co-operative alliances, is to moderate the risk of disloyalty from any of the parties. In gaining Sigurðr's fidelity through the swearing of pledges and days spent together forging strong bonds of brotherhood, the Gjúkung brothers overlook the possibility that disloyalty might come from other quarters and neglect the fact that other sensibilities need to be considered in the execution of the double-marriage scheme.

The fundamental compromise on Sigurðr's part – wealth and a wife as reward for duping Brynhildr into marrying Gunnarr – becomes clear as the party of young men visits Brynhildr:

> Unz þeir Brynhildar biðja fóru,
> svá at þeim Sigurðr reið í sinni,
> Völsungr ungi er vega kunni;
> hann um ætti, ef hann eiga knætti.[37]

The discrepancy between his sentiments and his actions foregrounds the notion of integrity, as the paragon of legendary warriors woos sincerely, but on behalf of another. The issue of trust comes to the fore in these stanzas, as the innocent Brynhildr is drawn unwittingly into the trio's scheme. Her blamelessness is unequivocal, according to the poet:

> Hon sér at lífi löst né vissi
> ok at aldrlagi ekki grand,
> vamm þat er væri eða vera hygði.
> Gengu þess á milli grimmar urðir.[38]

Another thirteenth-century version of the ancient event sheds light on how the integrity of a hero was imagined, and how culpable Sigurðr might therefore be regarded to be in deceiving Brynhildr. In Snorri's account in *Skáldskaparmál*, Sigurðr and Gunnarr exchange both appearances and names:

---

[37] *Sigurðarkviða in skamma* 3 'Until they went to ask for Brynhildr, and for this Sigurðr rode in their company, the young Völsung who knew the way, he would have married her if he could have'. The phrase 'er vega kunni' might also be understood as 'who knew how to fight'; see further von SEE: Kommentar Edda, 6: pp. 323-4.

[38] *Sigurðarkviða in skamma* 5 'She knew no wrong in her life nor harm in her future, no vice that was or could be imagined. The cruel fates intervened in this.'

> Þá ríðu þeir Sigurðr ok Gjúkungar . . . upp á fjallit ok skyldi þá Gunnarr ríða vafrlogann. Hann átti hest þann er Goti heitir, en sá hestr þorði eigi at hlaupa í eldinn. Þá skiptu þeir litum Sigurðr ok Gunnarr ok svá nöfnum því at Grani vildi undir øngum manni ganga nema Sigurði. Þá hljóp Sigurðr á Grana ok reið vafrlogann. Þat kveld gekk hann at brúðlaupi með Brynhildi. En er þeir kvámu í sæing þá dró hann sverðit Gram ór slíðrum ok lagði í milli þeira. En at morni þá er hann stóð upp ok klæddi sik, þá gaf hann Brynhildi at línfé gullbauginn . . . en tók af henni annan baug til minja. Sigurðr hljóp þá á hest sinn ok reið til félaga sinna. Skipta þeir Gunnarr þá aptr litum ok fóru aptr til Gjúka með Brynhildi.[39]

The prism of animal instinct helps to focus the social ethics of the situation. The only horse able to clear the flame hurdle, Grani, will only be spurred on by a rider named Sigurðr, his own performance as a fearless horse seemingly dependent on the known reputation of his rider. The double dealing Gunnarr and Sigurðr engage in might fool humans, but the horse is not tricked by a rider who just looks like his master: his equine sense apparently picks up the fact that Gunnarr, whatever his temporary appearance, is not the fearless hero he knows his master to be. In order to make good whatever the detail of the oath he has sworn to the Gjúkung brothers, Sigurðr has to lend not just his handsome form to Gunnarr but he has to take on the quest himself, in his own name. Sigurðr, looking like Gunnarr, but in all other respects himself, and still going by the name of Sigurðr, effects the quest and marries Brynhildr.

After marrying her, but promulgating non-consummation by placing a sword between them in the bed, Sigurðr returns to his companions and resumes his own appearance. But not before commemorating the event by an exchange of rings, the ring Brynhildr gives him, according to Snorri's account, recklessly –

---

[39] *Skáldskaparmál* I, 47/33-48/7, (Page and line numbers are to the 1998 edition of *Skáldskaparmál* by Anthony FAULKES.) 'Then Sigurðr and the Gjúkungs . . . rode up on to the mountain and Gunnarr was then meant to charge through the leaping flames. He had a horse called Goti, but it shied away from galloping through the fire. Then Sigurðr and Gunnarr swapped appearances, and names as well, because Grani would not move under any rider except Sigurðr. Then Sigurðr mounted Grani and rode through the leaping flames. That evening he married Brynhildr. But when they went to bed, he drew his sword Gramr from its sheath and placed it between them. In the morning when he got up and got dressed, he gave Brynhildr a gold ring as a morning gift . . . and he accepted from her another ring as a memento. Sigurðr mounted his horse and rode back to his companions. He and Gunnarr then changed back to their own forms and they returned to Gjúki with Brynhildr.'

bigomously – given by Sigurðr to his next wife Guðrún, who undoes the entire masculine subterfuge by boasting of it to Brynhildr some time later in a memorable scene by a river (*Skáldskaparmál* 48/9-22). Given that Sigurðr is said to have been *auðkennr* and Brynhildr later professes to have betrothed herself to him because his eyes and demeanour were so *unlike* the Gjúkung brothers ('varat hann í augu yðr um líkr, né á engi hlut at álitum' *Sigurðarqviða in skamma* 39), the deception is presented as having been consummate, his fearless manner convincing her that he was the man for her, despite the identity of the body through which he performed. Just as the eyes reveal the essential nature of his identity, so too the voice – which comes from deep within the body – might be understood to stem from the same being who has no fear and whose eyes shone brighter than a Gjúkung's. From Brynhildr's point of view then, the one who pledged his troth to her was, in all but outer appearance, Sigurðr. The fundamental ethical question thrown up by the plot, therefore, is whether Sigurðr is bound by the betrothal vow to Brynhildr which he has voiced while impersonating another. Perhaps earlier tradition exonerated Sigurðr, but later eddic poets, such as the poets of *Sigurðarqviða in skamma* (and *Grípisspá*, to which I will turn shortly), returned to the scene and restaged it. In re-imagining the dialogue, they subjected the ethical behaviour of heroic figures to a greater degree of scrutiny.

Sigurðr's split identity also has ramifications for another crucial aspect of the pact he has apparently made with Gunnarr: that while impersonating Gunnarr, he will not make love to Brynhildr. Yet on his death-bed, Sigurðr stakes his reputation on the fact that he kept his deal with Gunnarr, despite his betrayal of Brynhildr:

> . . . enn við Gunnar grand ekki vannk;
> þyrmða ek sifjum, svörnum eiðum,
> síðr værak heitinn hans kvánar vinr.[40]

In the eddic heroic tradition a false oath works as a kind of lever, prompting shifting perspectives on an individual's responsibilities and reputation. Responsibilities arising from the oaths between Sigurðr and the Gjúkungar are themselves contested between poems, Sigurðr reducing the scope of his deceit by

---

[40] *Sigurðarqviða in skamma* 28 '. . . and I caused no harm to Gunnarr; I preserved kinship, sworn oaths; I ought not have been called afterwards his wife's lover.'

claiming here that at the very least, he should not be called Gunnarr's wife's lover. In order to exonerate himself, however, he must blame Brynhildr:

> ... ein veldr Brynhildr öllu bölvi.
> Mér unni mær fyr mann hvern ... .[41]

In Sigurðr's view (in this poem), it is Brynhildr's determined attachment to him that is the source of the tragedy: it is her vow to marry a man without fear, and her subsequent oath of betrothal to that man, that he attempts to subordinate to the oaths he swore to the Gjúkungar, perhaps forgetting that a hero should recognise how ineluctable the will of a valkyrie-princess is. In Brynhildr's view (in another poem), being deprived of her chosen husband is not just the cause of personal sorrow, it is the very undoing of the oath-abiding character she is:

> Ek mun segja þér ...
> hvé gørðu mik Gjúka arfar
> ástarlausa ok eiðrofa.[42]

> ... þá varð ek þess vís, er ek vildigak,
> at þau véltu mik í verfangi.[43]

The importance of being trustworthy and behaving honourably to the probity and reputation of a young adult male is crucial, both in the ancient world in which eddic heroic poems were set and in the social world in which they were performed in later centuries. In the sequence of advice stanzas the valkyrie delivers to Sigurðr, being true to one's word is second only to being blameless in dealing with one's kin:

> Þat ræð ek þér annat, at þú eið né sverir,
>   nema þann er saðr sé;
> grimmar símar ganga at trygðrofi,
>   armr er vára vargr.[44]

---

[41] *Sigurðarqviða in skamma* 27-8 '. . . Brynhildr caused the whole misfortune. The girl loves me more than any other man. . .'.
[42] *Helreið Brynhildar* 5 'I will tell you . . . how the sons of Gjúki made me love-bereft and an oath-breaker'.
[43] *Helreið Brynhildar* 13 '. . .then I found out what I did not want to know, that they had deceived me in the taking of a husband'.

And there is no ignoring the responsibilities triggered by an oath, as Sigrún reminded her brother Dagr as she cursed him, predicting that the sworn oaths he had broken would *bíta* (*Helgaqviða Hundingsbana II* 31).

In the fragmentary poem that is preserved after the lacuna in the Codex Regius (known as *Brot af Sigurðarkviðu*), Sigurðr's two oaths become entangled as Brynhildr engineers his death for the false oaths he made with her and Gunnarr declares that he is the victim of Sigurðr's deception:

> Mér hefir Sigurðr selda eiða,
> eiða selda, alla logna;
> þá vélti hann mik, er hann vera skyldi
> allra eiða einn fulltrúi.[45]

Brynhildr denounces the Gjúkungar as well as Sigurðr as oath-breakers, predicting that this flaw will spell the end of their dynastic ambition:

> Svá mun öll yður ætt Niflunga
> afli gengin: eruð eiðrofa.[46]

Even Guðrún, who at first benefitted from her brothers' subterfuge in gaining the pre-eminent Sigurðr as her husband, lays the blame – with hindsight – for the collapse of her family's fortune on Gunnarr's behaviour:

> Svá ér um lýða landi eyðit,
> sem ér um unnuð eiða svarða . . .[47]

She condemns him for the deception conceived in the formulation of his oaths with Sigurðr, presumably because of his impolitic assessment of the risk involved in swapping appearances and trying to deceive Brynhildr.

---

[44] *Sigrdrífumál* 23 'The second piece of advice I give to you is do not swear an oath unless it be sincere; cruel consequences follow breach of troth, wretched is the vow-wolf'.

[45] *Brot af Sigurðarkviðu* 2 'Sigurðr has given oaths to me, oaths he gave, all were broken; then he deceived me when he should have been completely sincere in every one of his oaths'.

[46] *Brot af Sigurðarkviðu* 16 'And so the strength will drain from the entire dynasty of the Niflungar: you are oath-breakers'.

[47] *Guðrúnarqviða in fyrsta* 21 'So because of you the land and the people are devastated, as oaths were sworn because of you . . .'.

Earlier in the plot sequence of *Sigurðarqviða in skamma*, the poet dwells on the detail of the subterfuge perpetrated by the Gjúkung brothers to highlight its unconscionable nature. Once Brynhildr has discovered their treachery, the poet turns to the reactions of the two brothers. In anguish at the thought of losing her, Gunnarr ponders what the most honourable thing for him to do would be, or what would be best for him to do, for as the poet says, Gunnarr knew he had to get rid of the Völsung prince, and that Sigurðr would be a great loss. The network imperative of stabilising his family's power demands of Gunnarr an impossible move: to undo the network bond to Sigurðr without collateral damage. Gunnarr turned various plans over in his mind for a long time (*Sigurðarqviða in skamma* 13-14), before making a particularly dishonourable proposal to his brother Högni –

> Villdu okr fylki til fjár véla?[48]

– to which Högni replies:

> Samir eigi okr slíkt at vinna,
> sverði rofna svarna eiða,
> eiða svarna, unnar trygðir.[49]

Gunnarr may forget it, Sigurðr may try to obscure it, but as Högni enunciates, oaths matter. Even a raven is drawn into the debate (in another poem), crying out to Gunnarr after he had killed Sigurðr to warn him that the oaths of friendship he had now sundered will destroy him:

> ... hrafn at meiði hátt kallaði:
> 'Ykr mun Atli eggjar rjóða,
> munu vígská of viða eiðar'.[50]

To some poets, the naked sword which Sigurðr deployed to protect his reputation (and his pact with the Gjúkung brothers) becomes instead an emblem of his

---

[48] *Sigurðarqviða in skamma* 16 'Will you, for our sake, betray the prince for money?'.
[49] *Sigurðarqviða in skamma* 17 'It would hardly be honourable for us to do such a thing, sundering with a sword our sworn oaths, oaths we've sworn by, pledges we've made'.
[50] *Brot af Sigurðarqviðu* 5 '... a raven called out loudly from a tree: "Atli will redden sword-edges on you, oaths will destroy battle-hardened men"'.

compromise. So it is later in *Sigurðarqviða in skamma*, with Brynhildr insisting that the same decorated sword lie between their bodies in death because it was with them in the betrothal bed when they declared to each other that they were a couple:

> Liggi okkar enn í milli málmr hringvariðr,
> egghvast járn, svá endr lagið.
> þá er við bæði beð einn stigum
> ok hétum þá hjóna nafni.[51]

The iconic nature of the naked sword to some extent overdetermines Sigurðr's protested blamelessness: unsheathed it is potent and incriminating and a volatile emblem of his virile presence, albeit a presence that is not strictly his, but Gunnarr's. The implicit admission, however, that it would have been wrong for him to have a sexual relationship with Brynhildr while appearing to be Gunnarr makes it clear that the fundamental identity of the body lying on one side of the sword is Sigurðr's and not Gunnarr's. According to the poet of *Helreið Brynhildar*, Brynhildr's virginity was assured not by a token championed by Sigurðr, but by her own word:

> Sváfu við ok unðum í sæing einni,
> sem hann minn bróðir um borinn væri . . .[52]

For her part, Brynhildr lays the blame for her deception as much at the feet of the Gjúkung brothers as at Sigurðr's, taking a broader view of the strategic miscalculation of the Gjúkungar in assuming they could profit so handsomely from the more or less simultaneous marriage of both the daughter and son of the family to the preeminent marriage partners of their day. Brynhildr accuses Gunnarr of knowingly devising the deceit:

---

[51] *Sigurðarkviða in skamma* 68 'Lay between us again the ring-hilted sword, the edge-sharp iron, as it lay before, when we both got into one bed together and betrothed ourselves as a couple'.

[52] *Helreið Brynhildar* 12 'We slept and were content in one bed, as though he had been born my brother . . .'.

> Segja mun ek þér, Gunnarr – sjálfr veiztu gerla –
> hvé ér yðr snemma til saka réðuð;[53]
>
> Margs á ek minnaz, hvé við mik fóru,
> þá er mik sára svikna höfðuð;
> vaðin at vilja vark, meðan ek lifðak.[54]

She refuses to forget, let alone forgive, the treachery of the Gjúkungar against her and specifically identifies the loss of her *vilja* (her 'joy' or 'self-determination') as the catalyst for her retaliation. Like the Helgi poems, the poems presenting Brynhildr's life underscore the importance of marriages made in accordance with a woman's wishes.

The poem *Grípisspá* presents a particularly interesting perspective on the ethical crisis of Sigurðr's life, as the clashing oaths he made bring about his undoing. It is a dialogue poem in which the still-furled plot is revealed to Sigurðr through prophecy interleaved with his shocked reaction at the prospect of his own actions. Faced with the complex and often contradictory accounts of the dynastic networking of the Gjúkungar, the poet devises a way of interrogating Sigurðr at a point before he has made any of his compromising oaths, in order to articulate a strongly ethical view of how a young hero (and prospective husband) should behave. To Grípir's prescient observation –

> Iþ munuð alla eiða vinna
> ullfastliga, fá munuð halda . . .[55]

– he responds:

> . . . sér þú geðleysi í grams skapi?
> er ek skal við mey þá málum slíta,
> er ek allz hugar unna þóttumk.[56]

---

[53] *Sigurðarqviða in skamma* 34 'I will tell you, Gunnarr – though you know it yourself full well – how from the beginning you set out to cause strife'.
[54] *Sigurðarqviða in skamma* 57 'There is much I call to mind, how they behaved towards me, those who have bitterly betrayed me; I was deprived of joy during my life'.
[55] *Grípisspá* 31 'You two [Sigurðr and Brynhildr] will swear all oaths indelibly, few will you keep. . .'.
[56] *Grípisspá* 32 '. . . do you see lack of probity in the prince's character? if I should break my word with that girl whom I thought I loved with all my heart'.

Untarnished by the compromises yet to come, Sigurðr also expresses outrage, in prospect, at the deception involved in swapping appearances with Gunnarr:

> Hví gegnir þat? hví skulum skipta
> litum ok látum, er á leið erum?
> þar mun fláræði fylgja annat,
> atalt með öllu . . .[57]

At Grípir's revelation that he will affect Gunnarr's appearance and manner, but maintain his own *mælska* and *meginhyggja* ('eloquence' and 'powerful mind'), Sigurðr exclaims:

> Verst hyggjum því, vándr munk heitinn,
> Sigurðr, með seggjum, at sógüru;
> vilda ek eigi vélum beita
> jöfra brúði, er ek œzta veitk.[58]

Though the idealism of youth, and perhaps volition,[59] will later desert him, he is categorical in his denunciation of his predicted betrayal of Brynhildr. The laying of a sword between nubile bodies is not offered as a defence in this poem – though Grípir refers to Sigurðr as *hers oddviti* ('spearhead of the army', or 'leader') when he describes the three nights he sleeps with Brynhildr (st. 41). Instead, Sigurðr registers disbelief that Gunnarr could marry Brynhildr after she has spent these nights with him:

---

[57] *Grípisspá* 38 'What's the point of that? Why would we exchange our appearance and manner when we are on our journey? More treacherous conniving will follow there, utterly terrible...'.
[58] *Grípisspá* 40 'I think that the worst: I, Sigurðr, will be called repugnant by men for doing that; I would not wish to use deceit against the noble bride, whom I know to be best'.
[59] *Völsunga saga* (ch. 28) explains Sigurðr's neglect of his oath to Brynhildr as the result of a drink of forgetfulness given to him by Guðrún's mother Grímhildr; Grímhildr's culpability is also alluded to in *Grípisspá* 51. See JÓNSSON: Völsunga saga.

> Mun góða kván Gunnarr eiga,
> mærr, með mönnum – mér segðu, Grípir! –
> þóat hafi þrjár nætr þegns brúðr hjá mér,
> snarlynd, sofit? slíks eruð dæmi.[60]

To the poet of *Grípisspá*, behaviour such as Sigurðr's should not, in turn, serve as a *dæmi* of social conduct, or be viewed as exemplary by any means. Yet the poet contrives to redeem Sigurðr by representing him distancing himself vocally from his future actions, the poem as a whole exonerating him as a kind of confused accessory to fate. Despite the proleptic protests, the double marriage goes ahead, as Grípir foretells ('saman munu brullaup bæði drukkin', *Grípisspá* 43), and Sigurðr, still pondering the implications of what he has been told, realises that both men can hardly triumph after such treachery, and that each kin-group will undoubtedly suffer:

> Hvé mun at yndi eptir verða
> mægð með mönnum? mér segðu, Grípir!
> mun Gunnari til gamans ráðit
> síðan verða, eða sjálfum mér?[61]

When Grípir describes to Sigurðr how he will remember his oaths to Brynhildr but keep quiet about them (st. 45), Sigurðr openly acknowledges his responsibility for her misery:

> . . . hefir snót af mér svarna eiða,
> enga efnda, enn unat lítit.[62]

While the Codex Regius cycle of eddic poems introduces Sigurðr in the prose link following the Helgi poems as 'allra framarstr, ok hann kalla allir menn í

---

[60] *Grípisspá* 42 'Will Gunnarr marry the good woman, famous among men? – tell me, Grípir! – even though, for three nights, the warrior's bride, resolute in spirit, has slept beside me? – such a thing is without example.'
[61] *Grípisspá* 44 'How may these relationships-by-marriage bring pleasure to people afterwards? Will Gunnarr have enjoyment from this, or will I?'.
[62] *Grípisspá* 46 '. . . the lady has from me sworn oaths, none kept, and little contentment'.

fornfrœðum um alla menn fram ok göfgastan herkonunga',[63] there is, as we have seen, no consensus among the voices of ancient tradition about Sigurðr's culpability as a breaker of oaths. Poets appear to have returned to the issue again and again, as they scoured the plot for social values which their audiences might appreciate. It remains a paradox of eddic heroic poetry – so attuned to representing crucial scenes through dialogue – that the betrothal scene between Sigurðr and Brynhildr is shrouded in paraphrase and complexities of plot: the one conversation we might have liked to hear verbatim is instead spun into many fractured reports, laden with blame and attempted exculpation. In part this may be a consequence of the lacuna in the manuscript, into which so much poetry fell, but it is also in part characteristic of a story-line that excited so much interest among eddic poets over a considerable period of time – probably from the moment when the plot was first cast in alliterative measure in a Scandinavian language, to the repeated re-investigation of betrayals and reprisals and the detailed re-imagining, right through the twelfth and thirteenth centuries, of conversations between these ancient figures. The twisting of the many-stranded eddic plots into a more or less single thread by the author of *Völsunga saga* is, of course, a significant piece of evidence for the reception history of the Völsung tradition, but its flattened story-line necessarily loses the often startling dimensions of encounters portrayed in the eddic mode which create the space for poets to probe personal motivation and dynastic strategy in the forging of network ties.

The gambit of the Gjúkungar, to achieve advantageous marriage alliances simultaneously for a daughter and a son, by marrying the former to Sigurðr and betrothing the latter by means of Sigurðr, is not brought to a successful close. The compromises inherent in their stratagem materialise as risks which, in the end, are effectively out of their control: even once she is married and brought within the Gjúkung family, Brynhildr is strong-willed enough to threaten to return to her blood-kin (*Sigurðarqviða in skamma* 11) and nullify the arrangement made through deception. Had Gunnarr been content with his own modest level of fearfulness and aspired to marrying a less scrupulous bride than Brynhildr, the Gjúkungar might, hypothetically, have thrived on the strength of the excellent match between Sigurðr and Guðrún alone. To express this in terms of strategic marriage alliances, the Gjúkungar might have profited from securing

---

[63] '. . . then the most outstanding of all, and everyone in ancient tradition calls him foremost among men and the most magnificent of warrior-kings'.

one advantageous link at a time, extending their network in two independent directions. The choice of Sigurðr and Brynhildr as respective spouses for Guðrún and Gunnarr is unpropitious because they are already linked (either by prior engagement or by betrothal through impersonation, depending on the particular poetic representation). To choose two marriage partners who have just themselves formed a new family unit (verbally, at least) dissolves the lateral augmentation that was planned and takes network creation instead into a fatal *cul-de-sac* for the Gjúkungar.

As a consequence of the compact focus of eddic heroic poetry, the 'weak ties' of network theory are generally accorded very little importance in the playing out of dynastic plots, except insofar as treachery is sometimes sourced from beyond the family, from untrustworthy members of court such as Herkja (King Atli's mistress in *Guðrúnarkviða III*), Vingi (King Atli's duplicitous messenger in *Atlamál*) or Bikki (King Jörmunrekkr's counsellor who betrays Svanhildr according to *Sigurðarkviða in skamma* and the prose preface to *Guðrúnarhvöt*). Most often, treachery comes from within the tight network of the family and what is pursued with great interest by eddic poets is what might be termed the 'complicated tie', where a network reaches out to a new player who is from the beginning (or quickly thereafter) compromised in their loyalty to different members of the exisiting network. In the concentrated social networks depicted in eddic heroic poetry, the attention is in fact on the critical weakness of certain strong ties, particularly that between brother and sister.[64] The bond between sister and brother is a highly dynamic one, changing as loyalty ebbs and flows between siblings during their lives as their bonds with new families develop and events turn them towards or away from their natal kin. The fraught relationship between Sigrún and Dagr – the brother who killed his sister's husband as revenge for Helgi's killing of their father and who is consequently cursed by her (*Helgakviða Hundingsbana II*) – was mentioned earlier in this essay. Guðrún too is deeply disaffected by the behaviour of her brothers after they murder her husband Sigurðr (*Guðrúnarkviða I*), though the complications inherent in this tie twist around when she murders her second husband, Atli Buðlason, as revenge for his killing of her brothers (*Atlakviða*). Another interesting instance is the sibling relations of Brynhildr herself.

---

[64] For a full discussion of sibling relationships in eddic heroic poetry, see LARRINGTON: Sibling Drama.

Brynhildr's extant eddic biography is not straightforward: while she is described as the daughter of Buðli and the foster-daughter of Heimir, some of the events of her life run parallel to those of Sigrdrífa, a valkyrie whose kinship ties are not elaborated but whose domain seems closer to the mythological than the human. According to *Sigurðarqviða in skamma*, Brynhildr claimed not to have wanted to marry at all, until the Gjúkung brothers and Sigurðr rode into her court ('Né ek vilda þat at mik verr ætti . . .'; st. 35). Her brother Atli, however, threatened not to give her the inheritance she had been allotted as a child unless she married (*Sigurðarqviða in skamma* 36), a tactic designed to ensure the Buðlungar can exploit strategic advantages through marriage alliances of all their offspring. Brynhildr reconciled herself to Atli's demand, according to this poem at least, satisfying herself with the additional wealth she expected marriage to Sigurðr would bring:

> Létum síga sáttmál okkar;
> lék mér meirr í mun meiðmar þiggja,
> bauga rauða, burar Sigmundar,
> né ek annars mannz aura vildak.[65]

Crucial to her decision is the singularity of her chosen husband, a point she reiterates in the next stanza as she makes clear to Gunnarr that he had never been the husband she wanted:[66]

> . . . þeim hétomk þá
> er með gulli sat á Grana bógum;
> varat hann í augu yðr um líkr,
> né á engi hlut at álitum . . .[67]

---

[65] *Sigurðarqviða in skamma* 38 'We let our disagreement drop; I was more inclined to accept the treasure, the red-gold rings of Sigmund's son; nor did I want the money of any other man'.

[66] Editors since Sophus Bugge have rearranged the order of stanzas in this section of the poem, moving stanza 39 before stanza 36 (see von SEE: Kommentar Edda, 6: 39ff). In my reading of the poem I am following the order of the manuscript, which clearly describes Brynhildr betrothing herself to Sigurðr, since the antecedent of 'þeim' in stanza 39 is 'burr Sigmundar' of stanza 38.

[67] *Sigurðarqviða in skamma* 39 '. . . to that one I promised myself then, as he sat with the gold on Grani's back; he was not at all like you Gjúkungar about the eyes, nor in his appearance in any way. . .'.

The degree of volition on Brynhildr's part in marrying at all is represented rather differently in *Guðrúnarkviða I*, where Atli's greed is credited as the impulse that forced her into marriage:

> Þá kvað þat Brynhildr, Buðla dóttir:
> 'Veldr einn Atli öllu bölvi,
> of borinn Buðla, bróðir minn,
> þá er við í höll húnskrar þjóðar
> eld á jöfri ormbeðs litum . . .'[68]

The strength of Brynhildr's will matched with the pre-eminence of Sigurðr as a warrior-prince makes for an intense consideration of ethical issues in these poems, including the relative value of conflicting oaths and the possibility of self-determination among scheming kin groups, issues which clearly maintained a purchase on the imagination of audiences for many centuries. Brynhild is not the only eddic heroine who faced fraternal compulsion to marry. While grieving over her murdered husband Sigurðr, Guðrún is first offered compensation by her brothers for his death in a bid to re-establish the trust essential to good relations between siblings:

> Hverr vildi mér hnossir velja,
> hnossir velja ok hugat mæla,
> ef þeir mætti mér margra súta
> trygðir vinna, né ek trúa gerðak.[69]

The breach in trust has been too great, however, and Guðrún is no longer a biddable sister willing to be deployed by her family in their schemes for new marriage alliances, no matter how much emphasis is placed on selecting the very best of treasures for her. It takes drugs to make her compliant (*Guðrúnarkviða II*, 21-4), but even then her next marriage is against her will:

> Vilk eigi ek með veri ganga
> né Brynhildar bróður eiga . . .[70]

---

[68] *Guðrúnarkviða I*, 25-6 'Then Brynhildr, daughter of Buðli, said this: "Atli alone, born of Buðli, my brother, caused all this misery, when we, in the hall of the Hunnish people, saw the fire of the serpent's bed [> gold] on the prince. . ."'.

[69] *Guðrúnarkviða II*, 20 'Each wanted to select treasures for me, to select treasures and speak pleasingly, that they might win my trust despite the great sorrows, but I was unable to believe them'.

The marriage to Atli the Gjúkungar arrange for Guðrún seems ill advised on a number of counts, not least her own opposition to it. Rather than extending their dynastic network outwards to fresh family lines, the Gjúkungar turn again towards an already complicated tie, to an existing brother-in-law whose wife (their sister) has killed herself because of the deception perpetrated by them. While the offer of their sister to Atli might be interpreted as a form of appeasement, or even compensation, for the loss of his sister, the strategy of the Gjúkungar is at best a risky one. Rather than strengthening an established tie by reinforcing it, the social obligations accompanying the bond with Atli draw the Gjúkung brothers into lethal danger. The bad blood between the families darkens and the Gjúkungar lose both their sons Gunnarr and Högni to Atli's murderous scheming as well as seeing their daughter Guðrún turned into the antithesis of a dynastic bride. By murdering her sons with Atli she ensures there are no survivors who might avenge Atli, but she also truncates the Gjúkung line of succession and jeopardises the survival of the dynasty into the next generation. According to *Sigurðarqviða in skamma* 12, Gunnarr seems to have already killed Guðrún's first son at the time of Sigurðr's murder, and the daughter of that marriage is also murdered in due course by her mischievously misinformed husband (prose preface to *Guðrúnarhvöt*).

Such dismal prospects, born out of the tragic misjudgements of Sigurðr and the Gjúkung brothers, might have provided enough material for most eddic poets to mould into scenes of fury and grief. But at least one poet explores another strand of the tradition which posits an even more complicated tie between the family networks of the Gjúkungar and the Buðlungar. The poet of *Oddrúnargrátr*, another poem generally reckoned to be among the younger poems of the corpus, describes the fraught relationship between Atli and another of his sisters, Oddrún, who became Gunnarr's lover after her sister's suicide. Furthermore, the poem presents Oddrún's claim that her father had intended her to become Gunnarr's wife in the first place, instead of Brynhildr.[71] The underlying plot of the poem is complex and centres on the parallel affairs between Oddrún and Gunnarr and between another dynastic princess, Borgný, and her

---

[70] *Guðrúnarkviða* II, 27 'I do not myself want to go to another husband, nor to marry Brynhildr's brother . . .'.

[71] For a discussion of the order of stanzas in this phase of the plot of *Oddrúnargrátr*, see QUINN: Construing habitus.

lover Vilmundr, who is identified as Högni's slayer (st. 8).[72] The poem is structured as a lament by Oddrún after Gunnarr has been murdered by her family, with Oddrún vindicating her devotion to Gunnarr by revealing her father's dying wishes for his daughters:

> ... þat nam at mæla mál iþ efsta
> sjá móðr konungr áðr hann sylti.
>
> Mik bað hann gœða gulli rauðu
> ok suðr gefa syni Grímhildar...[73]
>
> Enn ek Gunnari gatk at unna,
> bauga deili, sem Brynhildr skyldi.
> Enn hann Brynhildi bað hjálm geta,
> hana kvað hann óskmey verða skyldu.[74]

Oddrún does not dwell on the deception of her sister by the Gjúkungar and passes lightly over the well-known consequences: 'Þat mun á hölða hvert land fara er hon lét sveltaz at Sigurði'.[75] Her focus instead is on the behaviour of her brother in the aftermath of Brynhildr's death, when the Gjúkungar offer reparations other than those described in *Guðrúnarkviða* II. Here, the Gjúkungar offer the Buðlungar handsome payment to facilitate the marriage of Oddrún to Gunnarr:

---

[72] The reading of *Oddrúnargrátr* presented here is based on the edition, translation and commentary published in QUINN: The Endless Triangles. Stanza numbers are to that edition, with the stanza numbers of the edition by Neckel and Kuhn given in square brackets.
[73] *Oddrúnargrátr* 12-13 [15] '... before he died the weary king began to speak of the highest matters. He said that I should be endowed with red gold and given to the son of Grímhildr in the south...'.
[74] *Oddrúnargrátr* 19 [16, 20] 'Yet I got the chance to love Gunnarr, the sharer of rings, as Brynhildr should have. And he said that the helmet should be given to Brynhildr, he said that she should become a wish-maid [valkyrie].'.
[75] *Oddrúnargrátr* 18 [19] 'It will have travelled to men in every land that she killed herself for Sigurðr'.

> Buðu þeir árla bauga rauða
> ok brœðr mínum bœtr ósmár;
> bauð hann enn við mér bú fimtán,
> hliðfarm Grana, ef hann hafa vildi.[76]
>
> Enn Atli kvaz eigi vilja
> mund aldregi at megi Gjúka ..[77]

But the attempt by the Gjúkungar to formalize Gunnarr's love affair with Oddrún into a marriage is thwarted by Atli, who will not countenance the alliance. In doing so, he presumably expects his sister to comply with his assessment of the best way to maintain family honour (by avenging their sister's death) and to forge strategic alliances (by his marriage to Guðrún and possibly by Oddrún's marriage to someone else, though speculation on this point goes beyond the bounds of the network presented by the poet). The precarious nature of the bonds scrutinised in the poems about Sigurðr and the Gjúkungar derive from their basis in sworn oaths; here in *Oddrúnargrátr* the poet homes in on a bond that is not expected to be so precarious: the indelible bond between brother and sister. As Larrington has described it, the intimacy between siblings is 'asymmetrical in its effects',[78] with a family's honour imperatives bearing more heavily on a sister than a brother, just as is shown in *Oddrúnargrátr*. Unable to resist her desire for Gunnarr, however, Oddrún secretly defies her brother's will and continues the affair (st. 21 [22]). Trusting in the strength of the tie between them – and trusting too much in the fundamental elements of a strong tie, of mutual confiding and reciprocal advantage[79] – Atli is blind to the risk his sister poses to the family.

His courtiers, however, gossip about his sister; still Atli assumes the tie between them guarantees that she will behave as he expects her to:

---

[76] *Oddrúnargrátr* 20 [21] 'Early they offered red-gold rings – no small compensation to my brother; and he [Gunnarr] offered fifteen farms for me, the side-load of Grani [Sigurðr's gold-hoard], if he wished to have it'.
[77] *Oddrúnargrátr* 21 [22] 'Still Atli said he would never want a bride-price from the sons of Gjúki . . .'.
[78] See LARRINGTON: Sibling Drama.
[79] For the elaboration of the constitution of strong ties, see GRANOVETTER: Strength of Weak Ties, p. 1361.

> Mæltu margir mínir niðjar,
> kváðuz okr hafa orðit bæði.
> Enn mik Atli kvað eigi myndu
> lýti ráða né löst gera.[80]

Atli's trust in his sister is poignant, but it is not as moving as Oddrún's unwavering devotion to Gunnarr, which lends the lament its emotional force and ethical gravitas. At the instigation of courtiers, rather than because of his innate suspicion of his sister, Atli organizes surveillance of his sister:

> Sendi Atli áru sína
> um myrkvan við, mín at freista;
> ok þeir kómu þar er þeir koma né skylduð,
> þá er breiddu við blæiu eina.[81]

The lovers' attempt to bribe the spies in order to defend their privacy comes to naught: they cannot safeguard the most ephemeral tie of all, between illicit lovers defying their powerful familes. Oddrún is betrayed and while she is away fulfilling her social duty at another court, Gunnarr is captured and thrown into a snake-pit. Oddrún's frantic attempt to return in time to save her lover's life, after she hears his desperate harp-playing from the pit, also comes to naught as Atli's mother sides with her son and kills Gunnarr before Oddrún can reach him.

While Oddrún's lament is for the loss of her lover, the discourse of the poem broadens into social reflection on desire that is at odds with familial will:

> . . . þeygi við máttum við munum vinna,
> nema ek helt höfði við hringbrota.[82]

> Enn slíks skyli synja aldri
> maðr fyr annan, þar er munuð deilir.[83]

---

[80] *Oddrúnargrátr* 22 [23] 'Many of my kinsmen talked, they announced we had been together. Yet Atli said I would not be responsible for disgrace, nor would I do wrong.'.

[81] *Oddrúnargrátr* 24 [25] 'Atli sent his messenger into the dark woods, to test me; and they came there where they should not have come, where we stretched out under one quilt.'.

[82] *Oddrúnargrátr* 21 [22] '. . . nor might we resist our desire – rather I lent my head against the ring-breaker [prince].'.

> Opt undrumk þat, hví ek eptir mák,
> línvengis Bil, lífi halda,
> er ek ógnhvötum unna þóttumz,
>   sverða deili, sem sjálfri mér.[84]

> . . . maðr hverr lifir at munum sínum,
> nú er um genginn grátr Oddrúnar.[85]

As mentioned earlier in this essay, *Oddrúnargrátr* is offered as solace to the audience who are assumed to be familiar with such conflicts of desire and familial duty. It is a strange twist in the plot of this poem, and in the biography of an eddic heroine, that despite the waywardness love inspired in her, Oddrún nonetheless had a keen sense of social duty, enforced by an oath she had made at some point in her life:

> . . . hét ek ok efndak, er ek hinig mælta
> at ek hvívetna hjálpa skyldak,
> þá er öðlingar arfi skiptu.[86]

She had sworn an oath to help dynastic families prosper and this is evidently the reason she has sought out Borgný, to use her magical medical powers to assist in the birth of her twins, fathered by Högni's murderer. Like her sister Brynhildr, she is faithful to her oath, even though in her case it means abetting the family line that has not served her own interests.

The intergenerational power dynamics represented in eddic heroic poetry demonstrate the considerable risk to a dynasty's status posed by strong-willed progeny, a social phenomenon of no less concern in the thirteenth century than in earlier ones. Though the entanglements of loyalty for Brynhildr and Guðrún are very different, in both cases their actions ultimately work to diminish the effectiveness of the social web formed through their marriages. *Oddrúnargrátr*

---

[83] *Oddrúnargrátr* 23 [24] 'Still such a thing should never be denied, by one person of another, where love is involved.'.
[84] *Oddrúnargrátr* 31 [33] 'Often I wonder, how I may still – goddess of the linen-pillow [woman] – keep living, when I thought I loved the swift-frightening one [warrior], – the sharer of swords [lord] – as I loved myself.'.
[85] *Oddrúnargrátr* 32 [34] '. . . each person lives according to their desires – now Oddrún's lament is finished.'.
[86] *Oddrúnargrátr* 10 '. . . I made a promise and kept it when I said in that place that I would help anyone who shared the inheritance of princes.'.

explores the strategies of risk containment that might be exercised to prevent wilful self determination damaging the family and achieves a curious balance through Oddrún's lament for her own personal loss offset by her social function in promoting the continuation of other families into the next generation.

This survey by no means exhausts the many relationships and strategic alliances depicted in eddic heroic poetry, nor does it treat all of the social issues the poems raise. I have analysed the manner in which the poems stage dynamic situations between members of networks in order to explore the risks inherent in creating and maintaining ties between them. In particular, I have focused on the maintenance of trust in alliances, both those forged through marriage and through friendship, and the co-operation of siblings to dynastic ends after each is involved in new family networks through their own marriages. Richard Gaskins (2005) has explored the new slant network theory provides for the analysis of social change as depicted in saga literature through the inference of cumulative political change from the typical action of saga characters. The inferences that might be drawn from eddic heroic poetry are less easily plotted against an historical time-line on account of the hazy prehistory in oral circulation of each of the written poems. Nonetheless the Codex Regius collection of heroic poems expresses in myriad forms the preoccupations of poets with trust, loyalty and the secure formation of marriage bonds between families. In so doing, the poems offer a rich source of social critique which it may be assumed was current within the milieu in which the poems were recorded in the mid- to late-thirteenth century. Far removed in style from saga narration, with its detached perspective and cool understatement of emotional impact, eddic heroic poetry dramatises individuals' horror at the implications of failed network links and the devastating impact on dynastic ambition of strategic miscalculation.

Bibliography

BARABÁSI, Albert-László: *Linked: The New Science of Networks*, Cambridge, MA: Perseus, 2002.

DRONKE, Ursula: *The Poetic Edda. Vol I: Heroic Poems,* Oxford: Oxford University Press, 1969.

FAULKES, Anthony (ed.): *Edda. Skáldskaparmál. 2 vols*, London: Viking Society for Northern Research, 1998.

FIDJESTØL, Bjarne and Odd Einar HAUGEN (ed.): *The Dating of Eddic Poetry.* Copenhagen: Reitzel, 1999. (= *Bibliotheca Arnamagnæana*; 41)

FINGERMAN, Karen L.: „Consequential Strangers and Peripheral Partners: The Importance of Unimportant Relationships", in: *Journal of Family Theory and Review* 1 (2009), pp. 69-82.

GASKINS, Richard: „Network Dynamics in Saga and Society", in: *Scandinavian Studies* 77.2 (2005), pp. 201-16.

GRANOVETTER, Mark S.: „The Strength of Weak Ties", in: *American Journal of Sociology* 78 (1973), pp. 1360-80.

HARRIS, Joseph: „Eddic Poetry", in: *Old Norse-Icelandic Literature. A Critical Guide*, eds. Carol CLOVER and John LINDOW, Ithaca and London: Cornell University Press, 1985, pp. 68-156.

HEUSLER, Andreas and Wilhelm RANISCH (eds.): *Eddica Minora. Dichtungen Eddischer Art aus den Fornaldarsögur und Anderen Prosawerken*, Dortmund: Ruhfus, 1903.

HEUSLER, Andreas: „Introduction", in: Codex Regius of the Elder Edda. Ms. no. 2365 4to in the Old Royal Collection in the Royal library of Copenhagen, Copenhagen: Levin & Munksgaard, 1937, pp. 7-35.

Guðni JÓNSSON (ed.): *Völsunga saga*, in: *Fornaldar Sögur Norðurlanda. 4 vols*, Akureyri: Íslendingasagnaútgáfan, 1954, I: pp. 109-218.

Stefán KARLSSON: „The Localisation and Dating of Medieval Icelandic Manuscripts", in: *Saga Book* 25:2 (1999), pp. 138-58.

LARRINGTON, Carolyne (trans.): *The Poetic Edda,* Oxford: Oxford University Press, 1996.

LARRINGTON, Carolyne. „Sibling Drama: Laterality in the Heroic Poems of the Edda", in: *Myths, Legends, and Heroes: Studies in Old Norse and Old English Literature in Honour of John McKinnell*, ed. Daniel ANLEZARK, Toronto: University of Toronto Press, 2011, pp. 169-87.

LINDBLAD, Gustaf: „Centrala eddaproblem i 1970-talets forskningsläge", in: *Scripta Islandica* 28 (1977), pp. 3-16.

LINDBLAD, Gustaf: *Studier i Codex regius av Äldre Eddan*, Lund: Gleerup, 1954.

NECKEL, Hans, (ed.), Hans KUHN (rev.ed.): *Edda. Die Lieder des Codex Regius nebst verwandten Denkmälern,* 4th edn, Heidelberg: Winter, 1962.

QUINN, Judy: „Betrothal and betrayal: the eddic tradition's treatment of Sigurðr", in: Agneta Ney, Henrik Williams and Fredrik Charpentier Ljungqvist (ed.): *Á austrvega. Saga and East Scandinavia: Preprint papers of The 14th International Saga Conference*, 2 vols, Gävle: Gävle University Press, 2009, II: pp. 783-87.

QUINN, Judy: „Construing habitus in eddic dialogue: the order of stanzas in Oddrúnargrátr", in: Susanne Kramarz-Bein (ed.): *Neue Ansätze in der Mittelalterphilologie/Nye Veier i middelalderfilologien. Akten der skandinavistischen Arbeitstagung in Münster vom 24.- 26.10. 2002*, Frankfurt am Main and Basel: Peter Lang, 2005, pp. 83-95.

QUINN, Judy: „The Endless Triangles of Eddic Tragedy: Reading Oddrúnargrátr", in: Maria Elena Ruggerini (ed.): *Studi anglo-norreni in onore di John S. McKinnell*, Caglieri: CUEC, 2009, pp. 304-326.

QUINN, Judy: „The Naming of Eddic Poems", in: *Parergon* 8/2 (1990), pp. 97-115.

QUINN, Judy: „The Realisation of Mythological Design: The Early Generations of the Völsung Dynasty", in: Annette Lassen, Agneta Ney and Ármann Jakobsson (ed.): *The Legendary Sagas: Myths and Reality. Studies in the Old Icelandic Fornaldarsögur*, Copenhagen: Museum Tusculanum, 2009, pp. 123-142.

QUINN, Judy: „Völuspá and the Composition of Eddic Verse", in: Teresa Pàroli (ed.): *Atti del 12° congresso internazionale di studi sull'alto medioevo. Poetry in the Scandinavian Middle Ages*, Spoleto: Centro italiano di studi sull'alto medioevo, 1990, pp. 303-20.

ROWE, Elizabeth Ashman: „Quid Sigvardus cum Christo? Moral Interpretations of Sigurðr Fáfnisbani in Old Norse Literature", in: *Viking and Medieval Scandinavia* 2 (2006), pp. 167-200.

SEE, Klaus von, et al.: *Kommentar zu den Liedern der Edda, 6 vols*, Heidelberg: Winter, 1993-2009.

MATTHIAS EWERING AND CHRISTIAN KROSING

Networktheoretical Approaches to Bandamanna saga and Færeyinga saga

Part I: An Investigation of Network-based Approaches to Old Norse Literature and Culture

Network theory in general examines complex patterns of various kinds. It is, more strictly speaking, the study of systems consisting of a large number of objects, and it is especially the study of these objects' connections to one another. In this context, we call the objects *nodes* and the connections *edges*, and nodes with extraordinarily many edges are called *hubs*. Networked structures can consist of virtually anything – friends, neurons, mathematicians, computers, characters in a play, and so forth. This article is rooted in the two authors' bachelor theses, and it seeks to investigate the potential of network theory applied in the study of Old Norse literature and culture. Both of them make use of network-based approaches in the study of Old Norse-Icelandic literature. We shall here present a range of scenarios for analyses in the field which we believe are likely to benefit from such an approach.

The first part of the article discusses several fields of the study of Old Norse literature, society, and culture which lend themselves to a network-based approach. In our theses, we were each concerned with one saga: *Bandamanna saga* and *Færeyinga saga*. The former is a fairly short narrative whose plot twists can very concretely be described in terms of network theory. The latter, on the other hand, is a longer text featuring a lot more characters with more complex interrelations with one another. Therefore, a network-based study of *Færeyinga saga* will have to focus on a small selection of characters. This kind of study forms the second part of this article, and because *Færeyinga saga* will be dealt with in detail further below, *Bandamanna saga* shall only be briefly addressed at this point, for it is useful to demonstrate what kind of networks we are dealing with when working with the sagas.

Network-based plot analysis

One of the major distinctive characteristics of Old Norse saga literature is the emphasis it lays on the individual as the chief constituent of society. Not only do many of the foremost examples of medieval Icelandic literary culture such as *Njáls saga* or *Egils saga*, to name two of the most prominent ones, bear the names of their main protagonists in their titles, but they really are stories about characters that have singular traits, preferences, and abilities to them, just as the old man Ófeigr in *Bandamanna saga* does. Only thereby do these stories unfold: they are propelled and given life by the characters whose stories they tell. This feature distinguishes them from the continental European literature of the time, whose protagonists – be they saints, kings, legendary heroes, or a blend of the three – can rather be regarded exemplary figures, generic idols or foes rather than actual characters. Since the dynamics of the diverse interrelationships between various saga protagonists is among the principal recurring themes especially of the *Íslendingasǫgur* genre, the designation of the society that unfolds in these sagas as a *network* has become a popular commonplace amongst scholars. The conception of the Icelandic society of the *sǫguǫld* as it is presented to us in the sagas therefore lends itself to an analysis based on network theory. It is, however, necessary in order to deepen our understanding of the effects of a networked society to take into account the dynamic nature of these networks rather than to perceive complex interrelated structures as stable once they are given.

Bandamanna saga tells the story of old chieftain Ófeigr Skíðason, who shrewdly assists his wealthy but overconfident son Oddr in his quarrel with a group of eight *goðar*, the eponymous *bandamenn*. He does so by skilfully playing his adversaries off against each other by means of bribery, flattery, extortion, appeals to personal honour, and so forth, thereby convincing them to side with himself, or at least to cease their attempts on Oddr. To this end, Ófeigr plans to arrange a wedding between his own son Oddr and a daughter of Gellir's, one of the eight *bandamenn*. In a wonderful dialogue with Gellir about this matter, Ófeigr says:

> Ek segi þér með sǫnnu at aldri giptir þú hana betr en svá, því at einmælt mun þat at hann sé menntr sem sá er bezt er, enda skortir hann eigi fé né ætt góða; en þú ert mjǫk féþurfi, ok mætti svá verða at þér yrði styrkr at honum, því at maðrinn er stórlyndr við vini sína.[1]

---

[1] MAGERØY: Bandamanna saga, p. 24.

This brief piece of advice contains a wealth of information on what saga networks typically consist of. Marriage, of course, is a prime means of manufacturing new edges to previously unconnected nodes in the form of new social ties. Another form of creating social ties is the formation of a *félag* similar to the type our *bandamenn* have conducted and which Ófeigr in turn seeks to break. *Bandamanna saga* has been credited for its display of an unusually high humoristic potential. This has largely been attributed to the cunning tongue of Ófeigr's, but it seems no less true that the very construction of the saga contributes to the reader's amusement. The whole story is a parody of the class of Icelandic chieftains and their dealings with each other. Indeed, the saga is very carefully arranged to cover this one theme, and it seems ironic that Ófeigr's ultimate success results from his strategy of successively turning a weakness into an advantage by crumbling his opponents' own network and dragging its members into his own. This way, network theory might contribute to an understanding of how the humour in the saga works. The strategy of manufacturing *weak ties* is a powerful instrument in social dynamics. Weak ties will be discussed below.

In his comment, the speaker also mentions friendship and the benefits that come with it. Oddr "skortir [...] eigi fé né ætt góða"[2], and both of these qualities will reflect on Gellir should he give his consent to the marriage Ófeigr dangles his son's monetary wealth and his respectable descent, and these features are good examples of what network ties within the saga society can be good for. They are carriers of resources, but much more do they form a resource in themselves. This resource is latent power, which increases all the more, the more extensive one's personal network grows.

Why dynamic networks are powerful

As Richard Gaskins has pointed out[3], the unique feature of literary network theory lies in the emphasis it places on the inherent *dynamics* of networked structures. Even though scholars have pointed to the importance of complex interconnections and interactions of fictional saga characters as well as historical persons, events, and entire texts, the significance of the nature of dynamic network structures as "essentially open-ended with no pre-determined out-

---

[2] ibid.
[3] Cf. GASKINS: Network Dynamics in Saga and Society.

comes"[4] has been widely neglected in pertinent analyses[5]. While it is true especially of Durrenberger's approach that Old Norse-Icelandic society and literature are regarded as unsteady rather than static settings, the aforementioned contributions would have profited from the use of a network-based model. Its characteristic features that facilitate typical patterns and transformations of these patterns are not to be neglected due to their potentially considerable explanatory power.

The characteristics and heuristically relevant features of structures organised as complex networks have been comprehensively described by Albert-László Barabási.[6] The implications of recent network theorists' findings for the study of Old Norse literature and culture seem potentially profound. This includes such diverse fields as the interior dynamics of saga plots, the distribution of manuscripts, the circulation of knowledge and power, and it may even propose a new perspective on the old debate about the value of the Icelandic Family Sagas as historical sources.

All of the networked structures have a number of striking features[7] in common, such as the famous six degrees of separation, or the 80/20 rule. What we would like to point out is the fact that these remarkably stable features facilitate highly dynamic developments. Thinking in terms of networks makes visible just how liquid the binding forces of society, as they are represented in the sagas, appear. This is because the single elements of a large network are fragile. People die, friendships end, and so forth. At the same time, children are born and grow older in order to participate in the big game themselves, making new ties, and so forth. This makes the whole structure prone to tremendous shifts, if one of the hubs suddenly disappears, or a new, competing hub emerges in its vicinity.

The networked logic of intertextual relationships

To this point, we have discussed network theory as an approach to investigate plot, which is a text-internal matter. We shall now take into consideration the various means of interactions which texts maintain with each other. The study of intertextual phenomena has a great tradition, but seldom has it focused on the aspect of network logic. In his brilliant study on the relation of orality to the

---

[4] ibid., p. 208.
[5] Cf. generally BYOCK: Feud and DURRENBERGER: Dynamics of Medieval Iceland.
[6] Cf. BARABÁSI: Linked.
[7] For a comprehensive overview, see BARABÁSI: Linked.

Icelandic sagas, Gísli Sigurðsson also talks about intertextual references between the sagas. Gísli counts four types:

- word-for-word copies of entire passages
- the same characters or incidents are described in more than one text
- one text is familiar with characters or incidents described in another text
- two or more texts use the same or similar wording, but in different scenes.[8]

Assuming that the production of texts was incumbent on an elite group of people, we can deduce which texts they knew, and which texts' styles they valued highly enough to incorporate it into their own works, or their remodelling of preexistent texts. In addition to the number of extant manuscripts of a particular text, we have here another quantifiable figure to work with. The conception of co-existing texts forming a network can reveal especially fruitful specimens, thereby giving information on their contemporary valuation through means other than sheer quantity in transmission. A different attempt has been made by Susanne Kramarz-Bein.[9] Her approach builds on the individuals who were concerned with the production and perpetuation of texts, and with the texts themselves. Kramarz-Bein is interested in the sphere of the translated *riddarasǫgur*, which emerged around the court of king Hákon IV. Hákonarson of Norway. By means of a network-based analysis of Old Norwegian and Swedish texts, she substantiates a range of connections between the West and East Norse traditions around Charlemagne and Dietrich of Bern. She concludes her study with the prospect of network theory as potentially offering "ein plausibles Erklärungsmodell für die sich epidemisch von Süd- nach Nordeuropa ausbreitenden höfischen Literatur-und Kulturtraditionen [...]."[10]

This seems plausible indeed. The increased interest in continental matter and traditions might be explained as a networked phenomenon, building on the need to be able to make contact, i. e. conversation, with power brokers within the social network. It was the king himself who endorsed the introduction of continental literary traditions to Norway, a person who undoubtedly was a huge hub in the web of personal ties among the noble society of the time. Therefore, fol-

---

[8] Cf. Gísli SIGURÐSSON: Medieval Icelandic Saga, p. 124.
[9] Cf. KRAMARZ-BEIN: Literarische Milieus.
[10] KRAMARZ-BEIN: Literarische Milieus, p. 233.

lowing the new fashion was an apt means of making or holding contact with nodes in his vicinity.

Social dynamics in the medieval and Viking Age North

The study of medieval and Viking Age Scandinavia is not only concerned with texts, but also with the historical developments that shaped the society in which these texts were productive. Since networked structures appear in a vast range of areas, network theory can also be employed in order to investigate certain historical phenomena. For our purposes, we shall formulate some ideas on how network dynamics affected the process of conversion to Christianity in early medieval Northern Europe. It is well known that this process was a long one, beginning in 10th-century Denmark and slowly coming to an end shortly after 1100 in Sweden. Especially in Iceland, the conversion took a peaceful course when the Althing decided in 999 or 1000 that all Icelanders were to become Christians, while pagan practices should still be allowed if carried out secretly. For the sake of simplicity, Przemysław Urbańczyk summarizes the various strategies the Scandinavian chieftains took facing the expansion of the new faith thus:

> A change of the religion itself was not [the pagan élites'] priority because their strategy was directed, first of all, at political and economic goals. [...] Some tried to actively oppose the 'inevitable', others remained indifferent, while others eagerly welcomed the new 'civilisation'. Usually, it is the last group only that was well recorded and memorised.[11]

Naturally, the victors were generally much more praised and remembered by posterity than were their pagan adversaries. But why were they victorious after all? Once again, the answer seems to lie in what Richard Gaskins called 'the strength of weak ties'[12]. It is the proponents of the new faith who are in a position to forge new edges with formerly unconnected nodes from the neighbouring lands of the South, where Christianity had already been implemented and established. From there, it was simply a matter of quantity: with their newly made contacts with players from outside Scandinavia, the progressive forces had a much more dense network at their disposal, which provided them with a strong latent power, since power can be defined as a *potential* to activate one's

---

[11] URBAŃCZYK: Politics of Conversion, p. 15.
[12] A term he borrows from the homonymous essay by Mark S. GRANOVETTER.

means. The reluctant or openly conservative chieftains, on the other hand, still had to make do with their traditional established ties in their vicinity. These ties, which supposedly were very strong ones, through marriage, neighbourhood, or traditional allegiance, in the end still found themselves to be in an inferior position to the sheer size of their opponents' newly created networks, which largely consisted of weak ties.

There is another characteristic of Christianity that helped support its successful expansion to the North. The possibility of becoming a part of a powerful network increases drastically when one is close to a powerful hub, or if one becomes a hub oneself. The structure of the church was fully suitable for this purpose:

> To perform Christian rituals it was necessary to construct sacral buildings that became **permanent religious centres**. These also were socio-topographic focal points and nodes for information-exchange, but the range was extended and specialised. Everybody who wanted to be informed on both the 'official' interpretation of the material world and the extra-sensual sphere, those who wanted to participate in common rituals and those who wanted to bury their dead properly, all had to come to a church, which thereupon defined a socially important centre.[13]

Thus, once there are enough worshippers of the Christian god in a particular area to raise and maintain a church, the logic of the network leads to an increase in the influence of those who have already converted anyway. The church centre provides the Christians with an impressive social resource which the pagans lack: a hub within the networked society which is itself connected to other hubs just like it, and typically even to a bishop's see as well.

A new perspective on the sagas as historical sources

The question of whether the *Íslendingasǫgur* are to be considered reasonably accurate historical accounts, mere fiction, or a blend of these two extremes has been extensively discussed amongst scholars for decades. This debate is only too well known to readers and commentators of the sagas and shall therefore not be recapitulated here. However, the view of the society of the saga world as a complex and dynamic social network yields further hints on how we may indeed extract valid information from these texts. Since the sagas undisputedly

---

[13] URBAŃCZYK: Politics of Conversion, pp. 18-19. Original Emphasis.

give close attention to the manifold ways people interact with one another, thereby – in many cases – consciously creating, modelling, and maintaining networks of power, often in fierce competition with rivals for the same social resources. Not only do the sagas seem to be aware of what Richard Gaskins called "the key forces of historical development",[14] but they also demonstrate how the characteristic dynamics of social networks deprive the protagonists of control over further developments. The tragic events described in *Njáls saga*, for instance, are allowed to take their course despite the various desperate attempts undertaken in order to secure the peace. In another instance, Ófeigr's efforts in *Bandamanna saga* prove successful. Further examples could be cited from many similar saga plots throughout the genre of the *Íslendingasǫgur*.

In this way, the focus in evaluating the sagas as historical sources shifts from the question of their precision and veracity in specific detail to a recognition of their observance of general strategies of power and their potential outcomes. We can thus use the texts as indices to how the people of the 13th century regarded their own past in the light of the world they lived in themselves. Consequently, the accounts assembled in the *Sturlunga saga* compilation emphasise struggles for power by network building as well. Since the turbulent Sturlung Age can be considered relatively well-documented in terms of accuracy as compared to the *sǫguöld*, we may deduce that the way both the *Íslendingasǫgur* and the Contemporary Sagas stress the network dynamics being at work as history proceeds do contribute to our understanding of how the saga writers perceived the current state of their society and the developments which led to its formation. The historical value of the sagas thus lies in the information they contain about the fashion in which social and political development took its course, rather than in their providing of singular facts which in most cases cannot be verified anyway. But the sagas do undoubtedly display a deep understanding of the importance of ties, their formation and preservation, to the functioning of the Icelanders' polity within their leaderless commonwealth.

Possibilities and limitations of literary network theory

A network-based approach seems to come naturally to the examination of plot construction. Indeed, plot analyses in terms of network theory have been suc-

---

[14] GASKINS: Network Dynamics in Saga and Society, p. 203.

cessfully done,[15] and the results give more than enough reason to endorse similar endeavours in the field of saga studies. Speaking about the method employed in his analysis of William Shakespeare's *Hamlet*, Franco Moretti states:

> [O]nce you make a network of a play, you stop working on the play proper, and work on a *model* instead: you reduce the text to characters and interactions, abstract them from everything else, and this process of reduction and abstraction makes the model obviously much less than the original object [...].[16]

Moretti's remark aptly explains what it is that network theory does to a text, be it a drama or a narrative in prose. Only if we reduce the masterpiece's diegesis to its bare technicalities by stoically quantifying the characters' appearances and their interactions with one another, we will be able to harvest the material necessary for the type of analysis endorsed here. This technique of reduction to a model constitutes the possibilities, but also the restrictions of network theory when applied to a text. What the abstract network model of a narrative lacks, is any information about the contents of the story. A character's *movens* will be invisible to such a study, as will weak, i. e. non-quantifiable information such as emotions, dreams, or any other internal activities. The method, however, is at its most impressive when it comes to the examination of quantifiable factors organised in complex networks. The diversity of these networks has been duly indicated above.

However, the range of possible scenarios for the application of network theory in the field of Old Norse literature, society, and culture as suggested in this article is by no means all-embracing, nor were the given ideas and examples discussed exhaustively due to the maximum possible scope in the format of an article. Nevertheless, we hope to provide an impulse towards an alternative way of regarding certain phenomena in our field of study. There is more than enough material out there suitable for investigation in terms of network theory. It is simply yet to be picked up.

---

[15] An excellent experimental, network-based study of Shakespeare's *Hamlet* and Cao Xueqin's The Story of the Stone has been delivered by Franco Moretti at the Stanford Literary Lab. See MORETTI: Network Theory.
[16] MORETTI: Network Theory, p. 4. Original emphasis.

Part II: Social Dynamics in the Sagas: the case of Færeyinga saga

When the situation in the first major chain of conflict calmed down, Þrándr realizes that the near future on the Faroe Islands will be a comfortable time under his domination. Moments ago the most powerful men on the isles killed each other in a struggle to restore stained honor. Þrándr's position in this conflict is dubious: on the one hand he does not actively participate in the battle, but on the other hand he plays a prominent role in pushing the escalation to the next level. In the course of this saga his character is the only one who is always involed in shaping the power structure of the isles over several generations. But how is it possible that a man who avoids every physical contention becomes such a person of influence? To approach this question a closer look at the potential application of network theory should be taken into account.

Network Theory and the Exposition of Social Dynamics

The narratives of sagas that are categorized as Íslendingasǫgur are fundamentally based on conflicts between individuals or groups. Several approaches regarding conflict-structures document the vivid interest in their reasons, developments and solutions.[17] Whenever conflicts between individuals are the core element of a narrative, feelings and emotions can be detected. Due to the fact that Íslendingasǫgur are defined by their effort to keep the narrative in perspective, which pretends a nimbus of objectivity[18], the psychological background that is connected to those conflicts is an idea that was pursued hesitantly for a long time. For a network-theoretical approach the motivations and ideas that further the shape of a social network should always be taken into account. However, the outcome of interacting characters within a text and its consequences for the construction of the social network can be identified as *Social Dynamics*. Attracted by the idea that networks always follow a specific set of rules, it would be interesting to check the range of this approach to analyse the ongoing changes in the constellation of characters.

The idea of detecting Social Dynamics in a saga is not new. One of the first attempts to systematically anaylse sagas from a network-theoretical perspective

---

[17] Especially BYOCK: Feud or MILLER: Bloodtaking and Peacemaking.
[18] This paper is based on the idea that saga narratives are not a complete reproduction of reality and in this respect it challenges the idea that the style of sagas indicates authetic objectivity. Here sagas are understood as literature without revaluation or devaluation of their content.

was made in 2005 by Richard Gaskins, in which he concentrated on power-building strategies in *Njáls saga*.[19] From this starting point this article wants to pursue the question how network theory can help to reexamine the relationship between the protagonists in a saga with an emphasis on subordinated characters within the narrative.

A useful example in this case is the *Færeyinga saga*, a rather neglected text within the corpus of Old Norse-Icelandic Saga Literature. Nevertheless, it offers three generations of struggle for power, outlines of Faroese-Norwegian relationships, complex family structures and different concepts of heroism; enough material for an extensive analysis, but just a few key features of this saga will be presented.

The anatomy of conflicts

As mentioned above, the saga offers considerable potential for conflicts which is result of the predominant struggle for identity. The main focus is on the powerful family of Gǫtuskeggjar, and the troublesome relationship between Þrándr and Brestir is the starting point for this analysis. To understand their differences general information concerning the power-structure on the Faroe Islands should be provided:

The constrast between Icelanders and Norwegians is a popular topic in the Íslendingasǫgur, and this possibility of conflict is transferred to Faroese conditions. The saga describes the situation on the islands as a kind of joint reign of three Faroese men under Norwegian administration. On the one hand, there is Hafgrímr, a liegeman of Haraldr gráfeldr Gunnhildarson.[20] Half of the islands are under his reign. On the other hand, there are the brothers Brestir and Beinir Sigmundarson, who are liegemen of Hákon Hlaðajarl Sigurðarson and govern the other half of the islands.[21]

---

[19] GASKINS: Network Dynamics in Saga and Society, pp. 201-216.
[20] HALLDÓRSSON: Færeyinga saga, p. 8. „Hafgrimr hed madr hann bío j Sudr ey j Færeyium hann var Rikr madr ok hard feín audigr at fe Gudridr het kona hans ok var Snæulfs dottir. Hafgrimr var hofdínge yfir helming eyíanna ok hellt þeim helminge j len af Haralldi konungi graf(elldi). er þa Red firir Noregi."
[21] HALLDÓRSSON: Færeyinga saga, pp. 5-9. „Sigmundr fadir þeirra ok Þorbeornn Gautu skeggr f(adir) Þrandar voru brædr þeir Brestir ok Bæinir voru agætir menn ok voru hofdíngíar yfir helminge eyíanna ok helldu þann j len af Hakoni j(arli) Sigurdar syni er þa hafde Riki nokkut jnn j Þrandheimi. ok voru þeir Brestir hirdmenn Hakonar j(arls) ok hínir kærstu vinir."

All of the three have a close tie to Norwegian rulers and benefit from being liegemen. Þrándr, however, is not interested in acting under orders of Norwegian rulers, and in the course of the saga he carries this aversion to extremes. The contrast of rejection and loyalty towards Norwegian rulers should be understood as one of the main conflicts in this saga; and this separates Þrándr and Brestir.

This might be a structuralist thought, but such a fundamental opposition shapes the identity of characters, on the basis of which conflicts are created. But there are not only family-internal conflicts (Þrándr and Brestir), there are also conflicts between powerful men (Brestir and Hafgrímr). It is remarkable that this saga offers a variety of conflict-patterns along with several methods of resolutions, including not only violent encounters but also brokerage and arbitrated resolutions.

The first chain of conflicts erupts while two men, Eldjarn and Einar, are disputing. In the course of this conversation, Eldjarn hits Einar with a stick, and Einar uses an axe in return. After the hit, Eldjarn faints. In consequence of this incident, Eldjarn needs legal support and chooses Brestir, because he is known for being clever and legally trained. Brestir accepts, and after a claim for compensation has failed, the case is disputed at the þing, the assembly of the Faroese people. Brestir wins the case, and Hafgrímr seeks openly revenge, but Brestir dismisses the threat; with disatrous consequences as the saga shows.

This example shows that conflicts are not stable. They are in flux and can move from a lower social level (Eldjarn and Einar) to higher social levels (Brestir and Hafgrímr). The first attempt to settle the matter by claiming for compensation was rejected by Hafgrímr. This leads to the decision at the þing. For Hafgrímr, this decision is an affront to his honour, and he rejects this arbitrated resolution which provokes a growing conflict between him and Brestir. The social dynamics transposes this conflict to higher social classes, thus making it ever more acrimonious.

Discarding the idea that a legal case could render justice, Hafgrímr, tries to find a way to take revenge on Brestir with the important addition that he wants to win honor with this action. This violent concept to restore honour poses several questions concerning the social code of this saga. Which are the motivations that influence decisions and create dynamics? Two aspects that are inextricably intertwined and should not be seperated from each other are honor and masculinity. They can be the cues for many escalations as *Færeyinga saga* shows.

Honor and masculinity as deliberate provocations

As shown above, this saga involves a complex net of powergames, opportunities, revenge, vengeance and restoration of honour. These are variations to underline the capability and position of characters within the society and social group. It is useful to look for the social code and motivations that legitimate such behaviour. Based on the major conflicts of this saga the constellation and social standing of characters should be analysed. The first striking aspect is the different concepts to gain power. On the one hand, there are characters like Brestir, Beinir, Sigmundr and Þórr, who represent an heroic ideal that is primarily based on 'going viking' which implies fighting skills and gaining good reputation with people in power, e.g. Norwegian kings. On the other hand, there is a character like Þrándr, whose strategical actions are well-considered and foresighted. He seems to know what impact impulsive actions and sudden revengefulness, can have on the stability and structure of the Faroese society in the long run. Therefore the question is: can Þrándr take any advantage of this matter of fact? The course of the first major conflict may offer some evidence.

When Hafgrímr tries to seek a possibility to kill Brestir without losing honour, he reveals two aspects: first of all, his strategic skills are anything but great because he is unable to think of a plan independently. In fact, his revengefulness and plan to kill Brestir meet with rejection from many sides, e.g. his father-in-law even tries to kill Hafgrímr. Þrándr, however, is an exception. He offers Hafgrímr help, and in return he demands a reward to ensure his economic situation even in case of Hafgrímr's death. Hafgrímr accepts immediately, and Þrándr takes care of planning the attack. The second aspect is vengefulness as motivation. Driven by his stained honour, he is vulnerable to any kind of provocation. This is a dangerous mixture for him and the society but Þrándr is able to seize the opportunity and manipulates him with a simple provocation.

During the single combat between Hafgrímr and Brestir, Þrándr does not intervene and observes the scene. Hafgrímr asks Þrándr to help him, but Þrándr accuses him of being a coward:

> „Þrandr svar(ar). Þu ert mannskræfa at meiri at þu getr eigi sott tua eina menn með tuenar tylftir manna. ok er þat hattr þinn at hafa iafnan aðra <at skotspæní> fyrir þer. en þu þorir lítt sealfr nærr at ganga ef nóckvr man raun er. Væri þat nv þitt *ef nóckvr dááð væri

iþer. at ganga fyrstr vpp aa klettinn at Bresti en aðrir fylgði þer. el-
la se ek at þu ert engv nytr."[22]

Þrándrs matured speech hits a very sensitive nerve. He challenges Hafgrímrs' honour and tells him to proof his masculinity. Compelled by dread, the accused decides to demonstrate his determination by attacking Brestir. During this last fray, both are losing their lives. Intended or not, Þrándr finds himself in a comfortable situation. All men in power on the Faroe Islands have died in this battle and their sons and heirs are too young to fill their fathers' shoes.
The social code of a saga tells a lot about the identities and motivations that are circulating within a society. In this case, honour and masculinity play a dominant role in the social standing of the protagonists. Any attempt to provoke someone on these accounts will result in a serious conflict that involves not only individuals but also whole groups and families. At this point, the dynamics of the society can be documented very well. A closer look at family ties should provide necessary information concerning family-internal relationships, with a special focus on brothers.

Fraternal hierarchies

A remarkable parallel that can be drawn between this saga and the Íslendingasǫgur is the frequent usage of the motif of two brothers. In this case, there are two men with close family ties but different from each other when it comes to physical features, attitudes or fighting skills. Susanne Kramarz-Bein has analysed these opposites in fraternal relationships and classified them as ‚polarisations'.[23] To follow up these ideas three fraternal constellations in *Færeyinga saga* are of particular interest in this context:

(1) Þrándr and Þorlákr
(2) Brestir and Beinir
(3) Sigmundr and Þórir

Little is mentioned about the relationship between Þrándr and Þorlákr. Þorlákr is the older brother, and their father is a rich and infuential man. After the death of their father, they share the inheritance, and Þrándr shows his economic skills.

---

[22] HALLDÓRSSON: Færeyinga saga, p. 15.
[23] The term used in her article is "Polarisierung". KRAMARZ: Zwei-Brüder-Motiv, pp. 444-465.

He insists on the father's homestead and lets out his inherited lands to several people and takes the highest rent. He goes abroad to Norway and Denmark to promote his career as tradesman.

At a market in Denmark, a purse with silver is stolen, and the Danish king forces the tradesmen to stay at the market until the thief is apprehended. The tradesmen are pressed for time, and so Þrándr submits an offer to the king. The offer is accepted by all parties: the king and the attendees agree to the offer, and Þrándr gets a large amount of money. He returns to the Faroe Islands as a man of wealth. From a network-theoretical perspective, he takes the opportunity of being in the right place at the right time. The market is a place where many characters (nodes) come together. The most powerful character in that scene, the hub, is the Danish king, because he is able to force the tradesmen to stay at the market. Now everything is focused on the solution to the problem, at which moment Þrándr interferes. His solution addresses the veneration for the king by suggesting that every man at the market should give some silver in honor of the Danish king. The thievery is not resolved but Þrándr finds a suitable compromise by respecting the social code. The resolution prevents everyone from losing their honour, and Þrándr's reputation grows.

The example above does not say much about the relationship of the brothers but it shows that standing up to one's own brother could be understood as a substantial aspect in Saga Litertature, especially in Íslendingasǫgur. A dominant position in this relationship can offer explanations for the course of a saga. The next two cases document how the hierarchy between brothers and some of its consequences are illustrated in this saga.

Brestir and Beinir share their power on the Faroe Islands. Both of them have extraordinary fighting skills and a good reputation. In fact, they differ just in very few characteristics, but Brestir is depicted as one of the main characters of the saga. His actions are always of particular interest, while Beinir's actions are mentioned only in passing, not in a deprecative way, because he is the weaker part in their relationship. In so far, it could be compared to the concept of "primus inter pares", literally "first among equals". No matter what Beinir is doing, Brestir always performs better than his brother, therefore he is the dominant part and his social standing grows.

Their sons and heirs Sigmundr and Þórir are cousins, but they are close like brothers. The saga documents their lives from childhood to men in power. As Gerd Kreutzer has pointed out, the description of children goes along with the depiction of upcoming heroes.[24] So let us take a look at the development of these characters.

Shortly after their fathers Brestir and Beinir die in the battle against Hafgrímr, the boys talk about their future situation. While Þórir is weeping for his father and their miserable situation, Sigmundr is determined and sure that the day of revenge will come and encourages his cousin. This is a recurring theme in this saga. Sigmundr is always the man of action; he is courageous, strong and never shows weakness, while Þórir is the more sensitive part. The boys are isolated from their family and are sold as slaves. They are disconnected from their native social network and can only rely on each other. In Norway, the trader who bought them, sets the boys free and gives them some money. Here they grow up and performe their first heroic deeds. Þórir accepts his role and admits various times that these deeds could only be performed by Sigmundr, e.g. when young Sigmundr kills a bear with an axe. With every action, their reputation grows; they meet powerful people and serve as liegemen for kings.

The Norwegian king Óláfr Tryggvason wants to convert the Faroese people to the Christian faith and chooses Sigmundr to execute this order. He succeeds, but in the course of events he and Þórir are attacked by a group led by Þrándr. They are able to escape and jump into the sea, but Þórir gets weaker and weaker, and finally addresses Sigmundr:

> "[…] þa mællti Þorir alla æfui okkra samuístu hefír ek nu fram lagit sligt er ek til færr vil ek at þu þítt líf vít frænde ef þu falltrazst vid mig."[25]

Sigmundr does not want to part with his fraternal friend Þórir and tries to save the life of his cousin, but when he reaches the beach with Þórir on his back, he is already dead. On the beach, the devitalized Sigmundr is killed by a group of men because they want the golden ring on his hand. It is remarkable that those heroic fraternal relationships end up with each party fighting side by side in their last battles. The ‚hero' of the saga is not supposed to continue his heroic deeds without his brother or fraternal friend, and shortly dies after him. Such characters as Beinir or Þórir might play a subordinate role in the saga, but in a larger context they are an essential part in the development of Social Dynamics. When their position within the social network is missing, the consequences for

---

[24] KREUTZER: Der Held als Kind, pp. 158-166.
[25] HALLDÓRSSON: Færeyinga saga, p. 85.

an interpretation of these texts are dire. In this respect, a network-theoretical approach underlines the importance of every character that is part of a social network.

Concluding remarks

As for initial question: how could Þrándr become such a powerful man in this saga? It can be maintained that strategical non-violent cleverness and well-considered decisions can have the same effects on saga networks as violent fighting activities do. A network-theorectical approach can support our understanding of complex hierarchies and interrelations of characters within the saga's society. In the Faroese case, it can be seen how an apparently minor incident between two men develops into a major conflict that leads to large-scale changes within that society and story Nevertheless, it is important to bear in mind that those activities that simulate Social Dynamics can primarily be found in conflicts that are the results of the identities and the social code of the saga-society. In a nutshell: network-theory offers a variety of models and tools to reinvestigate the complex relationships between characters in Old-Norse saga literature.

Bibliography

ANDERSSON, Theodore M.: *The Icelandic Family Saga. An Analytic Reading.* Harvard University Press, 1967.

BARABÁSI, Albert-László: *Linked: The New Science of Networks*, Cambridge, MA: Perseus, 2002.

BYOCK, Jesse: *Feud in the Icelandic Saga.* Berkeley: University of California Press, 1982.

DURRENBERGER, E. Paul: *The Dynamics of medieval Iceland. Political Economy and Literature*, Iowa City: University of Iowa Press, 1992.

GASKINS, Richard: "Network Dynamics in Saga and Society", in: *Scandinavian Studies* 77.2 (2005), pp. 201-216.

GRANOVETTER, Mark S.: "The Strength of Weak Ties", in: *American Journal of Sociology* 78 (1973), pp. 1360-80.

HALLDÓRSSON, Ólafur: *Færeyinga Saga.* Reykjavík: Stofnun Árna Magnússonar á Íslandi, 1987.

KRAMARZ, Susanne: "Das 'Zwei-Brüder'-Motiv in Droplaugarsona Saga", in: Otmar Werner (ed.): *Arbeiten Zur Skandinavistik: 8. Arbeitstagung Der Skandinavisten Des Deutschen Sprachgebiets, 27.9.-3.10.1987 in Freiburg I. Br.*, Frankfurt a.M.: Peter Lang, 1989, pp. 444-465.

KRAMARZ-BEIN, Susanne: "Literarische Milieus in der skandinavischen höfischen Literatur des 13. bis 15. Jahrhunderts unter dem Aspekt literarischer Vernetzung", in: Thomas Bein et al. (eds.): *mit clebeworten underweben. Festschrift für Peter Kern zum 65. Geburtstag*, Frankfurt a.M.: Peter Lang, 2007, pp. 213-234.

KREUTZER, Gert: „Der Held als Kind – das Kind als Held", in: Bernhard Glienke and Edith Marold (eds.): *Arbeiten Zur Skandinavistik: 10. Arbeitstagung Der Deutschsprachigen Skandinavistik, 22.-27.9. 1991. Am Weissenhäuser Strand*, Frankfurt a/M: Peter Lang, 1993, pp. 158-166.

MAGERØY, Hallvard: *Bandamanna Saga*. London: Viking Society for Northern Research, University College London, 1981.

MILLER, William Ian: *Bloodtaking and Peacemaking: Feud, Law, and Society in Saga Iceland*, Chicago: University of Chicago Press, 1990.

MORETTI, Franco: "Network Theory, Plot Analysis." *Literary Lab pamphlet* (2011: 2) → http://litlab.stanford.edu/LiteraryLabPamphlet2.pdf

SIGURÐSSON, Gísli: *The medieval Icelandic Saga and oral Tradition. A Discourse on Method*, Cambridge, MA: Milman Parry Collection, 2004.

URBAŃCZYK, Przemysław: "The Politics of Conversion in North Central Europe", in: Martin Carver (ed.): *The Cross goes North. Processes of Conversion in Northern Europe, AD 300-1300*, Woodbridge: York medieval press, 2003, pp. 15-27.

MASSIMILIANO BAMPI

Network Theory, Polysystem Theory, and Old Swedish Literature: An Experimental Approach

The aim of this essay is to compare the *network theory* as developed most recently by Albert-László Barabási, especially in his book *Linked: The New Science of Networks* (2002), with the *polysystem theory* advanced by the Israeli scholar Itamar Even-Zohar. As will be shown in the following sections, both theories display a number of interesting points of contact, which enable us to profitably employ them in order to study how one literature may link to other literatures, and how it then develops over time. The observations proposed in the first part of the essay will be applied to the analysis of the repertoire of courtly texts in medieval Sweden. Particular attention will be paid to the role played by the so-called *Eufemiavisor*, three romances translated into Old Swedish from different continental source texts at the beginning of the 14th century, in the shaping and subsequent development of a vernacular literature in Sweden during the Middle Ages.

The following comparison between *network theory* and *polysystem theory* is grounded first and foremost in the fact that both theories share a basic characteristic that is extremely relevant to the purpose of this study: indeed, they are concerned with describing the architecture underlying complex systems in which the network of relations between its components plays a key role for the development of the system itself.

Hence, before turning our attention to the major points of contact between the two theories, a brief overview of the polysystem theory will be given.

Even-Zohar's theory has been developed in a series of papers since the early 1970s.[1] It "offers a general model for understanding, analysing and describing the functioning and evolution of literary systems".[2] In recent years, its application to the study of translated literature has contributed to a lively discussion about the very notion of translation, although in the field of medieval studies the polysystem theory seems to have received very little attention so far.

---

[1] See especially EVEN-ZOHAR: Position of Translated Literaure and EVEN-ZOHAR: Polysystem Studies, for a short presentation of polysystem theory see SHUTTLEWORTH: Polysystem Theory.
[2] SHUTTLEWORTH: Polysystem Theory, p. 176.

The notion of the polysystem, which has been derived in its basic form from the Russian Formalists – and notably from the work of Tynjanov – is at the very heart of this theory.

The polysystem "is conceived as a heterogeneous, hierarchized conglomerate of systems which interact to bring about an ongoing, dynamic process of evolution within the polysystem as a whole."[3] The term *poly*system is used, among other things, to emphasize "the multiplicity of intersections and hence the greater complexity of structuredness involved."[4] The assumption underlying this theoretical position is that "semiotic phenomena (such as culture, language, literature, and society) could more adequately be understood and studied if regarded as systems rather than conglomerates of disparate elements", as Even-Zohar puts it.[5] This emphasizes the importance of considering the interaction between the elements that constitute the system.

Broadly speaking, the literary polysystem is made up of different systems encompassing various genres and types of text. Even-Zohar makes no distinction between *high* and *low* genres, the focus of his attention being on the interaction between the literary forms that make up a literary polysystem. Closely connected to the notion of genre is the (non-élitist) distinction between canonized and non-canonized strata within the polysystem. By canonized is meant "those literary norms and works (i.e., both models and texts) which are accepted as legitimate by the dominant circles within a culture",[6] whereas the term non-canonized refers to the norms and texts rejected by the dominant circles as illegitimate.

The above mentioned hierarchical structure of the polysystem entails that the elements that make it up are constantly competing with each other for the dominant position. According to Even-Zohar, a polysystem has a centre and a periphery, or rather more than one, since "several such positions are hypothesized."[7] Hence, competition plays a key role for the dynamic process of evolution of the polysystem as a whole. The evolution is determined by the struggle between the canonized and the non-canonized forms for the dominant position. Another facet of this competition is the tension between primary (innovative) and secondary (conservative) literary principles. After achieving canonized

---

[3] SHUTTLEWORTH: Polysystem Theory, p. 177.
[4] EVEN-ZOHAR: Polysystem Studies, p. 12.
[5] EVEN-ZOHAR: Polysystem Studies, p. 9.
[6] EVEN-ZOHAR: Polysystem Studies, p. 15.
[7] EVEN-ZOHAR: Polysystem Studies, p. 14.

status a primary form tends to become conservative and "attempts to fight off challenges from newer, emerging literary ideas."[8] Among the systems that make up the literary polysystem is the system of translated literature on which much of Even-Zohar's attention has been focused. Not unlike other systems, translated texts are closely related to other texts in the polysystem and interact with them.

Although translated literature tends to be a peripheral system, being subject to the influence exerted by central systems, Even-Zohar[9] identifies three sets of circumstances where it occupies a primary position:

a) when a polysystem has not yet been crystallized, that is to say, when a literature is "young," in the process of being established;
b) when a literature is either "peripheral" (within a large group of correlated literatures) or "weak," or both;
c) when there are turning points, crises, or literary vacuums in a literature.

As will be shown in the following sections, medieval Swedish literature in the vernacular at the beginning of the 14th century, when the *Eufemiavisor* were translated, falls into the first category.

The very concept of translation changes according to the position of translated literature within the polysystem. For instance, when translation plays a primary function the boundaries between original works and translated texts tend to fade, and the definition of translation becomes freer in that it comes to include imitations and adaptations.

A major aspect of the polysystem theory that is essential to our understanding of the mechanisms governing the development of a literature is that the literary polysystem, with its various genres, is understood as one polysystem within a wider whole which comprises other polysystems (e.g. the artistic, the religious or the political). Hence, literature comes to be viewed as part of a broader sociocultural polysystem which provides "a set of factors that govern the production, promotion and reception of texts."[10]

According to Even-Zohar,

---

[8] SHUTTLEWORTH: Polysystem Theory, p. 177.
[9] EVEN-ZOHAR: Polysystem Studies, p. 47.
[10] SHUTTLEWORTH: Polysystem Theory, p. 177.

> [...] if we assume that the literary system [...] is isomorphic with, say, the social system, its hierarchies can only be conceived of as intersecting with those of the latter. [...] The literary polysystem, like any other socio-cultural system, is conceived of as simultaneously autonomous and heteronomous with all other co-systems.[11]

In other words, what really matters in polysystem theory is the network of *intersystemic* and *intrasystemic* relations.

The features of polysystem theory briefly outlined so far invite comparison with Barabási's network theory. Before launching into a deeper analysis of the analogies that enable us to compare the two theories, I think it needs to be mentioned that the application of the network theory as developed by the Rumanian physicist to the subject of the present study is inevitably of a metaphorical kind since we do not know – as yet, at least – whether Old Swedish literature can be represented as a scale-free network. What is more, this essay does not take the whole literary repertoire of medieval Swedish literature into account. Only a detailed study of the literary polysystem would enable us to determine the full applicability of Barabási's theory to it.

I think it is possible to find four major points of contact between network theory and polysystem theory. First and foremost, as was mentioned earlier, both theories are devised to describe the architecture, the behaviour, and the characteristics of *complex systems* in which it is *the network of relations* among their components that plays a key role for the development of the system itself.

Secondly, such an architecture is *hierarchically* organized. In Barabási's theory, the nodes that make up the network do not play one and the same role. In particular, hubs – i.e. nodes with a considerably higher number of connections than other nodes – are most important because they constitute the pillar of the whole system, the pivot around which the system revolves. According to Barabási, "they dominate the structure of all networks in which they are present, making them look like small worlds:"[12] What is more, hubs are themselves hierarchized.[13]

Thirdly, the evolution of the system is dependent on the *competition* between the components of the system. Barabási explains the evolution of a scale-free

---

[11] EVEN-ZOHAR: Polysystem Studies, p. 23.
[12] BARABÁSI: Linked, p. 64.
[13] "The largest hub is closely followed by a smaller one, which acquires almost as many links as the fittest node. At any moment we have a hierarchy of nodes whose degree distribution follows a power law" BARABÁSI: Linked, p. 103.

network – and the existence of hubs – in terms of 'growth' and 'preferential attachment':

> As new nodes appear, they tend to connect to the more connected sites, and these popular locations thus acquire more links over time than their less connected neighbors. And this 'rich get richer' process will generally favor the early nodes, which are more likely to become hubs.[14]

The way in which the system evolves is determined by the result of such a competition. Fourthly, a major consequence of the tensions arising between elements making up complex systems is that such systems are *dynamic*, i.e. they develop over time.

These four major points of contact provide us with a basis on which a dialogue between network theory and polysystem theory can be established.

Here, the main objective is to provide a description of the behaviour of a complex system such as the literary one. As a (poly)system, literature can be viewed as a network in at least two ways. First, it is a network of interconnected texts. The way in which the texts are interconnected depends on a number of factors, such as the genre they belong to and the socio-cultural characteristics of the addressee. Second, as has been observed earlier, literature is also a network of intrasystemic and intersystemic relations within the broader socio-cultural polysystem. Hence, a literary fact comes to be viewed as the result of various factors, both literary and extra-literary, the interaction of which determines the development of the literary polysystem.

Broadly speaking, one can say that each system making up the polysystem is a network that is, using Even-Zohar's words, "simultaneously autonomous and heteronomous with other co-systems". Thus, in order to understand how a literary network works – be it one single system, encompassing a genre or related genres within the literary macrostructure of the polysystem, or the whole polysystem –, one has to look at the whole network of relations.

A polysystem can be described as a network of networks, represented by the single systems that make it up. Indeed, the adoption of a polysystemic perspective when studying the architecture of networks helps us understand how different networks interact with each other within a common framework.

---

[14] BARABÁSI-BONABEAU: Scale-Free Networks, p. 55.

Furthermore, the application of Barabási's theory to our subject of study, albeit with the caveats given earlier, raises at least two major questions that lead us to focus on some major aspects of the evolution of a literary polysystem. The first question regards the way a literature is linked to other literatures. The second question focuses on the development of the system: is it possible to detect 'textual hubs' within a literary polysystem?

These two questions will lead us into the second part of the analysis. The following sections will focus on the repertoire of courtly texts in medieval Sweden from a twofold perspective:

a) first, taking the Old Swedish literary polysystem as the centre of the discourse, attention will be directed *outwards* in order see how this young literary polysystem – as Even-Zohar would call it – begins to take shape by establishing a connection (both socially and literarily) with other coeval literary polysystems in Europe;

b) second, we will turn our attention *inwards* to determine how the literary polysystem – the new, growing network of texts – develops over time.

In order to propose some observations on both points, the study will focus on the role played by the *Eufemiavisor* in the emergence and subsequent evolution of the Old Swedish literary polysystem.

As was briefly mentioned above, *Eufemiavisor* is a collective name customarily employed to refer to three romances translated into Old Swedish from as many source texts from the continent at the beginning of the 14th century (between 1301 and 1312). It is known that they were translated at the instigation of Queen Eufemia (hence the designation *Eufemiavisor*), who was the wife of the Norwegian king Hákon V Magnússon (1299-1319), on the occasion of the betrothal of her daughter Ingeborg to Duke Erik, brother of the Swedish king Birger Magnusson, in 1302. The translated texts were probably meant as a gift to the couple.[15]

The *Eufemiavisor* represent the first example of secular narrative texts in the vernacular in medieval Sweden, the first major attempt to cross domestic borders and open up to new kinds of influence. As is widely known, before their

---

[15] On the *Eufemiavisor* as a whole see, among others, JANSSON: Eufemiavisorna and WÜRTH: Eufemia.

appearance the only genre in the vernacular that is known to have existed in Sweden is that of the provincial laws (*landskapslagar*).

Hence, the *Eufemiavisor* are of crucial importance for the evolution of the Old Swedish literary polysystem. The three romances are extremely interesting for the purpose of our analysis for two major reasons. First, they represent the first textual node in the literary network of courtly texts. Second, they can be viewed as a major instance of the role played by translation as a 'networking factor', i.e. a means to create new networks and/or to link literatures with each other. Indeed, very often it is by means of translation that literatures come to be interconnected, and the case of Old Swedish literature is certainly no exception.

A brief overview of the major philological questions about the three romances will help us make some further observations on their function within the literary polysystem.

In the case of *Herr Ivan lejonriddaren* and *Flores och Blanzeflor*, scholars have argued that they are most likely to have been translated from the Old Norse *Ívens saga* and *Flóres saga ok Blankiflúr* respectively.[16] Yet some of these scholars have also argued that copies of the French redaction of both romances have been used along with the main source texts. As far as the third romance is concerned – *Hertig Fredrik av Normandie* – it is generally assumed that it was translated from a Middle Low German source which is no longer extant.[17]

These hypotheses bring to the fore the fact that Norway, Northern Germany, and France are the cultures from which the three romances were imported into 14th-century Sweden, thus laying the foundations for the reception of both the ideological and the aesthetic set of values that characterized courtly literature on the continent, and strongly contributing to the development of a Swedish literary language.

The transfer of these texts from one culture into another has been made possible first and foremost by the existence of the network of political and social relationships between Sweden and Norway at the beginning of the 14th century.[18] As was mentioned earlier, the *Eufemiavisor* came into being thanks to the initiative of the Norwegian queen and to the fact that a connection between the two royal houses had been established through a betrothal. Hence, what determines the choice to create a link with other literatures is primarily a factor that is

---

[16] See JANSSON: Eufemiavisorna.
[17] See LAYHER: Origins.
[18] On these aspects see Susanne KRAMARZ-BEIN's essay in this volume.

placed outside the literary realm, though it is still closely connected with it. Indeed, the extra-literary dimension is of crucial importance to understand the dynamics of production, dissemination and reception of texts.

Dynastic connections not only make it possible to import new genres and new modes of narration into the Swedish literary polysystem, as the ties with the Norwegian court demonstrate, but they also contribute to the spreading of texts through the production of manuscripts. Indeed, the major miscellanies preserving literature in the vernacular in medieval Sweden belong to outstanding aristocratic families. A case in point is represented by two of such miscellanies, namely Cod. Holm. D 3 and Cod. Holm D 4 a.[19] As has been pointed out most recently by Per-Axel Wiktorsson,[20] the scribe of D 4 a is Sigge Ulfsson, brother of Märta Ulfsdotter, who is known to have owned the very same manuscript. Furthermore, Märta Ulfsdotter's daughter, Elin Gustavsdotter, is generally considered to be the owner of D 3. Both manuscripts preserve *Herr Ivan* and *Flores och Blanzeflor* and share a number of texts meant to serve different purposes, both for entertainment and for edification. All this makes it clear that the relevance of both interdynastic and intradynastic relationships for the process of development of the Old Swedish literature is undisputable. I think that applying Barabási's theory to the study of how such interrelations develop and expand might be very useful. One might say that it is even possible to build up a construct based on an interaction between these theories: whereas polystystem theory helps us explain the overall functioning of the whole system, network theory provides us with a tool to trace the development of the social relationships which are relevant for the development of the whole system.

Not only a single 'national' literature can be viewed as a complex network. In fact, the same can be said of medieval European literatures as a whole. It is interesting to point out that, according to Even-Zohar, "throughout the Middle Ages, Central and Western Europe constituted one polysystem, where the center was controlled by literature written in Latin, while texts in the vernaculars (either written or spoken) were produced concurrently as part of peripheral activities."[21] The capacity of attracting new connections by other literatures depends on the *authority* of the polysystem as a whole. By authority is meant not only the authority of the literary system as such, but also the social, the political and

---

[19] On both manuscripts see ÅSTRÖM: Manuscripts of Skemptan and CARLQUIST: Handskriften, 105-109.
[20] WIKTORSSON: Äktenskapsvisan, 5-8.
[21] EVEN-ZOHAR: Polysystem Studies, 24.

cultural authority. The more a literary polysystem appears as a model to other literatures, the more it reaches the status of something that is comparable to a hub in network theory.

The fact that some literatures, more than others, can be considered as hubs is more or less equal to saying that they come to occupy a position within the macro-polysystem that is closer to the centre than to the periphery. This enables such literatures to struggle for the dominant position, i.e. to acquire more and more connections.

The *Eufemiavisor* enable the Old Swedish literary polysystem to grow by attaching to those polysystems that played a key role for the production and dissemination of courtly literature. As was mentioned above, this growth is made possible first and foremost by the initiative of the Norwegian queen, in other words by the existence of a network of extra-literary relations.

Once the textual connection with such literatures has been established through the *Eufemiavisor*, it is even more interesting to look inside the polysystem to see what role they played for the subsequent growth of the literary network, especially as regards texts that were intended to address an aristocratic audience.

What can be observed is that the *Eufemiavisor* seemingly retained a key role in the following decades. This can be seen by looking at the relation between them and texts that were either composed or translated into Old Swedish from continental sources in the 14th and 15th centuries, and that were meant as texts for an audience made up of members of the Swedish aristocracy.

The comparison brings to the fore the influence of the *Eufemiavisor* on some texts, notably *Erikskrönikan*, redaction C of *Sju vise mästare*, and *Namnlös och Valentin*. It is not the scope of this paper to discuss in great detail the influence of the *Eufemiavisor* on these texts. However, some remarks are indispensable. *Erikskrönikan* is the most important and oldest example of rhymed chronicles (*rimkrönikor*) in medieval Sweden. It was composed some years after the translation of *Flores och Blanzeflor*, the youngest of the *Eufemiavisor*, between 1320 and 1335. Scholars have acknowledged a direct influence of the three romances on this chronicle, especially in terms of style.[22] There is no doubt that the *Erikskrönika* was meant to address an aristocratic audience. This is made obvious not only by the fact that it tells the story of Swedish kings and knights at a crucial period in the kingdom's development, but also by the fact that the text con-

---

[22] See especially LÖNNROTH: Det höviska tilltalet, p. 107.

tinued to be copied in manuscripts belonging to the aristocracy long after the topicality of the themes it dealt with was over.[23]

Sju vise mästare is the Old Swedish translation of the *Septem Sapientes*, a collection of exemplary tales of Oriental origin about wicked women and wise counsellors. The Old Swedish reception consists of three different translations. Redaction C was translated in all likelihood from a Middle Low German exemplar, very probably from an incunabulum printed in Lübeck by Lucas Brandis around 1478.[24] A comparison between the incunabulum and the Swedish translation brings to the fore a number of passages where the translator rewrote the text to adapt it to the reception by an aristocratic (probably female) audience. As I tried to show elsewhere, the changes made by the translator appear to follow the ideological principles that characterize the representation of the courtly world in the *Eufemiavisor*.[25] Furthermore, a number of formulae employed in the three romances crop up in this redaction of *Sju vise mästare*.

The same kind of analogies can be found in *Namnlös och Valentin*, a translation into prose from a Middle Low German exemplar (in verse) dating from around the middle of the 15th century. Scholars have spotted in it a considerable number of formulae taken from the *Eufemiavisor* that have been inserted into the translated text.[26] In addition to this, the same kind of translation strategy as that of *Sju vise mästare* can be observed: also in this text, certain passages, in which the representation of noble characters judged as inappropriate, are rewritten to adapt them to courtly norms.[27] Again, this is a feature that can be traced back to the *Eufemiavisor*.[28]

The fact that the *Eufemiavisor* are so relevant to the evolution of the literary polysystem can profitably be seen against the background of network theory. Indeed, it is fair to say that they become a textual hub in that they attract connections from younger nodes (in our case, the three texts mentioned above). Yet a distinction must be made between the node of the *Erikskrönika* and the nodes of the two translated texts, *Sju vise mästare* and *Namnlös och Valentin*. In the first case both the chronological distance and the social composition of the au-

---

[23] Two major examples are Cod. Holm. D 4 a and Cod. Holm. D 3.
[24] See SCHÖNDORF: Sju vise mästare.
[25] See BAMPI: Reception of the Septem Sapientes, pp. 91-113.
[26] See WOLF: Namnlös och Valentin, pp. LXXXII-LXXXIV.
[27] See WOLF: Namnlös och Valentin, pp. C-CI.
[28] See JANSSON: Eufemiavisorna, p. 47. On the translation strategy of *Flores och Blanzeflor* see also BAMPI: Translating Courtly Literature.

dience help us account for the fact that a clear influence from the *Eufemiavisor* can be observed. In polysystemic terms, when a literary system is in the process of being established – as is clearly the case with that of medieval Sweden – translation as an innovative force "participates actively in shaping the center of the polysystem", as Even-Zohar points out.[29] Hence, texts (both translated and original ones) produced during a period in which translation plays such a major role tend to adopt the models and the norms established by translated texts.

On the contrary, the case of *Sju vise mästare* and of *Namnlös och Valentin* tells us that the model of the *Eufemiavisor* was still influential a century and a half after they had been translated. Such an influence regards the thematic, the stylistic and the ideological levels. A different consideration should be made with regard to the formal aspect, since both *Sju vise mästare* and *Namnlös och Valentin* are in prose whereas the *Eufemiavisor* are written in knittelvers. However, such aspects deserve a more in-depth treatment which would exceed the scope of this paper.

Even-Zohar's theory helps us account for the long-lived centrality of the three translated romances. In particular, the concept of *dynamic canonicity* is most useful in considering this question. There is dynamic canonicity when

> [...] a certain literary model manages to establish itself as a productive principle in the system through the latter's repertoire. It is this latter kind of canonization which is the most crucial for the system's dynamics.[30]

Broadly speaking, if a text manages to establish itself as a model, it keeps exerting an influence on other texts over a long period of time because of its "exemplarity" within the system. Furthermore, this kind of canonicity enables the textual model to occupy a central position within the hierarchical structure of the polysystem.

I think it is safe to assert that what is called a model in polysystem theory can be equated with a hub in network theory. Hence, in the case under study the *Eufemiavisor* can be considered as a textual hub.

Another major question that is closely related to that of the position of translated texts within a polysystem is why the *Eufemiavisor* could remain so influential, especially if one considers that according to Even-Zohar translated texts tend to occupy a peripheral position in the long run. One possible answer to this

---

[29] EVEN-ZOHAR: Polysystem Studies, p. 46.
[30] EVEN-ZOHAR: Polysystem Studies, p. 19.

question can be reached if one looks at the network of relations within the polysystem. More specifically, judging from what is known to us of the Old Swedish literary repertoire, translated texts do not seem to set into motion a process of imitation that yields the composition of original works of the same kind and genre, based and modelled on them. In Sweden there is no such thing as the indigenous *riddarasögur* in the West Norse polysystem, which were partly patterned after the translated *riddarasögur*. This entails, among other things, that in the struggle for the occupation of the central position in the literary system made up of texts intended for an aristocratic audience, the *Eufemiavisor* as the very first example of translation of chivalric literature were not challenged by original works in the course of the development of the polysystem.

An exception is represented by the *Erikskrönika* and the later chronicles that took it as their model. As far as chronicles are concerned, also the *Erikskrönika* can be considered as a textual hub.

Furthermore, what has been observed thus far enables us to see translation as a networking factor not only between different literary polysystems, as was mentioned earlier, but also between different systems within the same polysystem, beyond any strict distinction of genre. The case of redaction C of *Sju vise mästare* is particularly interesting. Indeed, it is a collection of tales that were intended to provide material for the moral edification of a probably female aristocratic audience, possibly within the walls of the Cistercian nunnery at Askeby, in Östergötland. Thus, it is neither a romance nor a text meant to be used for the sole entertainment of the audience. Yet it shares with the *Eufemiavisor* both the ideological set of values that characterize the courtly world and the preoccupation to be also instructive through entertaining stories. Hence, the *Eufemiavisor* have probably been adopted as a model by the translator of redaction C of *Sju vise mästare* because they were still *canonic* – in polysystemic terms – to address an audience whose *Weltanschauung* still revolved around the social, the ideological and the moral values represented in those texts. Accordingly, in this case the *preferential attachment* described by Barabási can be explained mainly in social and ideological terms.

This leads us to propose some concluding remarks on what has been pointed out thus far. It seems to me that the case discussed in this paper enables us to say that the networking process by which a literature is connected to other literatures (and by which texts are connected to other texts) is first and foremost dependent on social, political and ideological factors that obviously have a bearing on literary facts.

As Even-Zohar points out:

> Texts and repertoire are only partial manifestations of literature, manifestations whose behaviour cannot be explained by their own structure. It is on the level of the literary (poly)system that their behaviour is explicable.[31]

In other words, literature as a complex semiotic phenomenon cannot be properly understood without taking into account its interrelations with other major aspects of the culture within which it comes to play a role.

Bibliography

ÅSTRÖM, Patrik: "The Manuscripts of *Skemptan*," in: Olle Ferm and Bridget Morris (ed.): *Master Golyas and Sweden. The Transformation of a Clerical Satire*, Stockholm: Sällskapet Runica et Mediævalia, 1997, pp. 235–256.

BAMPI, Massimiliano: "Translating Courtly Literature and Ideology in Medieval Sweden. *Flores och Blanzeflor*," in: *Viking and Medieval Scandinavia* 4 (2008), pp. 1–14.

BAMPI, Massimiliano: *The Reception of the* Septem Sapientes *in Medieval Sweden between Translation and Rewriting*, Göppingen: Kümmerle Verlag, 2007.

BARABÁSI, Albert-László: *Linked. The New Science of Networks*, Cambridge, Massachusetts: Perseus Publishing, 2002.

BARABÁSI, Albert-László and Eric Bonabeau: "Scale-Free Networks," in: *Scientific American* 288 (2003), pp. 50–59.

CARLQUIST, Jonas: *Handskriften som historiskt vittne. Fornsvenska samlingshandskrifter – miljö och funktion*, Stockholm: Sällskapet Runica et Mediævalia, 2002.

EVEN-ZOHAR, Itamar: "The Position of Translated Literature Within the Literary Polysystem", in: James S. Holmes, Jose Lambert and Raymond van den Broeck (ed.): *Literature and Translation. New Perspectives in Literary Studies*, Leuven: Acco, 1978, pp. 117–127.

---

[31] EVEN-ZOHAR: Polysystem Studies, p. 18.

EVEN-ZOHAR, Itamar: *Polysystem Studies*, Tel Aviv: The Porter Institute of Poetics and Semiotics, 1990.

JANSSON, Valter: *Eufemiavisorna. En filologisk undersökning*, Uppsala and Leipzig: Lundequistiska bokhandeln and Otto Harrasowitz, 1945.

LAYHER, William: "Origins of the Old Swedish Epic *Hertig Fredrik af Normandie*. A Middle Dutch Link?", in: *Tijdschrift voor Skandinavistiek* 21 (2000), pp. 223–249.

LÖNNROTH, Lars: "Det höviska tilltalet", in: Lars Lönnroth and Sven Delblanc (ed.): *Den Svenska Litteraturen. Från forntid till frihetstid, 800-1718*, Stockholm: Bonnier, 1987, pp. 93–123.

SCHÖNDORF, Kurt Erich: "Die altschwedische Version C von 'Sju vise mästare' und ihre mittelniederdeutsche Vorlage", in: Lennart Elmevik and Kurt E. Schöndorf (ed.): *Niederdeutsch in Skandinavien* III, Berlin: de Gruyter, 1992, pp. 49–69.

SHUTTLEWORTH, Mark: "Polysystem Theory", in: Mona Baker (ed.): *Routledge Encyclopedia of Translation Studies*, London and New York: Routledge, 1998, pp. 176–179.

WIKTORSSON, Per-Axel: *Äktenskapsvisan. En lustig visa om samgåendets vedermödor*, Stockholm: Sällskapet Runica et Mediævalia, 2007.

WOLF, Werner: *Namnlös och Valentin. Kritische Ausgabe mit nebenstehender mittelniederdeutscher Vorlage*, Uppsala: Svenska fornskriftsällskapet, 1934.

WÜRTH, Stefanie: „Eufemia. Deutsche Auftraggeberin schwedischer Literatur am norwegischen Hof", in: Fritz Paul (ed.): *Arbeiten zur Skandinavistik (13. Arbeitstagung der deutschsprachigen Skandinavistik 29.7.-3.8.1997 in Lysebu/Oslo)*, Frankfurt am Main and Basel: Peter Lang, 2000, pp. 269–281.

SUSANNE KRAMARZ-BEIN

Neuronal Networking in Literary Criticism as exemplified by Medieval Literary Milieus in Scandinavia

I. Introduction: Networked Literary Milieus in Medieval Scandinavian Chivalric Literature from the Thirteenth Century to the Fifteenth[1]

In Scandinavian culture and literature, the first tendencies of Europeanisation can already be found in medieval literature, this, however, being *avant la lettre*. Here, first appearances take place in the Old Norwegian chivalric literature of the 13th century, whereas, at the same time, a *claim* for Europeanisation by the Norwegian monarchy of the Sverrir dynasty was closely connected to it. According to first approaches of establishing a literary milieu under the dynasty's founder Sverrir Sigurðarson (r. 1177-1202), the formation of a literary basic milieu with European accentuation and a claim for political parity with the rulers of Continental Europe may first be found in the chivalric literary milieu of the Norwegian king (and grandson of Sverrir) Hákon IV. Hákonarson (r. 1217-1263). Under the aegis of Sverrir himself, the *Sverris saga* was written (around 1300) as one of the early kings' sagas, which, however, is not yet to be connected to the notion of Europe. On the other hand, during his long reign, which was influenced by Continental Europe, Hákon IV encouraged the genre of the so-called 'translated riddarasögur'/chivalric sagas, beginning with the genre-shaping translation of the Anglo-Norman chivalric novel of *Tristan* by Thomas de Bretagne (*Tristrams saga*, 1226), which he had commissioned. This happened on the basis of 'importing' continental chivalric themes to Norway within the scope of Hákon's cultural and educational policies. To these 'riddarasögur' belong, besides saga adaptations from the Arthurian subject matter, epic works such as the *Karlamagnús saga* and the *Þiðreks saga*, both written around 1250 in the literary milieu of Hákon. Hákon thereby initiated the chivalric phase of Norwegian literature from the 13th to the 15th centuries or, in other words, made the Norwegian contribution to European networking. An application of the literary network theory especially to this species of secular translated chivalric literature serves as a constructive theory model because of its further development, which (not least for dynastic reasons) spread 'epidemically' over

---

[1] For a general overview, see KRAMARZ-BEIN: Þiðreks saga im Kontext, pp. 68-101.

to the neighbouring countries, first of all Sweden. This theory model relates to the notion of Europe inasmuch as German cultural and literary traditions, established themselves in Scandinavia. Proceeding from France as the base of European chivalric culture, this happened in a first West Nordic phase of cultural transfer via England to the court of Hákon (first half of the 13th cent.) in Bergen, Norway, and in a second phase of development via Swedish East Nordic transmission to the court of Eufemia (end of the 13th to the first half of the 14th centuries) in Oslo. The East Scandinavian chivalric Eufemia milieu was continued by the daughter generation of Ingebjørg Hákonardóttir, who, on the paternal side, was the great-granddaughter of the Norwegian king and initiator of the chivalric milieu, Hákon IV. On the occasion of Ingebjørgs engagement and her later marriage to the 'courtly' Swedish Duke Erik Magnusson (d. 1319), Old Swedish literature received, subsequently, a chivalric impulse for a period of about 20 years (*Eufemiavisorna*, 1303, 1308, 1312, as well as *Erikskrönikan/ Eric's Chronicle*, c. 1320/21). A later 'reactivation' of this chivalric milieu finally took place in the middle of the 15th century at the partly German-speaking court of the Swedish King Karl VIII Knútsson (Bonde, 1408 or 1409-1470) in Stockholm, who was interested in German literature and culture. Besides the *Karlskrönika*, the commission of which was given by Karl VIII (probably for reasons of propaganda, legitimation of power or memorial culture). It was in his literary milieu that the Old Norwegian *Þiðreks saga*, which had developed in the 13th century in the Old Norwegian courtly-literary milieu of Hákon IV, was translated into Old Swedish (*Didriks Krönika*, around 1450). For the development of the latter, one has to consider similar and, furthermore, 'proto-national' motivations.[2] As an aetiological model to explain the chivalric culture proceeding from France and its epidemically spreading effect, which led to a networking of the whole of Europe from the South to the West to the North, the network theory is applicable in a methodologically profitable way. However, this current theory was originally developed in the American research discourse of natural sciences in order to serve the description of ecological systems (in biology) or - in medical research - a new discipline promisingly applied in order to fight epidemics (amongst others SARS- and influenza epidemics and the avian plague or bird flu). As the basic work of this recent direction of research, one can regard the publication by the Romanian professor of physics, Albert-László

---

[2] Cf. here, more precisely, KRAMARZ-BEIN: Karls- und Dietrichdichtung.

Barabási, who teaches at the University of Indiana and who is the leader of a body of research called "complex networks". In his search for universal principles of order, Barabási discovered some so-called "scale-free networks" in his analysis of organisms, which showed several 'nodal points' (amongst these many small and few large ones, so-called hubs), which can be identified as such via mathematical power laws.

I.1. Barabási's network theory

In the following, I will go into the network theory in more detail - largly according to Albert-László Barabási - as far as it contributes to a more profound understanding of the literary relations and cultural transmission to the Scandinavian countries. In his work *Linked: How everything is Connected to Everything Else and What it Means for Business, Science, and Everyday Life* (2003), the Romanian scholar and professor Albert-László Barabási describes how all domains of human communication are linked with one another and what this means for social and economic life. In his research, he discovers the omnipresent mode of action in networks: "Today we increasingly recognize that nothing happens in isolation. Most events and phenomena are connected, caused by, and interacting with a huge number of other pieces of a complex universal puzzle. We have come to see that we live in a small world, where everything is linked to everything else. We are witnessing a revolution in the making as scientists from all different disciplines discover that complexity has a strict architecture. We have come to grasp the importance of networks."[3]

According to Barabási, the starting point of the social network theory is the presumption that social networks can be met everywhere. "Networks are present everywhere. All we need is an eye for them. As you move from link to link within this book, you will learn to see society as a complex social network and to grasp the smallness of this great world in which we live."[4] Networks can be found in all areas of life. Barabási illustrates how they come into being, giving the example of a party with ten guests, not all of whom know one another. First, the guests begin to talk in small groups, the different groups still isolated from one another. Within the small groups, social connections develop successively, so that the guests in the other groups become outsiders. After some time, three guests merge into other groups, and a large cluster is formed. Although still not

---

[3] BARABÁSI: Linked, p. 7.
[4] BARABÁSI: Linked, p. 7.

all the guests know one another, there is now a social network including all guests. Each of these guests is now connected to all of the others via a cross-link: "The network, after placing a critical number of links, drastically changes. Before, we have a bunch of tiny isolated clusters of nodes, disparate groups of people that communicate only within the clusters. After, we have a giant cluster, joined by almost everybody."[5]

According to Barabási, there is a network among all people on earth. Even if they do not know each other personally, there is a guarantee that they are interconnected by cross-links via other people.

What's more, another network theorist, Mark Granovetter, differentiates between 'strong ties' and 'weak ties'. 'Strong ties' are mostly being represented by close friends, whereas 'weak ties' refer to more distant acquaintances. From the aspect of networking, this means that close friends are, as a rule, also friends with one another. Consequently, categorisation into "weak ties" or "strong ties" depends on the different degrees of intensity, expenditure of time or the intimacy of the relationship. Concerning the development of networks, it is important that particularly the "weak ties" play a central role because: "The weak ties, or acquaintances, are our bridge to the outside world, since by frequenting different places they obtain their information from different sources than our immediate friends."[6] Mark Granovetter examines the importance of the "weak ties" in connection with a study on people seeking employment. The result of this study was that the majority of the job seekers gained information about their new job from acquaintances - that is via "weak ties" -, which proves the power of the "weak ties", since it is these which network social groups.[7] Now, the formation of network structures works according to two criteria: 'growth' and 'preferential attachment', which means that every network starts with a small nucleus and expands with every new developing nodal point, or 'node'. When establishing new connections, however, these nodes especially prefer those nodes which have already developed many links - this is called 'preferential attachment': "We assume that each new node connects to the existing nodes with two links. The probability that it will choose a given node is proportional to the number of links the chosen node has. That is, given the choice between two nodes, one

---

[5] BARABÁSI: Linked, p. 18.
[6] BARABÁSI: Linked, p. 43.
[7] cf. GRANOVETTER: Strength of Weak Ties, pp. 1360-80; Furthermore, Holger Bienzle provided a remarkable introduction to Network theory in Germany (BIENZLE: Kunst des Netzwerkens).

with twice as many links as the other. it is twice as likely that the new node will connect to the more connected node."⁸ This, again, means that groups with many nodes become 'richer' still in their links, which is - in accord with the bible (Matthew 13:12) also called the Matthew Principle: "For whosoever hath, to him shall be given" (Matthew 13:12).

But what use is the application of this network theory to the examination of medieval Scandinavian literary relations? In how far is this theory model applicable to the medieval cultural transmission from Southern Europe to Scandinavia? "An application of the literary network theory especially to this type of secular translated chivalric literature serves as a constructive theory model because of its further development which (not least for dynastic reasons) spread 'epidemically' over to the neighbouring countries (first of all Sweden) [...]."⁹

Additionally, the marriage politics of the Scandinavian dynasties in question can be understood in the context of the mode of action of the network theory, too. The Norwegian King Hákon Hákonarson reigned over the Norwegian empire for 46 years, that is for a very long time, from 1217 to 1263. Under his reign, Norway expanded to a size larger than it had ever been. This is to say, the territory reached into West Atlantic areas, and even Iceland was under the Norwegian crown from 1262/64 onwards. This expansion, however, also served political and cultural purposes.¹⁰

In conclusion, it can be said that there were several possibilities and ways to transmit continental European literature to Scandinavia, including people as well as political structures and real historical contexts.

Based on the network theory by Albert-László Barabási, we discover that social networks can be found everywhere, which means that also in medieval Europe cross-links and social networks existed among different dynasties. Of special interest in the Scandinavian context is the relationship between the Norwegian Princess Ingebjørg and the Swedish Duke Erik. Through this marriage, a direct dynastic connection was established between the two royal houses, which, in any case, was beneficial for literary transmission. Furthermore, from the aspect of 'networking', Princess Eufemia of Rügen (German: Eufemia von Arnstein, who was of German descent) should be mentioned. Eufemia, who was raised in Northern Germany and who was very much interested in French literature, mar-

---

[8] BARABÁSI: Linked, p. 86.
[9] KRAMARZ-BEIN: Neuronale Vernetzung, p. 15.
[10] KRAMARZ-BEIN: Þiðreks saga im Kontext, pp. 68-81.

ried the Norwegian heir to the throne Hákon V, whereby a dynastic connection was established between Germany and Sweden as well. In any respect, Eufemia gained notable relevance to the Scandinavian literary milieu of the Middle Ages because of her profound interest in French literature. For instance, she had the so-called *Eufemiavisor* translated into Old Swedish - that is *Yvain* by Chrétien, *Hertig Fredrik av Normandie* and *Flores och Blanzeflor*. Here, it is important to note that these were not simply 'mere translations', but the works were given their own national traits, which means that they were edited especially for the Scandinavian public that had its own interests and expectations.[11]

Beside the reasons mentioned above, there were other historical factors which favoured cultural transfer in the Scandinavian area, among them the Hanseatic League. In this context, the Norwegian city of Bergen proved very important. With the different cities in several countries (e.g. England, Germany, The Netherlands), a loose net developed, in which trade relations took place. Consequently, the interest in the culture of the foreign country grew due to this cooperation of towns and the augmentation of trade relations. Additionally, it offered the possibility for merchants to take home foreign literature and communicate it there.[12]

Now, comparable mechanisms can also serve as fertile ground for literary criticism, as becomes clear in current research in the Dutch cultural area as well as in the research discourse in Dutch philology and the theory of 'epidemic' literary networks and examinations in the sense of 'network analysis', which was mostly developed there (e.g. Wouter de Noy). Such analyses and applications are currently being made and discussed both in medieval studies and modern comparative studies of different genres and epochs. Therefore, in connection with - in any way related - research in Dutch studies, this essay, too, is to be regarded as an attempt to make a constructive contribution to the description and the aetiological understanding of the networking of the chivalric literary and cultural traditions in Central and Northern Europe. Hence, it follows the example of the inter-cultural networking of literary milieus - which was motivated not least by dynasty - in the Old Norwegian and Old Swedish literature from the 13th to the 15th centuries. In the Old Norse field of research, one breaks relatively new grounds with this point of view. For such an application of this theory to Old Norse contexts there has been only one scholarly advance

---

[11] KRAMARZ-BEIN: Þiðreks saga im Kontext, pp. 265 ff.
[12] KRAMARZ-BEIN: Þiðreks saga im Kontext, pp. 68-101.

in American research discourse, by Richard Gaskins. Consequently, this is one more reason to further verify the capacity of this idea, using the example of the Old Norse transmission of the topics of Charlemagne and Theodoric the Great. Along with the suggestions concerning this network, there also are recent discoveries in biological and medical neurosciences that should be considered as a model in which the idea of 'neuronal networks' and here, the inquiry into 'biological synapses and their way of functioning', form a prevalent option literary criticism could profit from as well.

The material of the Old Norse epic poetry about Charlemagne and Theodoric the Great, which here forms the basis, is, for the North, a matter of translated chivalric literature on the threshold to heroic epic. The basic texts the Old West Norse *Karlamagnús saga ok kappa hans* and the Old East Norse *Karl Magnús' Krønike* will be compared and related to the Old West Norse *Þiðreks saga* and the Old East Norse *Didriks Krönika*, whereby the focus will, accordingly, be on the development and networking of central Scandinavian literary milieus from the 13th to the 15th centuries. Apart from its roots all over Europe, it is particularly German and Low-German sources which are of main interest in the case of the Scandinavian epic poetry of Theodoric and Charlemagne. Yet, in addition to its relevance to Old Germanic studies, the focus is on the Old Scandinavian literary context.

II. Medieval Scandinavian transmission of the subject matter of Charlemagne and Theodoric the Great

The medieval Scandinavian transmission of the subject matter of Charlemagne and Theodoric the Great is mostly preserved from the Old West Norse (i.e. Old Norwegian and Old Icelandic) language and cultural area. Here, the originally Old Norwegian *Karlamagnús saga ok kappa hans* and the Old Norwegian *Þiðreks saga af Bern*, represent the most substantial prose documents of their traditional subject matter. The Old East Norse references were written as translations from the Old West Norse originals, but with specific accentuations and interests. It seems advantageous to examine the East Scandinavian Charlemagne- and Theodoric-transmissions in this constellation together because these two subject matters have to be seen as central documents (of approximately equal length) of a common literary developmental milieu in the Old West Norse tradition and, within this milieu, show ideological affinities with one another. Along with other sagas from the Arthurian subject matter, *Karlamagnús saga* and *Þiðreks saga* respectively belong to the broader context of the Old Norwegian originally so-called 'translated riddarasögur'/chivalric sagas of the type of *matière de France* and *matière d'Allemagne* (Leach). These two types belong to the continent-based chivalric literary developmental milieu around the middle of the 13th century, which received its main impulse from the Norwegian King Hákon IV Hákonarson [r. 1217-1263] within the scope of his cultural and educational politics. As for the East Scandinavian literary context, it may be considered significant that well-established heroes of the West Scandinavian chivalric milieu such as Perceval, Theodoric the Great and Roland the Brave of the subject matter of the Charlemagne cycle were established and appreciated here. First of all, this was at the court of Eufemia in Oslo at the end of the 13th and the beginning of the 14th centuries, where they were commonly referred to in order to illustrate parallels between them and other heroes or sovereigns. Clearly, the (end-rhymed) *Eufemia-visa Herra Ivan Lejonriddaren* (1303) proves this with herra Ivan's superiority and bravery in battle being used intertextually by analogy with the above-mentioned well-established heroes of continental Europe, which he does not have to fear: "herra Percefal oc Diderik van Bærna/ them bestodhe han [herra Ivan] nw badhom gærna" (ll. 555f.) and "huath man sigher aff Roland/ han giordhe ey mera medh sinne hand/ a runzefal tha han var thær/ æn herra Iwan giordhe hær" (ll. 2521-2524).[13] Furthermore, in the prologue to *Herra Ivan* (ll. 15-18) a parallel is drawn between Charlemagne and King Arthur, with particular reference to their laudable services to the heathen mission. It is the fact that the subject of Theodoric and Charlemagne, as well as the heroes themselves, is repeatedly mentioned and discussed collectively that supports, in the East Scandinavian context, their belonging together, which is already familiar in the West Scandinavian area. Nevertheless, the cultural ways of transmission were specific in both cases: in the West, via Angevin cultural transmission (among this, above all, the chivalric *Tristrams saga* from 1226 as 'initiative'), and in the East, via (Northern) German cultural transfer. In contrast to the chivalric cultural traditions of Old West Norse or Old Norwegian, those in the Old East Norse or Old Swedish cultural area cannot be found before the period between the second half of the 13th to the middle of the 14th centuries, under the aegis of the Folkungar kings Valdemar (r. 1266-1275) and Magnus Ladulås (r. 1275-1290). Yet, a corresponding chivalric social class, following the continental German example, developed only successively in Sweden. Here,

---

[13] Cf. NOREEN: Herra Ivan.

chivalric literature is strongly linked with the name of the patron of literature, Eufemia of Rügen (Germ.: Eufemia von Arnstein; of German descent), who was, on the one hand, dynastically connected to Norway through her marriage with the Norwegian heir to the throne, Hákon V Magnússon in 1299, but, on the other hand, still orientated towards German literary examples. Likewise, this meant, as opposed to the Old West Norse saga prose, a preference of end rhyme, or rather *knittelvers* with rhyming couplets using a four-stress line in the chivalric *Eufemiavisor*, introduced and commissioned into Old Swedish by, and therefore named after, Eufemia. In a publication of 2000, Stefanie Würth made fundamental contributions to this East Scandinavian literary milieu of the Eufemia-court in Oslo; this serves as a reference here.[14]

Additionally, with regard to the Inter-Scandinavian dynastic relations towards the turn of the 14th century, it is important that for Eufemia's and Hákon's V daughter (and Princess of Norway) Ingebjørg, the engagement to the "courtly" Swedish Duke Erik Magnusson was arranged in 1302. It led to their marriage in 1312, at a time in which Old Swedish literature was in its chivalric phase, which lasted for about 20 years. Accordingly, the assumption is relevant to cultural politics that the chivalric *Eufemiavisor* can be connected to this (as an engagement or wedding present). Moreover, Würth differentiates between the literary particularities of the East Scandinavian tradition which uses rhymed couplets in *knittelvers* in accordance with German examples, and the West Scandinavian tradition. Quintessentially, the picture of the dynamic Inter-Scandinavian cultural transfer in the 13th and beginning of the 14th centuries is not least completed by the fact that both chivalric-literary milieus (the Old Norwegian one in Bergen in the 13th and the Old Swedish one in Oslo in the beginning of the 14th century) are dynastically connected to each other in the great-grandchildren's generation of Princess Ingebjørg Hákonardóttir.

Concerning the literary milieu of the court of Eufemia in Oslo, it was already in 1991 that Bengt R. Jonsson put forward extensive new theses supporting an earlier dating of the genre of ballads.[15] In linking its development with the court of Eufemia - his so-called 'Oslo theory' - and claiming it to have come into being between 1300 and c. 1320, he dated it much earlier than usual in tradition. In the context of the East Scandinavian epic poetry of Charlemagne and Theodoric the Great, the results of the Eufemia-court in Oslo are relevant inasmuch as

---

[14] Cf. WÜRTH: Eufemia.
[15] JONSSON: Oral Literature, Written Literature.

they can make substantial contributions to the East Scandinavian chivalric cultural and/or literary milieu of the early 14th century. Again, the later extensions of this can be related to the younger textual documents of the 15th century dealt with here, and, thus, the literary milieu of the court of Karl VIII Knútsson (Bonde, 1408 or 1409-1470).

Eufemia's son-in-law, Duke Erik Magnusson (d. 1319), was a politically influential sovereign at the beginning of 14th century Scandinavia. In accordance with the cultural temporary fashions of that time, he is "described as the incarnation of the chivalric ideal" in the Old Swedish *Erikskrönika* (1320/21), which was dedicated to him.[16] This is apparently owing to his confirmed particular bounteousness ("then milled"), by which the courteous term "generosity" is recalled, amongst other things. A relation to the East Scandinavian epic prose of Theodoric and Charlemagne does not least result from the *Erikskrönika* and its prologue about Sweden. Here, - hardly by accident - an analogy between the local heroes and Theodoric the Great is established with the intention to propagate their equality with the famous hero from Berne: "godha tiägna finder man ther (= in Sweden)/ ridderskap ok häladha godha/ the Didrik fan berner vel bestodo" (ll. 18-20).

Moreover, translations such as the Old Swedish *Didriks Krönika* and the Old Danish *Karl Magnus' Krønike* follow similar principles of translation and composition and a similar ideal in style. Concerning the East Scandinavian milieu, also at the time of the literary milieu at the court of Karl VIII, these principles lead, more generally, to hints about their belonging to a comparable milieu or school as the above-mentioned ones of the Eufemia-court.

All in all, this can be seen as a reason for the fact that the matière of Theodoric and Charlemagne belong together not only in the West Scandinavian but also in the East Scandinavian literary area, like in their West Scandinavian milieu- and school context of the 13th century. Comparing it with the Swedish *Karl Magnus* - which is relevant here as well -, but also with the Danish *Karl Magnus' Krønike*. Bengt Henning observes in his dissertation on the *Didriks Krönika* equal principles of translation and composition, which allow general conclusions about the principles of translation used in the East Scandinavian literary area. These were, for example, shortening or eliminating digressions and doublets and improving their (West Nordic) originals (i.e. the *Karlamagnús saga* and the *Þiðreks saga*) with regard to composition and the aim of sound stringency.

---

[16] Cf. WÜRTH: Eufemia.

For a better understanding of the networked development of the Scandinavian literary milieus from the 13th to the 15th centuries, which is of main interest here, a short digression concerning the literary activities of Hákon's IV descendants (sons and grandsons) will be inserted here.[17]

II.1. The impact of the kings of the Sverrir-dynasty on literary development

Hákon IV Hákonarson and the whole Sverrir-dynasty (beginning with the founder Sverrir Sigurðarson [r. 1177-1202], under whose aegis the *Sverris saga* [around 1300] was written as an early kings' saga), were of cultural political relevance to the genuine Old Norwegian literature and the literature translated into Old Norwegian, of the 13th and beginning of the 14th centuries. In order to convey the idea of this phenomenon, it is necessary to take into consideration the brisk literary initiatives of this Norwegian dynasty, which was of integrative value to the Old Norwegian literature. In the first place, it was Hákon IV Hákonarson himself who was the initiator of the literary milieu of translated literature from the Anglo-Norman Arthurian and the Frankish-Carolingian subject matters/areas. His sons and one of his grandsons continued this tradition. Accordingly, the name of his son and heir to the throne, Magnús Hákonarson *Lagabœtir*/ 'the Law-mender' (r. 1263-80), is closely connected to the record of the Old Norwegian allegiance law, the *Hirðskrá*, and he commissioned Sturla Þórðarson to write the *Hákonar saga*, the most well-known kings' saga about his father. Besides, many facts indicate that Magnús was also the commissioner of the *Alexanders saga* and *Gýðinga saga*. In literary documents Hákon's second son Hákon, who died early from an illness he had contracted while hunting, he is referred to by the affix 'inn yngri'/ the younger to distinguish him from his father. Additionally, Hákon inn yngri himself is believed to have worked as a translator of the *Barlaams ok Josaphats saga*. Finally, the youngest generation of the dynasty/ the Old Norwegian literary milieu ought to be mentioned: Hákon's IV grandson, Hákon V Magnússon (r. 1299-1319), who finished the Old Testament bible compilation *Stjórn* (shortly after 1300), which had been initiated by his father Magnús. The name Hákon V Magnússon is further related to the composition of the *Duggals leiðzla*, the Old Norse translation of the *Visio Tnugdali*. According to the prologue of the *Victors saga og Blávus*, an Icelandic "original riddarasaga" from the 15th century, he had written several riddarasaga translations from Greek and French to Old Norwegian, too ("ok hann liet venda

---

[17] Concerning this subject see KRAMARZ-BEIN: Neuronale Vernetzung.

morgum Riddara sogum j norænu uR girzku ok franzeisku mali").[18] Notwithstanding, Hákon V is believed to have known Latin and French himself. His wife Eufemia, the aforementioned Northern German Princess Eufemia of Rügen, made the chivalric epic blossom anew in the new Swedish context, as cited before, since she inspired the above-mentioned Old Swedish *Eufemiavisor* as a patron. A central point of my postdoctoral thesis (2002) is the idea that the Old Norwegian *Þiðreks saga* from the 13th century must also be seen in the context of Hákon's IV commissions and the literary milieu of his court in Bergen, but less than that of the Hanseatic office there. By way of conclusion about the active literary and at the same time cultural political interest of the Sverrir dynasty, one particular fact should be stressed once more: Apart from the cited male descendants of Hákon IV, there were also two women in the same time frame who made their contribution to the dynastic and literary historical networking, that is cultural transfer towards Old Swedish literature or - in network-terms - have to be regarded as connectors. These were Eufemia of Rügen, wife of Hákon V Magnússon, and their daughter, the Norwegian Princess Ingebjørg Hákonardóttir. As said before, the latter married the Swedish Duke Erik Magnusson in 1312 and contributed in this way to further Inter-Scandinavian networking of the literary milieus.

III. Conclusion and prospect

Between the creation of the *Þiðreks saga* as a model, which developed probably around 1250 and was codified just at the end of the 13th century, and the Old Swedish translation/ adaption there is a period of time of about 200 years. Not least does this mean that a different usage of passed-on knowledge, also historical knowledge, can be postulated for both versions. On the one hand, for the subject matter itself, this applies to the background of the migration period and heroic traditions. On the other hand, however, it also concerns the handling of courtly contexts of the 13th century, which already have to be presupposed as a level of meaning and palimpsest in the genesis of the Old Norwegian saga version as such. Apart from the level of meaning, which the Norwegian model already provides, special attention has to be paid when comparing the *Didriks Krönika* to the later form of the knightly culture in the 15th century, which shaped the Old Swedish chivalric literature. First of all, one has to consider the Eufemia court in Oslo (c. 1300-1320) and the context of the Swedish rhyme

---

[18] Cf. LOTH: Victors saga ok Blávus, 3.

chronicle - which was very courtly in some cases, but often political as well - and here, in particular the *Erikskrönika*. Additionally, in the 14th century, the Swedish milieu was oriented towards German cultural, and here especially also courtly contexts, - as opposed to the West Scandinavian - plays a significant role. Amongst others, contacts with the German courts, first of all Braunschweig, and with the Hanseatic League should be named as well as the preference for German literary verse metre and even a partly German-speaking literary milieu at the court in Stockholm in the 15th century. Moreover, besides the proto-national interest in the subject matter of the Wilzians/Veleti, which was relevant to Sweden, the backgrounds consisting in propaganda, the idea of supremacy, legitimation of power or memorial culture have to be taken into account in regard of the literary milieu of Karl VIII Knútsson, which is especially being discussed here with reference to the *Didriks Krönika*. Characteristically, unlike the - not least chivalric - level of meaning in the Norwegian 'model', in the *Didriks Krönika* representations of younger, that is late medieval and German chivalric culture, can be found, which did not yet exist in this style in the Old Norwegian version which is older by 200 years. Finally, such a change in the courtly style of representation is also documented by younger expressions from the chivalric sphere in the *Didriks Krönika*.

In comparing examinations of the Old Swedish style in the translations of *Karl Magnus* and *Didriks Krönika*, K.-I. Ståhle und Bengt Henning, for example, praised the more adequate, higher standard of the *Didriks Krönika* in contrast to the Old Swedish *Karl Magnus* translation, primarily because of the stereotyped fighting patterns of the latter.[19] Additionally, according to these medievalists, the translation of the *Didriks Krönika* is superior even in comparison to the Old Danish *Karl Magnus' Krønike*. The reason for this is, without any doubt, that its translation seems more self-contained, or more elaborate and 'creative' - as proved in the example "rakor huder oppa ærther". Independent of the mutual dependences in stemmatics of the Old Swedish and Old Danish transmissions of Charlemagne and Theodoric, which cannot be completely clarified, there was an important result from Bengt Henning's research: not only do the Old Swedish translations (*Karl Magnus* and *Didriks Krönika*) prove compatible with each other with regard to the method of translation used. What's more, translation works such as the Old Swedish *Didriks Krönika* and the Old Danish *Karl Magnus' Krønike* - both around the middle of the 15th century - follow – 'transna-

---

[19] Cf. WÜRTH: Eufemia.

tionally', so to speak - similar principles of translation and composition and a comparable, that is East Scandinavian, ideal in style. All in all, Bengt Henning has stressed the characteristic common features of the method of translation and composition in the epic poetry of Theodoric in Swedish and of Charlemagne in Danish. These features allowed general conclusions about the principles of translation used in the East Scandinavian literary area. As opposed to the West Scandinavian tradition, these consisted in shortening/eliminating digressions and doublets, that is improving their West Scandinavian originals - precisely, the *Karlamagnús saga* and the *Þiðreks saga* - with regard to composition and the aim of sound stringency.

In conclusion, it can be stated that the fact of the Theodoric and Charlemagne matters belonging together cannot be claimed for the West Scandinavian literary area of the 13th century alone, but also for the East Scandinavian chivalric literary context of the 14th and also of the 15th centuries. Likewise, there is a significant analogy between these milieu and school contexts notwithstanding the fact that both cultural areas are situated within different streams of influence of cultural transfer. From these observations one can deduce, first of all for the East Nordic transmission at the beginning of the 14th century, that the court of Eufemia in Oslo belonged to an East Scandinavian milieu traditionally following chivalric tendencies. Yet, in the middle of the 15th century, another younger, East Scandinavian literary tradition can be claimed, maintained at the court of Karl VIII Knútsson. This tradition illustrated the 'proto-national' traces in the *Didriks Krönika* - because of the positive judgement of the Swedish power relations already stated in its West Scandinavian original - and the traces of propaganda/legitimation of power/claim for Swedish supremacy or memorial culture in the *Karlskrönika* (corresponding to the sovereign Karl VIII). Hence, in both cases aspects are named which can, at the same time, shed light on the question of the 'setting in life'/ German: "Sitz im Leben", or the interest in writing down this secular literature. Nevertheless, concerning the East Scandinavian literary relations of the 14th and 15th centuries discussed here, one must not neglect the time span of about 150 years between the Eufemia milieu of the beginning of the 14th century and the developmental milieu of the *Didriks Krönika* and *Karl Magnus' Krønike* in the middle of the 15th century.

As initially proposed, an application of the "literary network theory" can in the first instance make a constructive contribution to the description and understanding of the Inter-Scandinavian milieu networking for dynastic reasons from the 13th to the 15th centuries. However, it could as well serve more globally as a plausible aetiological model of explanation for the courtly literary and cultural traditions spreading epidemically from Southern to Northern Europe in the late Middle Ages.

Bibliography

ALBERT, Mechthild: "Gesellschaftliche Symbolik bei Chrétien de Troyes: Zum Verhaltenscode von *chevalerie* und *courtoisie* im *Conte du Graal*," in: *Archiv für das Studium der neueren Sprachen und Literaturen* 154 (2002:2), 313-31.

ALMAZÁN, Vicente: "Translations at the Castilian and Norwegian Courts in the Thirteenth Century: Parallels and Patterns," in: *Mediaeval Scandinavia* 12 (1988), pp. 213-32.

BAGGE, Sverre: *From Gang Leader to the Lords Anointed: Kingship in Sverris saga and Hákonar saga Hákonarsonar.* Odense: Odense University Press, 1996, esp. pp. 147-55 (= The Viking Collection; 8).

BAGGE, Sverre: *The Political Thought of The King's Mirror*, Odense: Odense University Press, 1987, esp. pp. 97-112.

BARABÁSI, Albert-László: *Linked: How Everything Is Connected to Everything Else and What It Means for Business, Science, and Everyday Life*, New York: Plume, 2003.

BARNES, Geraldine: "Arthurian Chivalry in Old Norse," in: Richard Barber (ed.): *Arthurian Literature VII*, Cambridge: Brewer, 1987, pp. 50-102.

BARNES, Geraldine: "*Parcevals saga*: Riddara Skuggsjá?," in: *Arkiv för Nordisk Filologi* 99 (1984), pp. 49-62 (esp. 49, 52-54).

BARNES, Geraldine: "Some Current Issues in Riddarasögur Research," in: *Arkiv för Nordisk Filologi* 104 (1989), pp. 73-88.

BARNES, Geraldine: "The Riddarasögur and Medieval European Literature," in: *Mediaeval Scandinavia* 8 (1975), pp. 140-58.

BARON, F. Xavier: "Mother and Son in Sir Perceval of Galles," in: *Papers on Language and Literature* 8 (1972), pp. 3-14.

BARRON, William R. J.: *English Medieval Romance*, New York and London: Longman, 1987.

BEHRMANN, Thomas: "Norwegen und das Reich unter Hákon IV. (1217-1263) und Friedrich II. (1212-1250)," in: Susanne Kramarz-Bein (ed.): *Hansische Literaturbeziehungen: Das Beispiel der Þiðreks saga und verwandter Literatur*, Berlin and New York: de Gruyter, 1996, 27-50.

BIENZLE, Holger: *Die Kunst des Netzwerkens – europäische Netzwerke im Bildungsbereich*, Wien: Die Berater, 2007.

BRÜGGER BUDAL, Ingvil: *Strengleikar og Lais: Høviske noveller i omsetjing frå gammalfransk til gammalnorsk*. Bergen: University of Bergen, 2009.

BUSBY, Keith: "*Sir Perceval of Galles*, *Le Conte du Graal* and *La Continuation Gauvain*: The Methods of an English Adaptor," in: *Etudes Anglaises* 31 (1978), pp. 198-202.

CAMPION, John and Ferdinand HOLTHAUSEN (eds.): *Sir Perceval of Gales*, Heidelberg: Winter, 1913.

Chrétien de Troyes; Keith BUSBY (ed.): *Le roman de Perceval ou Le Conte du Graal*, Tübingen: Niemeyer, 1993.

COSMAN, Madeleine Pelner: *The Education of the Hero in Arthurian Romance*, Chapel Hill: University of North Carolina Press, 1966, esp. pp. 50-74.

DE NOOY, Wouter: *Exploratory Social Network Analysis with Pajek. Structural Analysis in the Social Sciences*. Cambridge; New York: Cambridge University Press, 2011.

GARDINER, Ann Broady: *Narrative Technique and Verbal Style in Parcevals saga ok Valvers Þáttr: A Comparative Study of the Old Norse Version of Chrétien de Troyes Perceval*, Philadelphia: University of Pennsylvania, 1977.

GLAUSER, Jürg. 2005. "Chapter 21: Romance (Translated *Riddarasögur*)," in: Rory McTurk (ed.): *A Companion to Old Norse-Icelandic Literature and Culture*, Oxford: Blackwell, 2005, pp. 372-87.

GLAUSER, Jürg: "Vorbildliche Unterhaltung. Die Elis saga ok Rósamundu im Prozeß der königlichen Legitimation," in: Walter Baumgartner (ed.): *Applikationen. Analysen skandinavischer Erzähltexte*, Frankfurt a.M. etc.: Lang, 1987, pp. 95-129.

GLAUSER, Jürg: *Isländische Märchensagas: Untersuchungen zur Prosaliteratur im spätmittelalterlichen Island*, Basel and Frankfurt a.M.: Helbing and Lichtenhahn, 1983.

GRANOVETTER, Mark S.: „The Strength of Weak Ties", in: *American Journal of Sociology* Vol. 78 (1973), pp. 1360-80.

GROOS, Arthur (ed.): *Perceval/Parzival: A Casebook*. New York and London: Routledge, 2002.

GUNNLAUGSDÓTTIR, Álfrún: "Um *Parcevals sögu*," in: *Gripla* VI (1984), 218-40 (esp. 228-30).

GUNNLAUGSDÓTTIR, Álfrún: 1985. "Quelques aspects de Parcevals saga," in: Régis Boyer (ed.): *Les sagas de Chevaliers (Riddarasögur): Actes de la Ve Conférence Internationale sur les sagas [...] (Toulon. Juillet 1982)*, Paris: Presses de l'Université Paris-Sorbonne, 1985, 217-33.

HALVORSEN, Eyvind Fjeld: "Problèmes de la traduction scandinave des textes français du Moyen Âge," in: Maurice Delbouille and Maurice Gravier (ed.): *Les Relations Littéraires Franco-Scandinaves au Moyen Age: Actes du colloque de Liège*. Paris: Les Belles Lettres, 1975, pp. 247-74.

HELLE, Knut: "Anglo-Norwegian Relations in the Reign of Håkon Håkonsson (1217-1263)," in: *Mediaeval Scandinavia* 1(1968), pp. 101-14.

JONSSON, Bengt R.: "Oral Literature, Written Literature: The Ballad and Old Norse Genres." In: Jospeh Harris (ed.): *The Ballad and Oral Literature*, Cambridge/London: Havard UP, 1991.

KALINKE, Marianne E.: "Norse Romance (Riddarasögur)," in: Carol. J. Clover and John Lindow (eds.): *Old Norse-Icelandic Literature: A Critical Guide*, Ithaca and London: Cornell University Press, 1985, pp. 316-63.

KALINKE, Marianne E.: "The saga of Parceval the Knight," in: Arthur Groos and Norris J. Lacy (eds.): *Perceval/Parzival: A Casebook*, New York and London: Routledge, 2002, pp. 219-36.

KALINKE, Marianne E.: *King Arthur, North-by-Northwest: The Matière de Bretagne in Old Norse-Icelandic Romances*, Copenhagen: Munksgaard, 1981.

KÖLBING, Eugen (ed./trans.): *Elis saga ok Rósamundu*. Heilbronn: Sändig, 1881.

KÖLBING, Eugen: *Riddarasögur: Parcevals saga, Valvers Þáttr, Ívents saga, Mírmans saga: Zum ersten Mal herausgegeben und mit einer literarhistorischen Einleitung versehen von Dr. Eugen Kölbing*, Straßburg and London: Trübner, 1872.

KRAMARZ-BEIN, Susanne: "Zur Darstellung und Bedeutung des Höfischen in der Konungs skuggsjá," In: *Collegium Medievale* 1 (1994), pp. 51-86 (esp. 62-64).

KRAMARZ-BEIN, Susanne: "Die altnorwegische *Parcevals saga* im Spannungsfeld ihrer Quelle und der mittelhochdeutschen und mittelenglischen *Parzival-Überlieferung*," in: Keith Busby, Bart Besamusca and Frank Brandsma (eds.): *The European Dimensions of Arthurian Literature*, Cambridge: Boydell & Brewer, 2007, pp. 135-56.

KRAMARZ-BEIN, Susanne: "Höfische Unterhaltung und ideologisches Ziel: Das Beispiel der altnorwegischen *Parcevals saga*," in: Stig Toftgaard Andersen (ed.): *Die Aktualität der Saga: Festschrift Hans Schottmann*, Berlin and New York: de Gruyter, 1995, pp. 63-84.

KRAMARZ-BEIN, Susanne: "Neuronale Vernetzung in der Literaturwissenschaft am Beispiel mittelalterlicher literarischer Milieubildungen in Skandinavien," in: Jürg Glauser and Susanne Kramarz-Bein (eds.): *Rittersagas – Übersetzung, Überlieferung, Transmission*, Tübingen: Francke, 2014, pp. 15-43.

KRAMARZ-BEIN, Susanne: "Zur altostnordischen Karls- und Dietrichdichtung," in: *Amsterdamer Beiträge zur älteren Germanistik* 62 (2006), pp. 99-121.

KRAMARZ-BEIN, Susanne: *Die Þiðreks saga im Kontext der altnorwegischen Literatur*, Tübingen and Basel: Francke, 2002, esp. pp. 173-93 (= Beiträge zur Nordischen Philologie; 33).

KRATZ, Henry: "Textus, Braull and Gangandi Greiði," in: *Saga-Book of the Viking Society* 19 (1977), pp. 371-82.

KRATZ, Henry: "The Parcevals saga and Li Contes del Graal," in: *Scandinavian Studies* 49 (1977), pp. 13-47.

KRETSCHMER, Bernd: *Höfische und altwestnordische Erzähltradition in den Riddarasögur: Studien zur Rezeption der altfranzösischen Artusepik am Beispiel der Erex saga, Ívens saga und Parcevals saga*, Hattingen: Kretschmer, 1982, esp. pp. 131-34.

LAYHER, William: *Queenship and Voice in Medieval Northern Europe*, New York: Palgrave Macmillan, 2010.

LEACH, Henry Goddard: *Angevin Britain and Scandinavia*, Cambridge: Harvard University Press, 1921 (= Harvard Studies in Comparative Literature; VI).

MARTI, Suzanne: *Kingship, Chivalry and Religion in the Perceval Matter: An Analysis of the Old Norse and Middle English Translation of Le Conte du Graal*, Oslo: Department of Linguistics and Scandinavian Studies, University of Oslo, 2010.

MCTURK, Rory (ed.): *A Companion to Old Norse-Icelandic Literature and Culture*, Malden, MA: Blackwell Publishing, 2005.

MEHL, Dieter: *Die mittelenglischen Romanzen des 13. und 14. Jahrhunderts..* Heidelberg: Winter, 1967 (= Anglistische Forschungen; 93).

NOREEN, Erik (ed.): *Herra Ivan – Kritisk upplaga*, Uppsala: Almqvist & Wiksells, 1931.

PETTERSSON, Jonatan: *Fri översättning i det medeltida Västnorden*. Stockholm: Acta Universitatis Stockholmiensis, 2009 (= Stockholm Studies in Scandinavian Philology; 51).

PSAKI, Regina F.: "Women's Counsel in the Riddarasögur: The Case of Parcevals saga," in: Sarah M. Anderson and Karen Swenson (eds.): *Cold Counsel: Women in Old Norse Literature and Mythology*, New York and London: Routledge, 2002, pp. 201-24.

SCHACH, Paul: "Some Observations on the Translations of Brother Róbert," in: Maurice Delbouille and Maurice Gravier (eds.): *Les Relations Littéraires Franco-Scandinaves au Moyen Age*: *Actes du colloque de Liège,* Paris: Les Belles Lettres, 1975, pp. 117-35.

TOGEBY, Knud: "La Chronologie des Versions Scandinaves des Anciens Textes Français," in: Maurice Delbouille and Maurice Gravier (eds.): *Les Relations Littéraires Franco-Scandinaves au Moyen Age: Actes du colloque de Liège*, Paris: Les Belles Lettres. 1975, pp. 182-91.

VELDHOEN, N.H.G.E.: "I haffe spedde better þan I wend: Some Notes on the Structure of the Middle-English *Sir Perceval of Galles*," in: *Dutch Quarterly Review of Anglo-American Letters* 11 (1981), pp. 279-86.

Victors saga ok Blávus. In: Agnete Loth (ed.): *Late Medieval Icelandic Romances,* Copenhagen: Munksgaard, 1962.

WEBER, Gerd Wolfgang: "The Decadence of Feudal Myth: Towards a Theory of Riddarasaga and Romance," in: John Lindow, Lars Lönnroth and Gerd Wolfgang Weber (eds.): *Structure and meaning in Old Norse Literature: New*

Approaches to Textual Analysis and Literary Criticism, Odense: Odense University Press, 1986, 415-54 (esp. 428-32).

WOLF, Kirsten (ed.) and Helen MCLEAN (trans.): "Parcevals saga & Valvens Þáttr," in: Marianne E. Kalinke (ed.): *Norse Romance II: The Knights of the Round Table*, Cambridge: Brewer, 1999, 103-216.

WOLF, Kirsten and Johanna DENZIN (ed.): *Romance and Love in Late Medieval and Early Modern Iceland. Essays in Honor of Marianne Kalinke,* Ithaca, New York: Cornell University Library, 2008.

WRIGHT, Glenn: "Þe kynde wolde oute sprynge: Interpreting the hero's progress in *Sir Perceval of Galles*," in: *Studia Neophilologica* 72 (2000), pp. 45-53 (esp. 52, note 3).

WÜRTH, Stefanie: „Eufemia. Deutsche Auftraggeberin schwedischer Literatur am norwegischen Hof", in: Fritz Paul (ed.): *Arbeiten zur Skandinavistik (13. Arbeitstagung der deutschsprachigen Skandinavistik 29.7.-3.8.1997 in Lysebu/Oslo)*, Frankfurt am Main and Basel: Peter Lang, 2000, pp. 269–281.

ZINK, Gaston: "Les Poèmes Arthuriens dans les Pays Scandinaves," in: Maurice Delbouille and Maurice Gravier (eds.): *Les Relations Littéraires Franco- Scandinaves au Moyen Age: Actes du colloque de Liège*, Paris: Les Belles Lettres, 1975, pp. 77-95 (esp. 82-86).

WILLIAM LAYHER

Network or Net?
Filtering the Political Voice in the *Revelaciones* of St. Birgitta of Sweden

One of the most prolific and influential female mystics of the later Middle Ages, St. Birgitta of Sweden (1303-1373) produced a corpus of almost seven hundred revelations. According to her *vita* her earliest visions came in childhood, but these were infrequent and she apparently did not speak of them to others. It was only in adulthood – as a wife, mother, and a widow – that her revelations came in greater numbers, and soon the vividness of her visions and the forcefulness of her rhetoric caught the attention of confessors and other ecclesiastical authorities in Sweden.[1] One early supporter, Magister Mathias of Linköping, who was said to be gifted in the divination of spirits, penned a spirited defense of the orthodoxy of Birgitta's revelations in the 1340s. It was surely not a coincidence that this treatise opens with a Biblical allusion that calls attention to the effect her words had on Swedish audiences: *Stupor et "mirabilia audita sunt in terra nostra"* ["strange and wondrous things have been heard in our land"] – a paraphrase of Jeremiah 5:30.[2] Called in a vision in 1344 to be a channel for divine witness, Birgitta left Sweden in 1350 for Rome, never to return to her homeland. She spent the final thirty years of her life recording and promulgating messages of piety and penitence, condemning vice, and announcing God's displeasure with kings and commoners alike. Upon her death, Birgitta's prophetic voice had become so well-known in devotional and political circles that the *vita* written for her canonization describes the occasion of her birth in pre-

---

[1] For more on St. Birgitta and her revelations see MORRIS: The Revelations of St. Birgitta of Sweden, Vol. 1; SAHLIN: Birgitta of Sweden and the voice of prophecy; MORRIS: St. Birgitta of Sweden; GILKÆR: The Political Ideas of St. Birgitta and her Spanish Confessor, Alfonso Pecha; FURUHAGEN: Furstinnan av Närke som blev Heliga Birgitta.
[2] The treatise written by Magister Mathias was used decades later to serve as the Prologue to Book 1 of her *Revelaciones*. For more on Magister Mattias and the Prologue, as well as on Birgitta's early years in Sweden, see MORRIS: St. Birgitta of Sweden, pp. 9-17; UNDHAGEN: Une source du prologue (Chap. 1) aux Révélations de Sainte Brigitte par le cardinal Jean de Turrecremata.

cisely those terms. The moment she first drew breath was the moment her *vox admirabilis* was made known to the world.[3]

The canonization documents prepared after her death in 1373 devote considerable attention to the integrity of that voice. Even the methods she used to record her visions were carefully noted in the record – a necessary step, perhaps, because up until the final dozen years of the 14th century Birgitta's revelations circulated almost exclusively in Latin translation rather than in her native tongue. According to a contemporary witness in Rome, Birgitta had some knowledge of Latin. Nevertheless, the source claims, Birgitta used the vernacular when she dictated her revelations or set them down in writing herself. As a rule these Old Swedish versions did not circulate, however, for they were quickly translated into Latin by her confessors and scribes, occasionally while Birgitta was still dictating them:

> Illa verba divinitus ei data scribebat in lingua sua materna manu sua propria, quando erat sana, et faciebat illa translatari in lingua latina fidelissime a nobis confessoribus suis et postea ascultabat illa cum scriptura sua, quam ipsa scripserat, ne unum verbum ibi plus adderetur vel deficeret, nisi que ipsa in visione divinitus audierat et viderat. Si vero erat infirma, vocabat confessorem et scriptorem suum secretarium ad hoc specialiter deputatum, et ... referebat ei verba illa in vulgari suo cum quadam attenta elevacione mentali, quasi si legeret in libro, et tunc confessor dicebat illa verba in lingua latina illi scriptori, et ille scribebat illa ibidem in sua presencia, et postea cum erant verba conscripta, ipsa volebat illa ascultare et ascultabat valde diligenter et attende.
> [The words that were given her from God she wrote down in her mother tongue with her own hand when she was well and she had us, her father confessors, make a very faithful translation of them into Latin. She then listened to the translation together with her own writing, which she herself had written, to make sure that not one word was added or subtracted, but was exactly what she had heard and seen in the divine vision. But if she was ill she would call for her confessor and a scribe ... whereupon ... she spoke the words to him in her native language in a kind of attentive mental elevation, as if she was reading them in a book, and then the confessor dictated these words in Latin to a scribe, and he wrote them down in her presence. When the words had been written down she

---

[3] COLLIJN: Acta et processus canonizacionis beate Birgitte, p. 75.

wished to hear them and she listened very carefully and attentively.]⁴

This anecdote underscores the unmediated nature of her witness in word and in writing, emphasizing that the visions transmitted under her name had been endorsed by Birgitta herself. The production of the *Revelaciones* as a text corpus was also her idea. Three years before her death in Rome in 1373, Birgitta asked her confessor, Alfons of Jaén, to collate her revelations and prepare copies of the Latin versions. This so-called "first redaction" of the *Revelaciones*, consisting of seven books and a laudatory preface, was completed in May of 1377, when Birgitta's canonization process began.⁵ The papal commission tasked with evaluating Birgitta's canonization used this preliminary corpus in their deliberations, but the process had hardly gotten underway when it was halted by the death of Pope Gregory XI in March 1378. Later that year the canonization inquiry was restarted under Pope Urban VI, and it continued, with sporadic interruptions, for another dozen years. As the process continued Alfons prepared a second redaction of Birgittine revelations in 1380, which expanded the corpus of revelations by adding additional material that had been overlooked or excluded just a few years earlier. Included in this second redaction were the *Liber celestis imperatoris ad reges*, the *Sermo angelicus* and *Quartor oraciones*, and the *vita* referenced above that was written by two of her confessors, Prior Petrus of Alvastra and Magister Petrus of Skänninge.⁶ Both of these men returned to Sweden after Birgitta's death. Magister Petrus went to Vadstena, the abbey devoted to the burgeoning cult of St. Birgitta, and served as its first Confessor General. Prior Petrus, who accompanied Birgitta's relics on their journey from Rome to Vadstena in 1374, continued to advocate for her canonization. Later in 1380 Petrus donated to Vadstena a corpus of Birgittine revelations in Latin he had personally collected that, for one reason or another, had never been taken up into any of the collections edited by Alfonso of Jaén.⁷

According to the testimony in the *vita* about Birgitta's use of the vernacular, the Latin translations do far more than preserve the substance of her revelations. Instead, the account shows Birgitta taking an active role in monitoring the

---

⁴ COLLIJN: Acta et processus canonizacionis beate Birgitte, p. 84. The English translation is from MORRIS: The Revelations of St. Birgitta of Sweden, p. 12.
⁵ MORRIS: The Revelations of St. Birgitta of Sweden, p. 18.
⁶ MORRIS: The Revelations of St. Birgitta of Sweden, pp. 18-19; HOLLMAN: Revelaciones extravagantes, p. 28.
⁷ HOLLMAN: Revelaciones extravagantes, pp. 28-29.

transmission of her words. Given the widespread acclaim that her *vox admirabiles* had won during her lifetime, it is significant that this posthumous account presents Birgitta's prophetic witness as an intrinsically vocalized phenomenon. Because she dictated her revelations aloud (in the vernacular) and insisted that the translated visions be read back to her, each vision is therefore set and secured not by the pen but by the process of speech. Birgitta – rather than her confessors – is characterized as the final arbiter of her prophetic witness: that which the ear hears, the eye sees, the tongue speaks and the hand writes is brought into perfect harmony. If the text of every vision contains "*nisi que ipsa in visione divinitus audierat et viderat*" ["exactly what she had heard and seen"] it is because the text contains exactly what she had spoken or heard recited back to her.

And yet, the voice is the weak link in this hermeneutic chain. Voice is intrinsically perishable. As an acoustic phenomenon it fades in an instant and is irretrievably lost, and it is only thanks to the medium of writing that the aftereffects of voice are preserved for the ages.[8] But how accurate an act of preservation is this? How "fixed" is the voice in the process of written transmission? Was Birgitta's prophetic voice considered inviolate once it was set down in writing? These questions take on an additional urgency when we examine some of Birgitta's revelations that took an expressly political rather than devotional edge, for it is in these visions that Birgitta's human voice – with all of its potential biases and shortcomings – seems most at risk of transgressing against the characteristic neutrality of divine revelation and causing a dissonant harmonic in the prophetic voice.

In this essay I examine the tensions between voice, writing and identity in some Birgittine revelations that were critical of the Swedish king and the royal family. The application of network theory draws our attention to the interlocking

---

[8] On the function of the voice in medieval literary practice see, for example, LAYHER: Queenship and Voice in Medieval Northern Europe; MEACHAM: Reading between the lines: compilation, variation and the recovery of an authentic female voice in the Dornenkron prayer books from Wienhausen; NICHOLS: Voice and Writing in Augustine and in the Troubadour Lyric; ZUMTHOR: The Text and the Voice. Some theoretical aspects of the voice as a medium are explored in DOLAR: A voice and nothing more; KOLESCH/KRÄMER: Stimme: Annäherung an ein Phänomen; KITTLER/MACHO/WEIGEL: Zwischen Rauschen und Offenbarung. On the female prophetic voice in medieval mysticism, see especially SAHLIN: Birgitta of Sweden and the voice of prophecy; OBERMEIER: The Privileging of Visio over Vox in the Mystical Experiences of Hildegard of Bingen.

groups of scribes, confessors, and translators in Sweden and in Rome that prepared the corpus of *Revelaciones* and other works, making them available to a broad European readership. The analysis suggests that the production of the *Revelaciones* involved far more than just the translation and collocation of her visions. In contrast to the characterization promulgated in the canonization documents, that the written texts preserved Birgitta's words in an uninflected and unmediated fashion, I argue here that some of her more outspoken revelations denouncing the Swedish king were deliberately altered by those networks during the process of transmission in Latin and in the vernacular. The rhetoric of the vision was sanitized and rendered less virulent, lengthier passages that ostensibly stemmed from Birgitta's mouth and pen were deleted outright. That this controversial material was caught up before it entered the corpus of the *Revelaciones* indicates that Birgitta's posthumous legacy was far from ironclad. Her vulnerability, especially during the period when her canonization was being debated, was not (exclusively) theological in nature – although she certainly had her detractors amongst the clergy[9] – but political. Although her revelations denouncing the wickedness of the Swedish royal family were topical and well within the mainstream of medieval European visionary discourse, they were also highly perishable. Some of her predictions and denunciations did not withstand the test of time, and occasionally the course of action Birgitta envisioned did not come to pass.

Looking back at her corpus with the benefit of hindsight, the networks in Vadstena and Rome were therefore confronted with a problem: what to do with these divinely-inspired words that seemed to have fallen short of the mark? When dealing with Birgitta's revelations, what had been said (and set down in writing) could not, of course, be unsaid – but it was possible, in many cases, to divert or halt the transmission of this material. By turning the network against itself, thereby preventing the widespread dissemination of controversial content, the network comes to resemble a net. The difference between a network and a net is functional rather than structural: if networks facilitate access and the transferal of information by providing multiple nodes of contact into and amongst the data (the metaphor is an extremely apt one for the production and transmission of the *Revelaciones* in late 14th-century Europe), a net utilizes that same connectedness in order to ensnare and isolate.

---

[9] For more on Birgitta's detractors see SAHLIN: Birgitta of Sweden and the voice of prophecy, pp. 136-168.

The prime witness in this inquiry is a rare holograph manuscript containing a revelation in Old Swedish that probably stems from Birgitta's own hand. The revelation, a stinging denunciation of the misrule of king Magnus Eriksson, who reigned 1319-1364, is a strange outlier in Birgitta's corpus. The vision was never taken up in its entirety into the corpus of the *Revelaciones*, which suggests that its content was somehow anomalous. And while the Old Swedish manuscript shows evidence of direct and substantial intervention by later redactors, including correction of misspelled words, interpolation, and erasure of text, the fact that the Latin translations deflect or omit some of the revelation's more extreme passages suggests that the networks were not immune from some degree of anxiety about the integrity of Birgitta's divine witness and the propriety of her outspoken political voice. This was felt most acutely, perhaps, once the canonization process was initiated in 1377 and her biography (including her political animosities toward the Swedish monarchy) came under renewed scrutiny by papal evaluators, whose task it was to discern to what extent sanctity and humanity coexisted in one body – or in one voice.

Manuscript

Cod. Holm. A65 (Stockholm, Royal Library, paper, second half of the 14th century) consists of two revelations that are believed to be written in Birgitta's own hand. The two visions are commonly known as Autograph A and Autograph B.[10] Autograph A is a revelation that Birgitta probably received in 1367. Autograph B dates to 1361.[11] Both revelations were written during Birgitta's stay in Rome. How and when these leaves returned to Sweden (and under what circumstances) is unknown.

---

[10] On the manuscript and its contents see HÖGMAN: Heliga Birgittas originaltexter. The paper leaves in Cod. Holm. A65 were subsequently folded or rolled, and there is evidence that both autographs were stored as *rotuli* at the Birgittine chapter in Vadstena. On the verso of Autograph A is an attestation written in an early 15th-century clerical hand, probably at Vadstena, that Birgitta had written the revelation herself: *Sancta birgitta scref thässa ordh mz sinne eghne hand som röre pawan oc cardenales*. The verso of Autograph B also features an inscription, likewise in a 15th-century hand: *fyrst vil iak ãik seya huru ãik æru andelik understandelse giuin*. This phrase is the incipit of the revelation itself. An analysis of the folds in the paper of Autograph A and Autograph B confirms that the two revelations were stored seperately. The lower margin of Autograph B (recto) contains additional notations by Swedish scribes: a rubricated *C:* followed by the word *scribatur*, and the phrase *Creditur scriptum esse p...* with the final words obliterated with ink. The significance of this passage is unclear.

[11] The dating of Autograph B is discussed in greater detail below.

The cramped and untidy presentation of the text in Autograph A and Autograph B bolsters long-standing suspicions that the revelations were indeed written by Birgitta herself, and not by a trained copyist or amanuensis. In terms of dating, the identification with Birgitta is on solid footing. The watermarks on the paper used in Autograph B confirm that the leaves are of Italian manufacture, probably from the period 1350-1370.[12] Even a cursory look at Cod. Holm. A65 reveals that the hand that wrote Autograph A and B is unusual. The letters appear mannered and irregular, quite different from what was common in contemporary Swedish scribal practice. This, too, speaks strongly in favor of Birgitta's authorship, in that the scribe of Autograph B did not use the Gothic cursive hand that was so prevalent in clerical circles in the latter part of the 14th century. Instead, the words were written in an angular style that was frequently used on wax tablets. The implication is that the person who wrote Autograph A and B was more familiar with the stylus than then pen.[13] It is significant that Birgitta was said to work with wax tablets while setting down her visions; perhaps she did so in this instance as well, exchanging the wax tablet and stylus for a paper leaf and pen.[14] Further evidence that the revelations in Cod. Holm. A65 were written by an unpracticed hand is found in the fact that the Old Swedish text contains just a handful of the abbreviations that are otherwise ubiquitous in 14th-century Swedish scriptoria, such as *mz* for *med* or the nasal stroke that indicates the endings *en / om / ung*. The lack of these refinements strongly suggests that the author was unfamiliar with the conventions of scribal practice.

Text

The revelation in Cod. Holm. A65 that denounces the misrule of Magnus Eriksson is one of several visions critical of the Swedish monarchy that Birgitta received during the latter decades of her life. What distinguishes this revelation from others of the same type is its complex political voicing. In order to isolate this phenomenon, the text must be examined in light of Birgitta's own biography. She was born into an aristocratic and influential family. Her maternal grandfather had been *lagman* or magistrate in Östergötland, and through her

---

[12] HÖGMAN: Heliga Birgittas originaltexter, pp. 13-14.
[13] On Nordic paleography (especially in the East Norse tradition) see WESTLUND: The development of Latin script III: in Sweden; JANSSON: Svensk paleografi. An up-to-date overview of medieval Swedish manuscript culture can be found in CARLQUIST: The history of Old Nordic manuscripts III: Old Swedish.
[14] MORRIS: The Revelations of St. Birgitta of Sweden, p. 34 note 42.

mother, Ingeborg Bengtsdotter, Birgitta was related to the ruling Folkung dynasty that held the Swedish crown from 1250 to 1364. Birgitta's father, Birger Persson, was a *lagman* in Uppland, and he had played an instrumental role in the codification of that provincial law code (*Upplandslagen*) in the final decade of the 13th century. Her husband, Ulf Gudmarsson, was a *lagman* in the province of Närke and a member of Magnus Eriksson's royal council – and it is through these family ties that Birgitta herself served at the royal court as a *magistra* and advisor to the new queen, Blanche of Namur, shortly after Blanche was wed to Magnus Eriksson in 1335.[15] As time passed, however, Birgitta's political loyalties changed dramatically. Once a courtier of Magnus Eriksson, she later became an outspoken critic of the king and his policies, and especially in the years following the ill-fated Swedish campaign against Novgorod in 1348, Birgitta saw Magnus' reign as corrupt.

Although Birgitta settled in Rome her distance from Sweden did not leave her isolated. Contemporary accounts indicate that she received a steady stream of visitors from the North who kept her reasonably well-informed about Swedish affairs. Internal evidence in the text of Autograph B suggests that the revelation was written down in 1361, when Birgitta had been living in Rome for over a decade. Its genesis seems to be linked to Birgitta's discovery that the southern province of Skåne had been lost to the Danish king Valdemar II in 1360, following years of skirmishing between Sweden and Denmark over this territory. The vision must have been recorded no later than the autumn of 1361, for it condemns the loss of Skåne to Denmark but makes no mention of the internationalization of the conflict and the involvement of the Hanseatic League in the dispute over Skåne's future that took place in early 1362. In addition, the revelation shows no awareness of the fact that Magnus Eriksson was briefly deposed in November of 1361 by a group of powerful Swedish barons. He was returned to the throne in February of 1362, and forced to share rulership with his son, Håkon Magnusson. Father and son ruled Sweden as co-monarchs until 1364.[16]

The revelation Autograph B, which Birgitta received from the Virgin Mary, paints a bleak portrait of the state of the Swedish monarchy. The king has stubbornly refused to heed Birgitta's counsel, and those who urge repentance and piety are turned away; his persistence in leading a life of sin will soon lead to

---

[15] MORRIS: St. Birgitta of Sweden, pp. 57-59.
[16] Hergemöller argues unconvincingly for a younger dating of Autograph B, to the middle or end of 1362. HERGEMÖLLER: Magnus versus Birgitta. Der Kampf der heiligen Birgitta von Schweden gegen König Magnus Eriksson, pp. 132-133.

his end. The revelation consists of three parts: a prologue, a transitional passage, and the revelation proper. The opening passage (vv. 1-6) discusses the variety of modes of divine revelation and clarifies the nature of Birgitta's prophetic abilities. She is told that some are granted the ability to know events before they happen or to formulate eloquent answers to questions that have not yet been asked, some can discern who is living or dead at any given moment, while others are able to predict the outcome of a battle before the troops take the field. Birgitta is granted the ability to hear or see spiritual things, but she is also charged with the responsibility of bearing witness to those audiences that need to hear her words. Although Magnus Eriksson has turned a deaf ear to her messages, this promises to be his undoing; another, wiser king will soon take his place and profit from her counsel.

Following the prologue the revelation takes on a sharper political tone. The vision recorded in Autograph B is far more than a revelation condemning political corruption in Sweden. It is, rather, a blueprint for a rebellion against the crown, for the revelation offers an elite readership theological and constitutional grounds for the renunciation of allegiances to Magnus Eriksson.[17] This justification is made explicit by Birgitta's recitation of a litany of sins that are laid at the feet of the king: as a man, a son, a monarch, and a child of God, Magnus Eriksson has failed to uphold his coronation oaths and the commandments of the church. What is remarkable about Autograph B is that these accusations were not intended to remain inert on the page. Instead, the revelation calls for the formation of a group of four Swedish noblemen who will take Birgitta's words and recite them in the king's presence. The final and lengthiest section of Autograph B addresses the four noblemen directly. Through Birgitta, the Virgin Mother instructs these men to confront Magnus Eriksson with four specific charges of misconduct and lewdness. In one such passage the group of four men is told exactly what to say to the king – phrases such as *oc sigin sua* [and say this] introduce the passages to be delivered verbatim – while elsewhere in the revelation the men are given some latitude on how they should speak. In one such phrase the men are instructed to capture the king's attention by announcing that his eternal soul is in peril, *oc mz flerum orāum til byrlekum æn idar āækis*

---

[17] The political dimensions of Autograph B are discussed in context in Lundqvist: Får man störta en usel kung? Den heliga Birgittas och de svenska reformatorernas skilda uppfattningar; FERM: Heliga Birgittas program för uppror mot Magnus Eriksson; CARLSSON: Heliga Birgittas upprorsprogram.

æn sua ar sensus [or with other words to this effect, which seem proper to you, but that is the underlying sense [of it]].[18]

The political scenario described in this revelation suggests that Autograph B was intended for use in Sweden in the year 1361. This would imply that the manuscript was supposed to be sent back to that kingdom and placed into the hands of a group of sympathetic barons. The plan was envisioned in such detail that the text of Autograph B provided the names of these four noblemen – or at least, at one time, it used to. The names had been scratched off of the paper in Cod. Holm. A65 and are now irrevocably lost. While it remains a mystery who these men were, and what their relationship to Birgitta might have been, the erasure demonstrates unequivocally that Autograph B underwent a process of intervention, correction, emendation and erasure during its transmission. In a metaphorical sense these are the fingerprints of the networks involved in setting her visions before a broader readership, and thus we must turn our attention to the text itself and examine how Birgitta's prophetic voice is represented there.

The text below follows Högman's diplomatic transcription of Autograph B. In order to accurately reproduce the look of the text I have maintained the line breaks and spellings as in the original, but for ease of comprehension the abbreviations have been expanded. Marginal and interlinear corrections are indicated through superscript or text strikethrough. Occasionally a slanted line is used as a punctuating subdivision in the text or to separate two adjacent words that were originally copied (erroneously) as one word.[19]

1   fyrst vil iac ãik sighia huru ãik æru andelik vnder-
    standilse gifin sea oc hora
2   sumi hafão ãæn hælghanda sua at ãe visto timan sum pro-
    fetin saghe til konunge ãæn dagin koma
3   sænde-boãan oc mange visto huat ãem skulle suaras fyr
    æn ãe taã talaão sumi visto oc vtan man
4   kyniles mana kynilse suma ãem ãær æru varo lifande ælla
    døãe oc visto ãe fyr æn stiãin byriadis
5   huru hon ændaãis ãik ær eg mer lofat at vita æn se oc
    høra andelika oc æpte ãy sighia
6   eg oc vita huat ãe æru lifande ælla døãe ãot ãem bius
    skrifa ãik æru fiærre eg oc huat

---

[18] HÖGMAN, lines 26-27. Further references to this edition will be made parenthetically by line number.
[19] For a detailed explanation of Högman's editorial practice see HÖGMAN: Heliga Birgittas originaltexter, p. 73.

7	ãe vilia lyãa ælla gøra ãe ãæt hera hafãe ãu vitit at ko-nungin ville eg lyãa ãa hafãe ãu ge egi urit
8	varit sua væl viliugh honum alt æpte ãy ãu hørãe at sigha ãot huaro at konungi ãæt for
9	smaãe oc burtkastaãe ãa skal annar konunge ãæt nytia for heãar taka oc vælzytia
10	C. ãik skal synas sum fyre/mine vini fore mik standande ãæn ãe ãær än æru lifande en af ãem
11	ær ãæn konungin lyde ãa han var værælslikar oc hataãe han furst han byrãade at varãa
12	guãleka ãæsse fyre namnas æpte sino værulzslko valle [...]²⁰
13	C. siãan ãotte mik sum iumfrun til ãera talaãe oc sin orã byrãade C. iac ær ãe ængiln saghe he
14	ave gracia plena for ãy min naã ãæn skul biuãas vt mina/ãaã naãe allum viãar ãyrtug
15	um ãær ãem vlia hafa / iac byuãar idar mira hiælp til idar rikis styrkilse mote guzs o
16	vinum ændelekum oc likamlekum iac biãar idar at i maghin arfuda at rikit finge ãæn konung ãy
17	matte hiæpa til guãleka gærniga oc høfiska siãuanno iac varal idar viãar at guzs
18	ræt viso domba skal kunung oc hans af kørnd viã ãæt rike / skilia²¹ en an annan annan man i rike
19	no in fødar ãætta sin o næmdar af guãi til konung valdar han skal rikeno styra æpte
20	guz vina raãum oc rikis ãarfum gyrin sum iac idar raãar til ãæs at flere fære fin
21	go skaãa oc i mattin flere til idar skaãa dragha hafin ãæta raã hemelikt i fyre
22	iac nu sigar baãe fore guzs vinum oc hans ouinum bør idar ãæt løna vtan i finnin ãæn sua vil
23	sum i æt riket matte i guz heãær ãyr styrkiæs oc goã siãuenia byrias oc vpnyas oc ãæt
24	kronan hafar mist vnder hona lægias byrin sua til / en af idar ælla flere gange
25	til konungs magnus oc sigin sua vi hafum nokot ãæt sigia ãæt idra siæl varãa oc sua sum

---

[20] The words in the remainder of this line were scratched off of the paper.
[21] This line shows clear evidence of correction by another hand The word *skilia* was written as an interlineal interpolation by a different scribe, and the same writer changed *en* to *be* in that line and corrected the faulty spelling in the line above by altering *varal* > *vara*.

26	skriptamal biãium vi idar ãæt lena oc mz flerum orãum til byrlekum æn idar ãækis æn sua ar
27	sensus i hafin ~~haf~~ ãæt fulastu frægã i rik oc vtan ãæn kristin man ma haua ~~nat~~ at i
28	hafin hapt natura bland mz manum os ãikkis ãæt vara likt sano ãy i ælskin me men en
29	gud ælla idra egna siæl ælla idra egna husfru / annat at vi eg vitum eg huat i hafin
30	rætta tro ællar eg ãyt i uarin af kirkiun forbuãit at høra mæso ãær gafin i
31	ingte vm vtan gingin i kirkiu sum fyr oc hørin mæsor ãriãar i ærin / vara krono
32	røuare lans oc gozs fiærãa ihafin varit idra ãiænisto/manna oc vnderdana ~~forraãa~~
33	forraãare skanuga idar oc idrum syniãiænto viliandis idar oc idrum syni ãiæna oc landit
34	til vara krono mz ræt halla oc kronona ovinum skaãa gøra i anduarãen ãem i hændar sinum
35	høxta ~~vin~~ ouini suat ãe æru aldrigh mæã han lifar gozs ælla lif felughe vilin i synde
36	ena bætra oc landit atar vina ãa vilium vi / idar gærna ãiæn vilin i eg siælue ãa fan/us
37	idan sun sut i burt farin ælla oc honum kronona opanurãii mz surnum eãe ãæt han
38	vili vart land atar vinna sino raãe oc sinum ãiænistomanum lyãa oc almaogin til
39	ræt styrkia ãot huaro at ãæn ær annar guzs kungar skal vara ãylar ma han
40	mæã ãoleko framkoma mz minsta vaãa ãyt guã ægar sua val ifir ãean vnga sum ãæn
41	gambla lif stækia alla af lande köra sua nu sum ãa vtan han vil æfte sinum skipaãum dom
42	al ãing hafa langiæ ælla stækia / kan sua vara ãæt ãe vilia eg lyãa ãa letin hemelika
43	idar vini ãa ãe i hauin nokra ãem ~~mæf~~ af ridar skapino mz idar halla ãa sigin ãem
44	opinbarleka ãæt i saghin konungi hemelika oc sigin at i vilin ængum kættara ãiæna
45	ælla forraãara oc eg hans syni æn han ~~vil~~ vil sins faãurs gærnigum fylghia oc
46	takin idar siãan en for man ãær a kronunu vægna ~~strið~~ ørloghar i lægin til ãæn
47	igiga oc rað ær ãæt min sun hafar valt ãa vaãar han fulkumnaãar ære eg han

48	ãa vaãar han skal ɔka af skipaãar i lægin til raã oc paniga iacl iac lægar til ãuru
49	oc manlekit hiærta at ãæn eg vil han skal
50	vil konungin a landit fara ængin af idar skal honum følgia

C. scribatur Creditur scriptum esse p....

Networking Birgitta's voice

If Autograph B was indeed written by Birgitta, as seems likely, what does the text reveal about the process of composition? Important clues are found in the text's many errors. The high frequency of scribal oversights and so-called "Flüchtigkeitsfehler" in Autograph B may indicate that the text was a rough draft of a revelation that Birgitta received and set down herself on paper, and some have forcefully defended the notion of primary, unmediated authorship for this text.[22] Whether Autograph B was a presentation copy meant for a Swedish readership remains less certain, however. The profusion of errors, deletions and marginal emendations suggests that this sole surviving manuscript may not have represented the final version of the text, but surety on this issue remains elusive. One of the curiosities surrounding Autograph B concerns its fragmented transmission across the corpus of Birgittine revelations. The revelation as we know it from Cod. Holm. A65 never appeared *in toto* in Latin translation. Instead, only portions of the vision were translated into Latin. The opening passage of vv. 1-9, a prologue to the revelation itself, was separated from the bulk of the text. The Latin translation of the prologue appears, incongruously enough, as the conclusion of chapter 56 in the *Liber celestis imperatoris ad reges*, an entirely different revelation.[23] The visions in this collection concern the proper exercise of worldly authority, and a number of them, including chapter 56, are critical of Magnus Eriksson. It is unsurprising to see some text from Autograph B taken up into this context, for the rubric of chapter 56 indicates that the revelation concerns not only the king of Sweden but also Birgitta's attempts to soften his heart: *Deus pater declarat sponse et ostendit ei seriose processum terribilem divini iudicii factum contra quendam ingratum regem adhuc viuentem et inobedientem diuinis consiliis* ["God the Father speaks to his bride and reveals to her in grave earnestness the program of divine and terrible justice that will be meted out against a certain ungrateful king who is still alive and remains disobedient of divine counsel."] The prologue to Autograph B provides a fitting conclusion

---

[22] HÖGMAN: Heliga Birgittas originaltexter, pp. 22-30.
[23] AILI: Sancta Birgitta Revelaciones Book VIII, pp. 212f.

to chapter 56 of the *Liber celestis imperatoris ad reges* because it validates the integrity of Birgitta's prophetic gifts, referring not only to their divine origins but also to the foolishness of kings who reject her counsel:

> Sed licet iste rex contempserit verba mea, veniet vtique alius, qui recepturus est ea cum reuerencia et honore, et fruiturus est eis ad salutem suam.
> [But although that king may have rejected my words, certainly another will come who will accept them with reverence and honor, and he will delight in them to his benefit.][24]

The *Liber celestis imperatoris ad reges* exists in ten manuscripts, the oldest of which is an Italian codex dating to 1377-79.[25] This early date is significant, for it confirms that the full text of Autograph B was known in Rome at the time when Birgitta's canonization process was begun. The revelation was nevertheless not taken up into the so-called first redaction. Only a small and largely apolitical section of it (the prologue) was included in the second redaction.[26]

It was not until several years later that the main portion of Autograph B appeared in Latin translation as chapter 80 of the *Revelaciones extravagantes*. According to Morris the *Revelaciones extravagantes* is comprised largely of material that "had been omitted by Alfonso, either deliberately on sensitive political or theological grounds, because they were obscure or cast a negative light on Birgitta, or because they had been left in Sweden and never passed through his hands."[27] This version omits the prologue to Autograph B and begins with the phrase *Virgo Maria, mater Dei, loquebatur sponse Christi: 'Ego sum, ad quam angelus dixit: 'Aue gracia plena...'*, which corresponds to line 13 in the original text (*iac ær ãe ængiln saghe ave gracia plena*). It is clear that the Latin translation in the *Revelaciones extravagantes* was designed for a broader European readership, because the text omits several details in the Old Swedish autograph that were directed towards a specifically Swedish readership or that would have been comprehensible only to those familiar with the political situation in Northern Europe. For example, the Latin version in the *Revelaciones extravagantes* substitutes the word *rex* for *konung Magnus*, replaces the noun

---

[24] AILI: Sancta Birgitta Revelaciones Book VIII, p. 222.
[25] Manuscript M498, New York, Pierpont Morgan Library; see AILI: Sancta Birgitta Revelaciones Book VIII, p. 25.
[26] AILI: Sancta Birgitta Revelaciones Book VIII, p. 9.
[27] MORRIS: The Revelations of St. Birgitta of Sweden, p. 19.

scanunga 'inhabitants of the province of Skåne' with a paraphrase that refers to *terra Skanie*, and clarifies the reference to *idar rikis* 'in your kingdom' by replacing it with the Latin phrase *regni in quo tu nata est*. A third and unique witness of the Latin text is found in Cod. Holm A77 (ca. 1400), a vellum manuscript of unclear provenance. This version differs from its counterpart in chapter 80 of the *Revelaciones extravagantes* in a number of minor ways, but in the main the text corresponds to the Latin archetype.[28]

There is evidence that Autograph B had returned to Vadstena by the beginning of the 15th century, if not earlier. The text left its mark in an Old Swedish revelation that appears in Cod. Holm. A5a, a Vadstena manuscript from around 1425. This revelation, a vernacular "re-translation" of the canonical Latin text transmitted as chapter 80 in the *Revelaciones extravagantes*, is unique in that the translator had access to Autograph B and used that text when preparing his Old Swedish translation. The Old Swedish text in Cod. Holm. A5a avoids a highly localized translation error that all of the Latin versions of chapter 80 hold in common. The mistake concerns the word *regimen* in the Latin phrase *Ego exhibeo adiutorium meum ad regimen regni, in quo tu nata es, contra inimicos Dei corporales et spirituales* ["I offer my help for the governing of that kingdom, in which you were born, against the spiritual and corporal enemies of God."] The corresponding phrase in Autograph B reads *iac byuðar idar mina hiælp til idar rikis styrkilse* ["I offer my help for the strengthening of your kingdom"] (15). This minor shift in meaning reveals that the Latin translator who prepared the text for the *Revelaciones extravagantes* misread the vernacular word *styrkilse* [strengthening] as **styrilse* [governing] – an error that the translator who produced the version in Cod. Holm. A5a did not replicate.

It is significant that only the prologue to Autograph B – the portion devoted to the varieties of prophetic witness and to Birgitta's particular gifts – was taken up into this collection. Its inclusion in this context is sensible, for the prologue contains one of the most direct statements in Birgitta's entire corpus about the divine nature of her abilities. We can well surmise that the case for canonization was strengthened by the claims articulated here by the Virgin Mary, in whose voice this prologue speaks – that Birgitta was one of the *sancti dei* who was granted the power to hear and see spiritual things (*spiritualia audire et videre*) and, moreover, that Birgitta was charged with the responsibility of writing and

---

[28] HOLLMAN: Revelaciones extravagantes, pp. 201-203. On ms. A77 see also HÖGMAN: Heliga Birgittas originaltexter, pp. 54f.

declaiming the things she has seen (*et illa, que vides, scribere et dicere illis personis, quibus tibi precipitur*).[29]

These passages from Autograph B offer a clear defense of the orthodoxy and legitimacy of Birgitta's prophetic powers. And yet, the Latin translation diverges from its source in a way that suggests the authority of voice was perceived to be insufficiently clear in Birgitta's original. Autograph B, which has no preamble, opens the words *fyrst vil iac ãik sighia huru ãik æru andelik vnderstandilse gifin sea oc hora* (1), 'First I wish to tell you how you are granted [the] spiritual understanding to see and hear.' Although the relationship between speaker and auditor is established from the outset by pronouns such as *iak* 'I' and *ãik* 'you' – and Birgitta is clearly the 'you' – the identity of the speaker is not immediately apparent. It is only in much later, in verse thirteen, that Autograph B clarifies that the source of the revelation is the *iumfru* 'the Virgin.' This ambiguity has been eliminated in the Latin translation of the revelation. The material from Autograph B that appears in chapter 56 of the *Liber celestis imperatores ad reges* begins at the 97th sentence with the introductory phrase *Post hec autem virgo, que sedebat cum agno, loquebatur ad me dicens: Ego indicare tibi volo, quomodo data est tibi intelligencia spiritualium visionum*, 'Thereafter the virgin who sat with the lamb spoke to me, saying: I wish to disclose to you in what manner the perception of spiritual visions has been given to you.'[30] The opening passage about the Virgin and the lamb is not found in Autograph B, but the amplification is minor; it simply makes explicit that which Autograph B reveals only indirectly. The emendation is nevertheless significant because here, again, the issue of voice proves to be undesirably complex. The Latin translator(s) of this revelation worked repeatedly to draw clearer distinctions among the voices – not only in the opening passages, but also later on, when Birgitta's endorsement of an uprising against Magnus Eriksson shifts into high gear.

When viewed in light of the goals of the canonization inquiry, namely to weigh Birgitta's sanctity against any potential demerits, the remainder of Autograph B sounds a dissonant note. Its fervid denunciation of Magnus Eriksson is coupled with a strategy of confrontation that could lead to the overthrow of the Swedish king. Politics and divine intervention intermix here in curious ways, and if Autograph B does indeed contain the words Birgitta wrote with her own hand, it is telling that the network of confessors and translators took exception to two pas-

---

[29] AILI: Sancta Birgitta Revelaciones Book VIII, p. 222.
[30] AILI: Sancta Birgitta Revelaciones Book VIII, p. 222.

sages in that text that had significant and controversial political impact. The first passage is found in line twelve of Autograph B. In this portion of the revelation Birgitta describes a vision granted her by the Virgin Mary (10-14) about four honorable Swedish noblemen, who were charged with the task of chastising the king and leading him onto a path of repentence and just rule. The imagery is clear, but the complex syntax of this passage makes it difficult to discern how Birgitta envisioned her own involvement in this vision and its intended effect. Not only is revelatory discourse in Old Swedish characterized by the frequent use of the passive and reflexive voice – as is the case here – but Birgitta's narrative phrasing shifts in and out of different personae. In the opening sentence of this passage Birgitta is revealed to be the recipient of the vision, while the Virgin Mary is represented in the first person. In the very next sentence, however, the first-person "I" refers to Birgitta, but only for a moment; immediately afterwards she quotes the Virgin Mary again, and the discourse reverts to a citational nature. The difficulties posed by the fluctuations in Birgitta's narrative voice are highly relevant here, because the troublesome issue in line twelve concerns the identity of the four Swedish noblemen whom the Virgin Mary has singled out. At one time the text of Autograph B named their names – but who was responsible for revealing them? Was it the Virgin Mary, or was it Birgitta herself, speaking as an aside to the readers and auditors of this revelation?

> C. ãik skal synas sum fyre/mine vini fore mik standande ãæn ãe
> ãær än æru lifande en af ãem
> ær ãæn konungin lyde ãa han var værælslikar oc hataðe han furst han byrãade at varãa
> guãleka ãæsse fyre namnas æpte sino værulzslko valle […]
> C. siãan ãotte mik sum iumfrun til ãera talaãe oc sin orã byrãade C.
> iac ær ãe ængiln saghe he
> ave gracia plena for ãy min ãã ãæn skul biuãas vt mina/ ãã naãe allum viãar ãyrtug
> It will seem to you as if four of my friends were standing in front of me, they are still alive and one of them is the man the king listened to when he was in the secular realm but hated when he entered the Church. These four are named according to their worldly rank […]
> Then I sensed that the Virgin spoke to them, and her words began "I am she of whom the angel said Ave gracia plena…" (10-14)

Autograph B claims that the names of the four men are listed in line twelve, but hardly any trace of the letters remains.[31] When the erasure occurred, and by whom, is unknown.[32] Given the laudatory claims about the *vox admirabilis* of St. Birgitta, the truncation of line twelve – the stilling of that voice on the textual level – is striking, but it was not an isolated incident. In the Latin translation as well as the Old Swedish redaction of it, the names are likewise absent and nearly every reference to the group of four noblemen has been omitted. Only on one occasion does the Latin translation of Autograph B still refer to "you four" as the primary recipients of Birgitta's witness (*Vos igitur quatuor faciatis secundum consilium meum…*)[33] but it does so in a haphazard and unprecedented manner, almost as if by accident. Who these four men are, and what role they are expected to play, is never explained.[34]

What could have prompted such a drastic intervention in the text of Autograph B, when other errors or oversights in the same manuscript were simply corrected on the spot? What justification can be found for this irreversible violation of the integrity of Birgitta's vision? In order to fully address those questions, the network's second intervention into the revelation known as Autograph B must be taken into account. In this latter case, the text of Birgitta's revelation was not damaged in the codicological sense, but her phrasing was nonetheless sanitized

---

[31] HÖGMAN: Heliga Birgittas originaltexter, pp. 17-18.

[32] Attempts to read the deleted text under a quarz lamp or through infrared photography were unsuccessful. Did the deleted passage actually contain four names? Högman argues that there was insufficient space in line 12 to list the names of four Swedish men in sequence, especially if the names were prefaced by a title such as *hærra* [sir] or the like. Perhaps Birgitta abbreviated the names. HÖGMAN: Heliga Birgittas originaltexter, p. 18. This hypothesis is endorsed by CARLSSON: Heliga Birgittas upprorsprogram, p. 101 note 25, who suggests that the paper leaf did offer sufficient space for the identification of four men.

[33] HOLLMAN: Revelaciones extravagantes, p. 202.

[34] It remains a parlor game in medieval Swedish history to guess at the identity of the four men. Two of the leading hypotheses involve members of Birgitta's own family. One hypothesis would link the four men to the group of four that were dispatched by the Swedish court in 1361 to negotiate a marriage with the house of Holstein. These men were Bengt Filipsson (a son-in-law of Birgitta), Karl Ulfsson (Birgitta's son), Herman von Vitzen and Diderich Vieregge, the latter pair representing Mecklenburgian interests. CARLSSON: Heliga Birgittas upprorsprogram, pp. 91-93. The second hypothesis would associate Birgitta's group of four with the four knights described in a Swedish charter as *dilecti et fideles consiliarii* 'devoted and loyal advisors' of king Håkon in May 1362, namely the knights Nils Turesson, Karl Ulfsson von Tofta, Bengt Filipsson, Trotte Petersson. LILJEGREN: Diplomatarium Suecanum VIII, nr. 6625, p. 189.

and rendered harmless in Latin translation – an analogous process of cleaning up, not by erasure but by emendation.

In this second example, as in the first, the narratological fluctuations inherent in Birgitta's use of the prophetic voice render her statements about the necessity of political action problematic. At issue here is the final directive of the Virgin Mary, that the four noblemen charged with confronting Magnus Eriksson elect a fifth man, a native-born Swede, to act as their marshal and military leader if the negotiations with the king break down. Autograph B, in other words, sews the seeds for an insurrection against the lawful monarch of Sweden and calls for the election of a commander who might well serve as the eventual protector of the realm or even its next king. The troublesome aspect of this passage concerns Birgitta's use of the phrase "my son" when referring to this man. A literal reading of Autograph B offers little indication of whether the Virgin Mary was speaking metaphorically about a devout and upstanding Swedish knight or, in contrast, whether Birgitta was advocating for the inclusion of her eldest son Karl Ulfsson (1327-1372), a leading nobleman of the kingdom, as one of the key figures of the rebellion:

> takin idar siãan en for man ãær a kronunu vægna ~~striã~~ ørloghar ~~i lægin til ãæn~~
> ~~igiga oc raã~~ ær ãæt min sun hafar valt ãa vaãar han fulkumnaãar ære eg han
> ãa vaãar han skaleka af skipaãar i lægin til raã oc paniga Then you shall elect a foreman who shall battle for the crown. If my son has chosen him (?) then he shall be perfect in all ways. If he is not he shall be dismissed at once. (46-48)

The question mark in the translation is necessary because the sentence containing the words "my son" is not as unambiguous as it appears. The Old Swedish text may be defective here, as a crucial pronoun seems to be missing from the beginning of line 47. Some critics suggest providing the pronoun *ãæn* so as to produce the phrase **ær ãæt ãæn min sun hafar valt ãa vaãar han fulkumnaãar*.[35] If we accept this interpolation a number of textual ambiguities are cleared up, for the revised version of the phrase reads 'if it [the leader] is the one my son has chosen, then he shall be perfect in all ways.' With this emendation the speaker is revealed unambiguously to be the Virgin Mary, so the phrase

---

[35] HÖGMAN: Heliga Birgittas originaltexter, pp. 67-68, my emphasis.

"my son" could only refer to Christ, who has already selected a leader for the Swedish barons; it now falls to the four noblemen to discern Christ's will and elect the proper candidate for the task at hand. The emendation is not unreasonable, but caution is nevertheless warranted. Given the wealth of errors and corrections in the text of Autograph B, it is curious that this error (if it indeed is one) was not caught and corrected by Birgitta or any of the other scribes involved in the production of Autograph B. By design or coincidence, the passage remained as Birgitta wrote it.[36] My purpose with calling attention to the persistence of this error in Autograph B is not to suggest that Birgitta deliberately let an ambiguous passage stand in her revelation, but rather to highlight the fact that after her death her network was confronted by a text in which Birgitta's intent – not the Virgin Mary's – was difficult to discern. And because the confusions inherent in this passage turn on the proper interpretation of whose "son" is being referred to, the networks in Rome and Vadstena found themselves forced to address the possibility that Birgitta's political voice had slipped into an improper register: that the Swedish noblewoman was speaking for the benefit of her own family and offspring and not for the greater glory of God. If we read the passage as written, as Birgitta's posthumous network undoubtedly did, then the statement about "my son" drifts uncomfortably close to the interpretation alluded to above, that Birgitta's call for a uprising against Magnus Eriksson presupposed the close involvement of her eldest son in the process of selecting the leader of the armed rebellion.[37] What is at risk, in other words, is Birgitta's status as an impartial witness to heavenly wisdom.

Reading the phrase *min sun* as suggestive of Karl Ulfsson is not just a modern critic's farfetched view. There is an historical basis for the notion that Karl Ulfsson wielded too much political influence in 14th-century Sweden. Already by the 1340s, according to the canonization testimony prepared after Birgitta's death, Swedish elites were concerned about her attacks on the monarchy and the

---

[36] Högman's discussion of this passage in Autograph B argues that the text was indeed corrected by the same hand. He points to the word *ãæn* in line 47, and suggests that the final letter was changed from *n* to *t* – changing it, in other words, from *ãæn* to *ãæt*. This word does have a smudge over the final letter, but even after examining the text under great magnification I cannot recognize a terminal *n* underneath the *t*; and at any rate Högman's reconstruction still leaves the passage one pronoun short. HÖGMAN: Heliga Birgittas originaltexter, p. 82.

[37] Högman interprets the words *min sun* metaphorically, suggesting that they refer to Birgitta's warning to elect only a man who is spiritually in line with her precepts: her spiritual offspring, as it were. HÖGMAN: Heliga Birgittas originaltexter, pp. 67-68.

perceived conflict of interest that could place one of her own kinsmen on the throne. Prior Petrus, for example, recalled an anecdote that took place in Sweden in which Birgitta's powers of prophecy were openly mocked. Her accuser was Håkon, duke of Halland, the half-brother of king Magnus Eriksson.[38] One of the charges that Håkon leveled against Birgitta belittled her prophetic abilities (an accusation that she would face repeatedly during her lifetime) but it is notable that Håkon's secondary accusation took on an explicitly political edge. The implications of this encounter suggest that the prestige of Birgitta's own family – especially Karl Ulfsson – was seen as a threat to the monarchy:

> The witness also said that he had been present and had seen it with his own eyes when, in the castle of Bohus located in the diocese of Oslo, the younger brother of the king, Lord Håkon, a worldly nobleman, asked one morning when he met Birgitta ... whether there was going to be rain or fair weather – or will your sons be kings and we will be deprived of the kingdom? Birgitta, undaunted and fully inspired by the Holy Ghost, said: if you do not improve your way of life, neither will you be king nor will you live long, and you will see neither your first nor your second generation. Moreover no mother will rejoice in you and the memory of you will be short. Therefore humiliate yourself publicly in the face of God, and you will find His mercy. The aforesaid was troubled and died after a short time, without progeny and without kingdom, just as had been predicted by Lady Birgitta.[39]

Håkon's first question, concerning Birgitta's ability to prognosticate about the weather, calls her divine inspiration into question by associating it with the types of practical divination that witches were often accused of doing. The second question in this anecdote – concerning the political future of Birgitta's sons – differs from the first. Here Håkon is confronting the prominent political status

---

[38] Magnus Eriksson's father, Erik Magnusson, the duke of Södermanland, married Ingeborg of Norway in 1312. Erik Magnusson was murdered in 1319, leaving two children: Magnus Eriksson (1316) and a daughter named Eufemia (1317). In 1327 Ingeborg remarried, taking as her second husband the Danish nobleman Knut Porse. This union produced two children, Håkon and Knut – half-brothers to king Magnus Eriksson – both of whom died in 1350.

[39] *Haquinus ... derisorie dixit ei, utrum erit pluuia an serenum, aut filij tui erunt reges et nos priuabimus regno.* COLLIJN: Acta et processus canonizacionis beate Birgitte, p. 514. My translation is slightly adapted from that found in WILSON: Medieval women writers, p. 248.

of Birgitta's aristocratic family. Birgitta's uncle, Knut Jonsson of Aspenäs, had served as the marshal of the kingdom of Sweden, and after his death Birgitta's brother Israel assumed the office. Her family had strong ecclesiastical ties as well, for an uncle of Birgitta's father, Jacob Israelsson, had been the archbishop of Uppsala, and several of his descendants remained prominent clerics in that diocese.

Additional testimony by lady Juliana, wife of the knight Nicolai Dannes, indicates that a number of Swedish noblemen resented Birgitta's influence with Magnus Eriksson during the 1350s but were unable to move openly against her. Noblemen loyal to the king sought to silence Birgitta, or even to kill her, but these plans came to naught because the noblemen feared retaliation from Birgitta's powerful kinsmen.[40] Recognizing their weak political stance, the noblemen sought instead to defame her as a witch and seductress.[41] Further incidents of grumbling by prominent men of the realm are recorded elsewhere in the canonization documents.[42]

The turbulences surrounding the issue of *min sun* complicated Birgitta's holy vision for the restoration of the monarchy, even decades after the fact. Accordingly, the network took steps to minimize the disturbance. In the transmission of this revelation in Latin, as well as in the younger Old Swedish versions that were based on the Latin translations, the passage in question is emended so as to remove any hint of personal or familial bias. The Latin translation, which ap-

---

[40] Qui non credentes ei faciebant derisiones et detracciones de ea et murmurabant fortiter tali modo, quia intrepide reprehendebat eorum vicia, quod, si ipsa non fuisset tanti generis, interfecissent eam, sed timentes magnos dominos filios et fratrem et consanguineos eius permittebant eam. COLLIJN: Acta et processus canonizacionis beate Birgitte, p. 313.

[41] *...dicentes eam esse sortilegam et seductricem.* COLLIJN: Acta et processus canonizacionis beate Birgitte, p. 66.

[42] According to the *vita*, Birgitta remained in Sweden after the death of her husband and received a number of revelations proclaiming God's disfavor with the wickedness of Magnus Eriksson and queen Blanche and other notables of the realm: *habuit aliquas revelaciones divinas, in quibus Deus precipiebat sibi, quod accederet ad regem et reginam et alios maiores regni et prediceret eis ex parte Dei maximam iram et justiciam Dei in brevi et in proximo venturam, nisi se emendarent cito de certis peccatis in eisdem revelacionibus contentis.* Later in the canonization documents, another witness recounts a similar anecdote but expands upon it to speak of Birgitta's piety and humility in the midst of the political backlash against her: *Ipsa vero omnes oblocuciones, detracciones et derisiones, que fiebant contra eam, pacientissime sustinebat orando Deum pro eis, qui talia sibi inferebant.* COLLIJN: Acta et processus canonizacionis beate Birgitte, p. 492. See also SAHLIN: Birgitta of Sweden and the voice of prophecy, pp. 148-151.

pears in chapter 80 of the *Revelaciones extravagantes*, renders the problematic phrase *min sun* elliptically rather than literally: *Qui electus si fuerit amicus meus, perfectus erit*, 'if the one elected is my friend, he shall be perfected [or: it shall be accomplished].' This locution clearly served as a model for the derivative Old Swedish version in Cod. Holm A5a from around 1425, where the same passage readers *Är then sami min vin som valdir vardhir tha vardhir han fulkompnadhir oc stadhfästir*, 'if this one who is elected is my friend, then he shall be complete in all ways and strengthened.'

From a theological as well as a political standpoint, the substitution of "my friend" for "my son" in this passage is altogether satisfactory. The emendation underscores the agency of the Virgin Mary, the ostensible source of this revelation, by stressing her independence from Christ, the Son, as an agent of divine guidance. The Latin translation of the passage also has a secondary benefit, in that it reinforces the connection between piety and political success. By elevating the Virgin Mary into the position of the one who is first chosen by the military leader before he in turn is elected by his peers – note that the phrase now reads "if [he] is my friend..." – the revised text of the revelation presents the military leader as a man whose authority is predicated upon the pureness of his heart rather than the strength of his arms. The reciprocity envisioned here between heavenly favor and earthly devotion stands in marked contrast to the ways in which the *Revelaciones* characterize the corrupted lordship of Magnus Eriksson and the royal family, where power and authority are said to lack every foundation in godliness. Birgitta claims that the elected marshal of the military forces shall be entirely unlike a king in that sense.

Perhaps most importantly, however, the emendation to the text of Autograph B removes any hint of nepotism with regard to Birgitta's own son. Neither the Latin translation nor its vernacular analogues can be construed so as to implicate Karl Ulfsson in the divine plan for the restoration of the Swedish monarchy. And yet, despite the fact that the network took steps to shift attention away from Karl Ulfsson in the transmission of this revelation, the phrase *amicus meus* still retains an element of ambiguity: who is *meus* here? Once again, the intermixing of the prophetic voice with the divine voice forces the issue of interpretation. While we cannot know for certain how late 14th-century audiences understood the revelation and its message, the words *amicus meus* could apply to Birgitta as well as to the Virgin Mary in equal measure. In a doctrinal sense, what it meant to be devoted to the Virgin Mary seems clear enough, and in return for this devotion stems the promise of military advantage (*perfectus erit*). But in the political sense, to be a "friend" of Birgitta during the reign of Magnus Eriksson was likewise beneficial. There was no penalty to be paid for standing allied with those who supported her message and urged the monarchy to respect the laws of God and the kingdom. Thus the ambiguities in this passage resolve themselves in a single conclusion. According to the Latin translation of Autograph B, both Birgitta and the Virgin Mary opposed Magnus Eriksson, and in the latter half of the 14th-century it made little political difference which of them was "befriended" in the public eye. In either case the desired outcome – a reformed king or a new one – was the same.

Networks and Readership

Let us consider one further example in the vernacular tradition. This case helps illuminate some of the political complexities with which the networks were operating, for as we shall see, the steps that were taken to minimize or interdict controversial statements in the *Revelaciones* were not universally applicable. In some instances, Birgitta's jagged-edged condemnations were allowed to stand in the written transmission. As I suggest below, I link this phenomenon to the assumptions held by the network of scribes and translators about the intended readership of the revelations. For some readers, filtering was apparently not necessary.

As explained above, the Latin translations of Birgitta's visions represent the primary account of her prophetic activity. The Old Swedish corpus of her revelations, which began to appear towards the end of the 1380s in Sweden, represents a secondary account, because these texts had been retranslated back into the vernacular from the canonical Latin versions that had been prepared by her confessors and the other scribes in Rome. Because the Old Swedish *Uppinbarelser* hold close to the phrasing and syntax of their Latin sources, they transmit the sense but not the essence of what Birgitta had spoken or written in the vernacular; her prophetic voice has been streamlined, retrofitted into Latinate constructions and parallelisms, and rendered more obvious.

There is, however, an independent branch of the vernacular transmission that appears to have bypassed any Latin intermediaries. A single paper manuscript from around 1400 contains twenty-five revelations of St. Birgitta that were written in a hybrid Swedish/Norwegian dialect known as Bigittinernorsk. It is believed that the manuscript, Stockholm E 8092, was prepared in Vadstena for a readership in Bergen that was connected to the Benedictine monastery at Munkeliv, which in the years around 1400 was coming into the Birgittine orbit.[43] Textual analysis of the revelations in E 8092 confirms that the Norwegian scribes preparing the translations used Old Swedish sources, some of which were otherwise unattested; a few of these may have been autographs from Birgitta's own hand. In cases where a Birgittinernorsk revelation does have a counterpart in the Old Swedish or Latin corpus, we see that the Birgittinernorsk versions of the revelations preserve a more archaic wording, a more colorful lexicon, a rougher syntax. They also convey a much sharper sense of Birgitta's political engagement in Swedish politics during the 14th century – an engagement, moreover, which was embittered in tone and shrill in its denunciation of the wickedness of the Swedish royal line.

E 8092 contains a revelation that denounces Magnus Eriksson's mother, Ingeborg of Norway, as a venomous snake. We can compare this revelation with its counterparts in the Latin corpus (where it appears in the *Revelaciones* Book VI, chapter 32) and with the canonical Old Swedish version that is found in Cod. Holm. A5a. The text in E 8092 seems to preserve an archaic version of the revelation, for its style is angular and headstrong, the diction elliptical. In its subsequent redactions in Latin and Old Swedish, however, this revelation was stripped of much of its emotional intensity. While the revelation – in all versions – is sharply critical of Magnus Eriksson's mother and the children by her second marriage to a Danish nobleman, the Birgittinernorsk version showers the queen mother and her sons with invective and declares them to be accursed, worthy of excommunication:

> E 8092: Ãolkin är ään **banzatte** ormunghin han är födhir af eirom orme **bansattom** säm är iordnadhir i heluit. ok af enne ydhlo säm nu stundar eptir ormenom fara. hwad är värre eitir än höfärdhin mz äässo komo ormen ok ydhlan saman Ormen hafde ... mykla giri til världhinna heidhir. han sa ydhlonna fägrind. ok geirnadhis meira hona en mik Ormbren sa at ydlan var faghir. ok girnadhis iämmykit

---

[43] On the Birgittinernorsk transmission see GILKÆR: The 'Birgittiner-norske' Texts: Purpose and Tradition; MOBERG: Heliga Birgitta på birgittinnorska. Några språkliga iakttagelser; WOLLIN: Två språk och två skikt: Uppenbarelsernas tradition. The manuscript is described in WESSÉN: Svensk Medeltid. En samling uppsatser om svenska medeltidshandskrifter och texter, pp. 95 ff. A few other isolated cases of vernacular transmission in Old Swedish, independent of Latin intermediaries, are identified in MORRIS: St. Birgitta of Sweden, p. 8, note 26.

til henna. Af ãässom lustanom komo **bansatta** somon mz alle högfärd […]⁴⁴

This man is the **accursed** youngling snake. He is born of a **damnable** snake that lies buried in Hell, and of a serpent that now stands ready to follow after him. For what is a worse poison than pride? Thus the snake and serpent came together. The snake … lusted the things and rewards of this world. He saw the beautiful serpent and desired her more than me. The snake saw that the serpent was beautiful and desired her greatly. On account of that lust these **accursed** ones united in all pride.

Cod. Holm. A5a: Tholkin är thän mannin som thu känne thy at han är suasom orm vnge föddir aff ormslicom fadhir oc ormslike oc etirlike qvinno thy at badhin thässin saman komo mz värsta etre som är höghfärdhin hulkin fordömelicare skadhir siälina än licamlikit etir kroppin Visselica thänne ormbir hafdhe owirmatto astundan til hedhir oc oskällica giri oc bran til qvinnona lusta Hon skodadhe han vara sniällan ok faghran ok bran mz jämpnom älskogha til ormin thy saman komo the mz höghfärdh …⁴⁵

This is the man that you recognize because he is like a youngling snake born of a snakelike father and snakelike and venomous woman. The two of them were united by the deadliest poison that is pride, which surely imperils the soul more than poison does to the body. Indeed, this snake held high ambitions for worldly honor and desires, and he burned with lust for women. She regarded him as courtly and handsome, and burned with an equally strong desire for the snake. Thus they came together because of pride.⁴⁶

The canonical Old Swedish revelation in Cod. Holm. A5a corresponds so closely to the Latin version that it was probably translated from that source. None of the invective that was characteristic for the Birgittinernorsk version remains.⁴⁷

---

⁴⁴ KLEMMING: Heliga Birgittas uppenbarelser, efter gamla handskrifter IV, p. 484, my emphasis.

⁴⁵ KLEMMING: Heliga Birgittas uppenbarelser, efter gamla handskrifter IV, p. 74.

⁴⁶ The deletion of words like *forbanadher* in the canonical Old Swedish version has been noticed previously; see WESSÉN: Konungen och helgonet. Magnus Eriksson och Birgitta Birgersdotte, p. 140.

⁴⁷ Talis est ille homo, quem tu nosti. Est enim sicut natus serpentinus, quia de patre serpentino et femella serpentina natus est. Nam isti ambo conuenerunt cum pessimo veneno, idest superbia, que dampnabilius nocuit anime quam corpori venenum materiale. Ipse denique serpens, cum nimium haberet ambiendi affectum et cupiditatem inextinguibilem, arsit in concupiscenciam femelle. Que considerans eum sapientem, formosum et strenuum ardebat in serpentem amore equali. Ideo cum omni superbia

The brief excerpts quoted above give the flavor of the text as a whole. The comparison could easily have been extended, for the term *forbanadher* and its cognates is used repeatedly in this revelation as an epithet to damage Ingeborg's character. Far from appearing only as an isolated occurrence, the word serves as the moral anchor point for an extended denunciation of Ingeborg's perceived wickedness, and this consistency (in terminology as well as tone) stands as a reliable indicator of Birgittine authorship. The bluntness in this revelation could hardly have been the work of a willful scribe at Vadstena. As a unique witness in the textual history of Birgitta's revelations, the texts in E 8092 bear a special relevance for our understanding of how the networks dealt with controversial content. Networks appear to be responsive to political considerations. For an elite readership in late 14th-century Norway, where unfavorable memories of Ingeborg's self-serving political machinations probably lingered long after her death, the use of words like *forbadadher* – even in a divine revelation – could still be seen as appropriate. For other readers outside of Norway, unaware of this historical context, the fervor of Birgitta's diction evidently went beyond the pale. The revelation was therefore sanitized for all other audiences save the one near Munkeliv.

Filtering

In closing let us return to the lone status of Autograph B. It is puzzling that the revelation, which is highly critical of unjust kingship, was not taken up into the *Revelaciones ad reges* when so many other revelations condemning royal misrule found their way into those pages. Instead the revelation was assigned a place amongst the supplementary visions in the *Revelaciones extravagantes*. I submit that the network of scribes and confessors that prepared Birgitta's work for wider distribution may well have recognized that the revelation as it exists in Autograph B contained a troublesome intermixing of prophetic voices that calls into question Birgitta's status as a neutral vehicle for divine revelation. Although two papal committees had attested in 1377 and 1379 that her revelations were *autentice atque veritate plene et a Dei spiritu veraciter edocte* ["authentic as well as filled with truth and truly instructed by the spirit of God"], the au-

---

contempto timore meo conuenerunt isti et de venenato genere venenatum generauerunt serpentem. AILI: Sancta Birgitta Revelaciones, VI, chapter 32.

thenticity of a voice is determined by its singularity.[48] Birgitta's reputation as a blessed and impartial voice for God's plan for the Church and for Sweden was called into question by the double-voicings in several key passages in that vision. The network, it seems, was compelled to invene.

The passage of time is a critical factor, too, for her canonization process began fourteen years after the events of 1361. By the time the *Revelaciones extravagantes* appeared in 1380, seven years after Birgitta had died, it was clear that nothing of what she had called for at that time had come to pass. Skåne had not been reclaimed for the glory of Sweden, and Magnus did not repent of his defiance of the Church. The Swedish barons did not band together in rebellion against their king in 1361, nor is there any record that the king had been chastised by a group of noblemen and compelled to better himself. Birgitta's hope that Magus Eriksson's son Håkon would emerge as the suitable alternative king for Sweden turned out to be unfounded as well. Even the short-lived dethroning of Magnus Eriksson in 1362 was not by any measure a fulfillment of divine prophecy, for the events of 1362-64 revealed Håkon to be as duplicitous as his father. The young prince was not the Swedish-born nobleman foretold to assume the throne and reign in accordance with God's precepts and the laws of the kingdom (*en annan man i rikeno in födar.... han skal rikeno styra æpte guz vina raðum oc rikis āarfum*, 18-20). Measured against the yardstick of history, the revelation in Autograph B proved to be as overheated as it was inaccurate.

But was the network justified in expecting accuracy from a mystic? The premise seems unreasonable on its face, for one of the characteristics of revelatory discourse is its reliance on idiosyncratic and highly symbolic imagery. That which is seen by the mystic must be interpreted for others, and Birgitta does this, for example, in the revelation about venomous snakes in E 8092 when she explains that the "poison" in the royal family is pride (*hwad är* värre eitir än höfärdhin).[49] Yet since Birgitta claims in Autograph B to have the ability to see and hear spiritual things (*ãik æru andelik vnderstandilse gifin sea oc hora*, 1) but not to know with certainty what the future might hold (*ãik ær eg mer lofat at vita æn se oc høra andelika*, 5), it is unlikely that the network found fault with the revelation because of the nature of the vision she received. If we judge the revelation by that which was filtered out of it – most prominently, the names

---

[48] UNDHAGEN: Une source du prologue (Chap. 1) aux Révélations de Sainte Brigitte par le cardinal Jean de Turrecremata, p. 224.
[49] KLEMMING: Heliga Birgittas uppenbarelser, efter gamla handskrifter IV, p. 484.

of the four noblemen and nearly every allusion to them, together with her reference about *min sun* – then it appears that the text was perceived as damaging to Birgitta's reputation because of its incongruous specificity. In its original state the revelation named the names of Swedish noblemen and hinted, albeit awkwardly, that Birgitta's son might play a central role in the upcoming confrontation with the king. That the Virgin Mary would show such concern with the problems afflicting the Swedish monarchy, that she would provide the names of those she had chosen to lead the rebellion in a public document, seems farfetched. The same, however, could not be said for Birgitta, who as the daughter of an illustrious and well-connected aristocratic line and the mother of an influential nobleman was closely knit into the fabric of 14th-century politics in Sweden. The topic of this revelation and her remedy for the ills of the monarchy lay too close to her own interests – and especially for the period during which her canonization was subjected to papal inquiry, any potential mark on her sanctity was of serious concern for the network committed to moving her canonization forward. The Birgittinernorsk revelations, in contrast, were copied for use in Norway after the canonization was complete. There was no need to defend Birgitta's reputation any more, not for this marginal readership far away from the ecclesiastical centers of power of Norway. In this instance her voice remained unfiltered.

The reception and transmission of Autograph B and the revelations in E 8092 reveal new dimensions of Birgitta's status as an authoritative figure in 14th-century Sweden. Her voice and her influence were typically described with superlatives. According to the Bishop of Linköping, for example, when the Spirit of God was upon her "truth and goodness" flowed from her mouth (*ex ore ... veritas et bonitas redundat*).[50] What the fate of Autograph B reveals is that this *vox admirabiles* also had its limits.

Bibliography

AILI, Hans (ed.): *Sancta Birgitta Revelaciones Book VIII. Liber celestis Imperatoris ad reges*. Stockholm: Almqvist & Wiksell, 2002.

AILI, Hans, Ann-Mari JÖNSSON, Birger BERGH and Carl-Gustaf UNDHAGEN (eds.): *Sancta Birgitta Revelaciones*. 8 vols. Uppsala: Almqvist & Wiksell, 1967-2002.

---

[50] SCHÜCK: Nicolaus Hermanni, Rosa rorans: Ett Birgitta-officium, p. 37.

CARLQUIST, Jonas: "The history of Old Nordic manuscripts III: Old Swedish," in: Oskar Bandle, Lennart Elmevik a. Gun Widmark (ed.): *The Nordic languages: An international handbook of the history of the North Germanic languages*, Berlin/New York: Walter de Gruyter, 2002, pp. 808-816.

CARLSSON, Gottfried: "Heliga Birgittas upprorsprogram," in: Ingvar Andersson (ed.): *Archivistica et mediaevistica Ernesto Nygren oblata*, Stockholm: Svenskt arkivsamfundet, 1956, pp. 86-102.

COLLIJN, Isak (ed.): *Acta et processus canonizacionis beate Birgitte*, Samlingar utg. av Svenska fornskriftsällskapet. Uppsala: Almqvist & Wiksell 1924-31.

DOLAR, Mladen: *A voice and nothing more*, Cambridge, Mass.: MIT Press, 2006.

FERM, Olle: "Heliga Birgittas program för upprör mot Magnus Eriksson," in: Alf Härdelin (ed.): *Heliga Birgitta - budskapet och förebilden. Föredrag vid jubileumssymposiet i Vadstena 3-7 oktober 1991*, Stockholm: Almqvist&Wiksell, 1993, pp. 125-143.

FURUHAGEN, Hans: *Furstinnan av Närke som blev Heliga Birgitta*, Stockholm: Norstedt, 1990.

GILKÆR, Hans: "The 'Birgittiner-norske' Texts: Purpose and Tradition," in: Bridget Morris and Veronica O'Mara (ed.): *The Translation of the Works of St. Birgitta of Sweden into the Medieval European Vernaculars*, Turnhout: Brepols, 2000, pp. 75-86.

GILKÆR, Hans Torben: *The Political Ideas of St. Birgitta and her Spanish Confessor, Alfonso Pecha. Liber Celestis Imperatoris ad reges: A Mirror of Princes*. Vol. 163, Odense: Odense University Studies in History and Social Sciences, 1993.

HERGEMÖLLER, Bernd-Ulrich: *Magnus versus Birgitta. Der Kampf der heiligen Birgitta von Schweden gegen König Magnus Eriksson,* Hamburg: HHL-Verlag, 2003.

HÖGMAN, Bertil: *Heliga Birgittas originaltexter*. Vol. 205, SFSS, Uppsala: Almqvist & Wiksell, 1951.

HOLLMAN, Lennart (ed.): *Revelaciones extravagantes*, Samlingar utgivna av Svenska fornskriftsällskapet, Ser. 2, Latinska skrifter, Uppsala, 1956.

JANSSON, Sam: "Svensk paleografi," in: Johannes Brøndum-Nielsen (ed.): *Palæografi A: Danmark og Sverige*, Stockholm: Nordisk kultur 1943, pp. 82-134.

KITTLER, Friedrich, Thomas Macho a. Sigrid Weigel: *Zwischen Rauschen und Offenbarung : zur Kultur- und Mediengeschichte der Stimme*, Berlin: Akademie Verlag, 2002.

KLEMMING, Gustav, (ed.): *Heliga Birgittas uppenbarelser, efter gamla handskrifter*. 5 vols, Stockholm: P.A. Norstedt, 1857-84.

KOLESCH, Doris a. Sybille Krämer: *Stimme: Annäherung an ein Phänomen*. Vol. 1789, Frankfurt am Main: Suhrkamp, 2006.

LAYHER, William: *Queenship and Voice in Medieval Northern Europe*. New York: Palgrave, 2010.

LILJEGREN, J. G. (ed.): *Diplomatarium Suecanum*. Stockholm: div. publ, 1867-.

LUNDQVIST, Elisabeth: "Får man störta en usel kung? Den heliga Birgittas och de svenska reformatorernas skilda uppfattningar," in: Hans-Albin Larsson (ed.): *Forskningsfronten flyttas fram: utbildningskultur och maktkultur*, Bromma: HLF Förlag, 2003, pp.140-165.

MEACHAM, June: "Reading between the lines: compilation, variation and the recovery of an authentic female voice in the Dornenkron prayer books from Wienhausen," in: *Journal of Medieval History* 29, (2003:2), pp. 109-128.

MOBERG, Lennart: "Heliga Birgitta på birgittinnorska. Några språkliga iakttagelser," in: Börje Tjäder (ed.): *Smärre texter och undersökningar*, Uppsala: SFSS, 1998, pp. 9-31.

MORRIS, Bridget: *St. Birgitta of Sweden*. Vol. 1, Studies in Medieval Mysticism, Woodbridge: Boydell Press, 1999.

MORRIS, Bridget: *The Revelations of St. Birgitta of Sweden, Vol. 1*, Oxford: Oxford University Press, 2006.

NICHOLS, Stephen G: "Voice and Writing in Augustine and in the Troubadour Lyric," in: A.N. Doane and Carol Braun Pasternack (ed.): *Vox intexta. Orality and Textuality in the Middle Ages*, Madison: University of Wisconsin Press, 1991, pp. 137-161.

OBERMEIER, Anita: "The Privileging of *Visio* over *Vox* in the Mystical Experiences of Hildegard of Bingen," in: *Mystics Quarterly* 23 (1997), pp. 137-167.

SAHLIN, Claire L.: *Birgitta of Sweden and the voice of prophecy*. Vol. 3, Studies in medieval mysticism. Woodbridge/Suffolk/Rochester/NY: Boydell Press, 2001.

SCHÜCK, Henrik: "Nicolaus Hermanni, *Rosa rorans: Ett Birgitta-officium*," in: *Meddelanden från det litteraturhistoriska seminariet i Lund* 2 (1893), pp. 29-53.

UNDHAGEN, Carl-Gustaf: "Une source du prologue (Chap. 1) aux Révélations de Sainte Brigitte par le cardinal Jean de Turrecremata," in: *Eranos* 58 (1960), pp. 214-226.

WESSÉN, Elias: "Konungen och helgonet. Magnus Eriksson och Birgitta Birgersdotter," in: *Nordisk Tidskrift* 44 (1968), pp. 117-44.

WESSÉN, Elias: *Svensk Medeltid. En samling uppsatser om svenska medeltidshandskrifter och texter. II. Birgitta-texter*. Vol. 10, Kungl. Vitterhets historie och antikvitets akademiens handlingar : Filologiska serien. Stockholm: Stockholm, 1968.

WESTLUND, Börje: "The development of Latin script III: in Sweden," in: Oskar Bandle, Lennart Elmevik a. Gun Widmark (ed.): *The Nordic languages: An international handbook of the history of the North Germanic languages*, Berlin, New York: Walter de Gruyter, 2002, pp. 841-49.

WILSON, Katharina M. (ed.): *Medieval women writers*. Athens, GA: University of Georgia Press, 1984.

WOLLIN, Lars. "Två språk och två skikt: Uppenbarelsernas tradition," in: Tore Nyberg (ed.): *Birgitta, hendes værk og hendes klostre i Norden*, Odense: Odense University Press, 1991, pp. 407-34.

ZUMTHOR, Paul. "The Text and the Voice," in: *New Literary History* 16 (1984:1), pp. 67-92.

II: Modern Networks: 19th and 20th Century

BIRGE HILSMANN

Interlacing Subjects. Networks in Uppsala Romanticism

The main title of this essay, mysterious as it may seem at first, attempts to express in a nutshell that which makes network analysis and Romanticism such a good combination. Hopefully, this will have been convincingly explained at the end of the following text.

The subtitle – Networks in Uppsala Romanticism[2] – is obviously easier to grasp; still, it mirrors the complexity of our endeavour: the subtitle is in one respect too wide and in another respect too narrow.

As we are going to concentrate on Travel Writing by two of the main protagonists of Uppsala Romanticism without grasping the whole 'movement' or all their writing, the subtitle is too wide.

But with these travel writings as a starting point, we will see that it is rather inadequate to work on Uppsala Romanticism alone, as if this were a strictly isolated phenomenon, both locally and temporally. The closer one looks, the clearer it becomes that neither Uppsala nor Romanticism are boundaries which would be easy to define – all the more so as we are examining networks. In this sense the subtitle is clearly too narrow.

Even more thrilling a step to undertake and to present than reconstructing networks within Uppsala Romanticism and between Swedish and German Romanticism in a socio-topographical, empirical sense is asking the question: which were the individual, the specifically literal and, finally, the specifically Romantic features (one would rather say: threads) of these networks and their dynamics?

So, apparently, we have to ask first about the individual, personal, emotional motivations and implications of networking.[3] What is the personal motivation of

---

[1] In this essay the term network analysis refers broadly to those concepts developed in the field of natural sciences and specifically to their description in BARABÁSI: Linked.

[2] The term *Uppsala Romanticism* is a common name for the Romantic movement that started at Uppsala University and evolved around the poetic societies *Musis Amici* resp. *Auroroförbundet* and Malla Silfverstolpes salon, though it was closely intertwined with the Romantic circles surrounding *Götiska förbundet* in Stockholm. For a first introduction into this period, see for example OLSSON/ALGULIN: Litteraturens historia, pp. 178 ff.

[3] Of course we will not treat this matter completely in a socio-psychological sense, but only from a literary studies' point of view, although it might be fascinating and fruitful

individuals to become part of a network? What are the special motivations of hubs and connectors?[4] How does their role in the network correspond to their self-images? Are they aware of their central role? And then, finally: how does all that correspond to being a poet and a Romanticist?

Of course, these first questions cannot be answered from a point of view of literary studies without another question: how are these networks, including their individual implications, represented and constructed within texts? We cannot talk about networks on the one hand and then about their literary representation on the other. We only know about the literary constructs of networks. We do not examine complex human psyches but their literary reflections. But as we are talking about Romantic poets, these two aspects – personal implications and literary representation – form a symbiosis just the same.

One of the demands of a Romantic existence is to push back the boundaries between Life and Literature. A true Romanticist is expected to devote his whole life to serving Poetics and Poetry, *Poesie*, as the German Romanticists called it. *Poesie* not only means texts and the production of texts, but also denotes the metaphysical realm, from where poetic inspiration originates.[5] An attempt at conveying this aspect of the German term rather than cutting it off by use of the term poetry has been made by the rare English term poesy,[6] which I will use in the following.

So, if someone rightfully claims to live a romantic life, it would not even make sense to try and learn of the real motivations behind the textually claimed ones. By writing them down, transforming them into literature, they achieve relevance, they become romantically true. In German Romantic terms, this symbiosis is called 'Romantisieren', which may be translated into English as 'romanticizing'[7]. It is vitally important to understand that 'Romantisieren' in this sense has no connotation of glorification in the sense of euphemism or repression.[8] It means nothing more and nothing less than to transform things according to Ro-

---

to try and cooperate with psychology to get deeper and new insights into the issue of social-network-motivation. However, such collaboration will be postponed to another essay.

[4] For further explanation of the terms *node, link, hub* and *connector* in network theory see BARABÁSI: Linked, pp. 55-64.
[5] See KREMER: Romantik, pp. 89-113; SAFRANSKI: Romantik.
[6] SAUL: Cambridge Companion, pp. 2 ff.
[7] See SAUL: Cambridge Companion, p. 11.
[8] See the article *romanticize* in Webster's 1993, which implies that the English term is commonly connected with this kind of blind glorification.

mantic ideas. So we can say: the Romanticists' aim was to *romanticize* their own lives and to *romanticize* the world.

The eagerness to *romanticize* has its root in Idealistic Philosophy, especially, but not exclusively, in Schelling's aesthetics.[9] It rests on the pantheistic idea that the basic principle of existence, called the Ego or the Self, inheres in virtually any entity, living or dead, in the universe. Following Schelling's argumentation, human beings can gain conscience of this Self, but only so in fleeting moments, by means of *poiësis*, that is: creation of art.[10] Conscience of the Self, though, is the only way to reach the Divine Infinite. The realm of poesy is thus the one part of the Divine Infinite which human beings can enter. Romanticizing everything is such an important task for a Romanticist, because the desire to resolve one's self in the Divine Infinite is the main characteristic desire of the Romantic period.[11]

---

[9] It is not the megalomaniac ambition of this essay to explain in detail this notoriously complex concept, which does not at once correspond to our contemporary discourses. We cannot even try and squeeze a qualified introduction to German Idealism and Romantic Aesthetics into it. Instead, we will have to just accept, heuristically, these seemingly strange ideas as facts, or to grant forgiveness for the rather coarse outline of this complex matter, respectively. Still, it is necessary to have at least a vague concept of Romantic thought, if we want to truly understand the motivations of our protagonists. (A still very short but convincing overview of this period in German philosophy and its input on Romanticism is given in SAUL: Cambridge Companion, pp. 9 ff.)

[10] Introductions to Schelling's philosophy abound. For example: WHITE: Schelling, BAUMGARTNER/KORTEN: Schelling; Concerning Schelling's concept of Genius and his aesthetics in general: GETHMANN-SIEFERT: Ästhetik, pp. 183-186, 189-193.

[11] AARSETH: Romantikken, p. 36, cit. Nilsson: „[...] det djupast utmärkande för den romantiska rörelsen är dess idealistiska strävan att betrakta världen som en enhetlig levande organism [...]" (= "[...] the deepest distinction of the Romantic movement is its idealistic striving to regard the world as a unified, living organism [...]"); AARSETH: Romantikken, p. 39: „[...] det mest framtredende elementet tvers igjennom [...] [er] en romantisk kontinuitet i form av uendelighetslengsel og individualisme [...]" (= "[...] the most evident element throughout [is] a Romantic continuity appearing as desire for infinity and individualism [...]"); AARSETH: Romantikken, p. 40: „[...] Individets unendelighetslengsel kan arte seg som et behov for å omfatte, gjennomtrenge og beherske altet, eller som en trang til å frigjøre seg fra det samme altet for å nå det absolute, idéens verlden." (= "[...] the Individual's desire for infinity can express itself as a need to embrace, penetrate and control the universe or as an urge to free itself of the same universe in order to reach the Infinite, the realm of ideas."); ATTERBOM: Minnen, p. 100: „[...] bemödandet att upphöja det oändligt lilla Jag [sic!] till Poesiens kärna [...]" (= "[...] the endeavour to raise the infinitely small I to the core of poesy [...]")

All translations from German, Swedish and Norwegian in this and the following footnotes and the main text are mine.

1. Cast and corpus

Amongst the group of Uppsala Romanticism there are two protagonists with whose travel writing this essay will deal more closely.

First, there is the poet Per Daniel Amadeus Atterbom, who is rightfully reckoned to be one of the founders of Swedish Romanticism (albeit not the one and only founder); second, there is Malla Silfverstolpe, hostess of one of the important Romantic *salons* in Uppsala.

They serve as examples not only due to their role within Uppsala Romanticism. Whereas it would be imprecise to state that the whole of Swedish Romanticism follows German Romantic poetology, a strong German influence on the beginnings of Uppsala Romanticism is a fact,[12] and is strongly tied to these two in point of their biographies: Atterbom is a disciple of the German Idealistic philosopher Schelling and has been thoroughly inspired by contemporary German aesthetics and poetics in general.[13]

Malla Silfverstolpe's *salon* is not only closely modelled on German examples, but is even initiated by a visitor from Weimar, Amalia von Helvig, who remains some kind of muse and patron for Uppsala Romanticism and the *salon*, even after her return to Germany.[14]

1.1. Per Daniel Amadeus Atterbom

Per Daniel Amadeus Atterbom was born in 1790 as a low-rank clergyman's son in rural Middle Sweden. At Uppsala University, Atterbom and several fellow students soon became enthusiastic about German Romanticism.[15] In 1809, they founded a literary society, *Aurora-Förbundet*, and a journal, *Phosphoros*, in order to establish Swedish Romanticism and establish themselves as prominent Romanticists.

---

[12] This often stated fact of literary history has been linguistically examined and proved by Charlotta Brylla (see BRYLLA: Rezeption and BRYLLA: Överföring). See also any of the Atterbom biographies by HELLSTEN-WALLIN, TYKESSON, AXBERGER, who can also serve as a witness for any other fact on Atterbom's life reported in this essay.

[13] See for example HELLSTEN-WALLIN: Atterbom, with interest of Atterbom's Schelling-reception and -enthusiasm especially pp. 12-15.

[14] See HOLMQUIST: Vänskap och kärlek, p. 209.

[15] Concerning the velocity of their Romantic education see RISBERG: Tyska förebilder, who proves that Atterbom for example did not become familiar with the German sources until 1807, and TYKESSON: Atterbom, p. 55, who characterizes this phase in Atterbom's life as one of 'intellectual ecstasy'.

Atterbom stayed abroad from 1817 to 1819, spending the spring and summer of 1818 in Italy, but otherwise travelling through Germany and, shortly, Austria. The motives for his departure from Sweden were mixed. On the one hand, it was the traditional ambition of an educated bachelor from Northern Europe to visit Italy as the cradle of European culture; for the Romantic traveller, it is important that this is the Christian Culture as opposed to ancient heathen Greece.[16] Furthermore, Atterbom obviously longed to visit some of his literary and philosophical idols in Germany and in the empire's capitol Vienna, whose works and thoughts had become so important for his life in only a few years' time.

On the other hand, fate gave Atterbom the opportunity to feel like a kind of martyr or exile, driven from his mother country by the enemy establishment. Indeed, although Atterbom was only one of the founders of Swedish Romanticism, he clearly was its main and most polemic propagandist against the preceding Classicism, which had degenerated into a kind of epigonic stiffness, but was still the predominant power within Swedish literature and within the Swedish Academy.[17] In a manner of speaking. Atterbom had not made friends among the Swedish Academy, and they neither liked to be opposed and attacked nor seemed to understand the fantastic, radical and seemingly anti-enlightened thoughts imported from Germany.

Their anti-propaganda helped to cast suspicion on Atterbom to be either Catholic or a Pantheist or an Atheist, which are of course not the same things from a theological point of view, but meant practically the same for the suspect from a legal point of view: namely, they all meant not being a Swedish protestant, which was legally forbidden in Sweden on the possible pain of exile. (Which – in parenthesis – was a bit awkward at that time, as the country was in the process of getting a newly elected king, field marshal Jean Baptiste Bernadotte from France, baptized Catholic, who converted, but his wife, the future Queen of Sweden, refused to leave the Catholic faith.) Thus, there were quite grave

---

[16] See for example ATTERBOM: Minnen, p. 305: „[...] den *äldsta* kristna kyrkans trosartiklar, traditioner och legender äro ett arv, som hon [= Rom, Bi.Hi.] lämnat åt [...] den kristna församlingen [..]!" (= "[...] the articles of faith, traditions, and legends of the eldest Christian Church are an heirloom, which she [= Rome, Bi.Hi.] has left to [...] Christendom [...]!"); p. 425: Constantine the Great, the first Roman Emperor who converted to Christianity, saw a cross descending from heaven near Pons Milvius; pp. 531-533: Atterbom describes numerous Christian buildings which stand upon antique foundations. – See as well LEWAN: Drömmen, pp. 52-54.

[17] See for example OLSSON/ALGULIN: Litteraturens historia, pp 173-183.

accusations brought against Atterbom. Although it may be exaggerated to say he was in actual danger of arrest, it seemed advisable to get out of the country, that is: out of the focus of public interest, out of reach of his opponents. If we read some of his comments in his letters from Germany, it seems as if it were by no means only the Classicists who could not leave Atterbom alone as long as he was in their range of sight: it is quite obvious that Atterbom himself could not stop picking fights as long as the members of *Svenska Akademien* were in his reach.[18]

The journey could never have been realized without personal networks. The afore-mentioned German writer Amalia von Helvig used her good relations for fund-raising. Atterbom himself lacked the financial possibilities for such a long journey; and even with the help of his friends in Sweden he would not have come as far as he did.[19]

Right from the beginning of his journey, Atterbom planned to publish some kind of travel book in a typical Romantic style, consisting of mixed prose and verse, narration and reflections, letters and essays. Although some of his poems and essays were published during his stay abroad or soon after his return, a more or less complete book, more or less according to his plans, was published only posthumously in 1859, the so called *Minnen från Tyskland och Italien* (= Reminiscences of Germany and Italy).[20]

---

[18] ATTERBOM: Minnen, p. 102: „Vi [...] tröttna dock snart att predika för åhörare, som med alla sina sinnen oupphörligt dväljas i narrspel och oreda." (= "We [...] do get tired though of preaching to an audience who doesn't cease to stay with all their senses in folly and confusion."); during his journey Atterbom's aggression and mockery do cool off somewhat, see for example: ATTERBOM: Minnen, p. 104: „Säg nu ej, att jag ju åter själv sammanskrivit ett stycke polemik: det är blott en polemik emot polemiken." (= "Don't say now, that I have again scribbled down a piece of polemics myself: this is nothing but polemics against polemics."); p. 560: Atterbom talks about making peace, but is sure that „fabriken av dumma in- och utfall kommer väl ej att upphöra." (= "the manufacturing of stupid ideas and attacks is not going to stop.") Context makes clear, that those are stupid ideas and attacks **against** Atterbom (not **by** him). Nevertheless, a regular peace-offer to Classicism can be found in the poem *Fridsrop* (= Call to Peace) at the end of Atterbom's *Minnen*, i.e. pp. 666 ff.

[19] This aspect worries Atterbom nearly constantly, but especially after his return from Italy, as can be seen for example: ATTERBOM: Minnen, pp. 547-552. His impatience with Amalia von Helvig's constant promises to send him money only proves the importance of her financial support for his journey.

[20] See the anonymous preface to ATTERBOM: Minnen, pp. 3-11.

1.1.1. Travelling in Search of Recognition

In contrast to Atterbom's claim that he quite likes to be alone and does not care too much for company and social life,[21] the *Minnen*texts show his desire to be in contact with people. This becomes even more evident if we take into account how we learn about the course of events on Atterbom's journey: mostly by letters he sent to his friends and relatives in Sweden. Thus the main part of the *Minnen*texts bear witness to Atterbom's longing to communicate; not only to communicate with anyone, but to communicate with people who hold him in high esteem.

The importance of this last aspect, the desire for appreciation, can be seen in Atterbom's descriptions of most of his encounters. While he uses his stays in the cultural centres to visit as many prominent artists and scholars as possible, he is not content with just having met them in person. One question is foremost on his mind: what do these people know not only about Sweden, but about Atterbom himself?

He is pleased when some Italian librarian speaks a bit of Swedish,[22] but Atterbom is really thrilled when the highly-acclaimed author Jean Paul or the Queen and Prince of Bavaria tell him to have known him beforehand as a Swedish poet of some importance.[23] By reporting on these appreciations in letters and his diary, Atterbom manages to make otherwise fleeting moments of acknowledgement last – and to make them last in a public conscience.

Thus, the *Minnen* reveal how networking serves as a means of affirmation and self-affirmation. Atterbom uses his networks, especially his newly established networks with German celebrities, as a means to verify and improve his self-image as an important Swedish poet.

As we are interested in the details of human networking, we have to keep in mind that personal networks are not only a financial precondition of Atterbom's journeys.

---

[21] See ATTERBOM: Minnen, p. 632: „[...] det verkligen beror på mig själv, att tumla mig om i den mest glänsande rymden av Berlinervärlden [...]. Men mitt lynne är [...] för ingen del egentligen riktat åt societets- och konversations-livet, varföre jag håller mig undan så mycket jag förmår [...]." (= "[...] it really is up to me to hang around in the most glamorous spaces of Berlin-Society [...]. But my mood actually is in no way directed towards a life of society and conversation, which is why I keep as much to myself as possible [...]")

[22] See ATTERBOM: Minnen, p. 398.

[23] See ATTERBOM: Minnen, pp. 169 and 181, pp. 439-440 for the royal appreciation; Jean Paul's acknowledgement is mentioned pp. 138-139.

Another aspect has to be taken into account which furthers Atterbom's interests: In the early 19th century, it is obviously not difficult to gain access to the private homes of writers and philosophers – as long as one can present letters of recommendation by respected members of society. Atterbom is well-endowed with such references: mostly thanks to the strong and widespread social networks of his friend and patron, the writer Amalia von Helvig. She is on good terms as with classicists and nobility in Weimar as well with Romanticists in Jena, and artists, aristocrats and officers in Berlin.[24] After the first contact has been made possible by these references, sometimes Atterbom manages to establish frequent contacts or even friendships, as is the case with his idol Schelling or the poet Ludwig Tieck, for example. We can see here how networks are built on networks, Atterbom's on Amalia von Helvig's.

1.2. Malla Montgomery Silfverstolpe

Malla Montgomery Silfverstolpe, born 1782 as a daughter of Finland-Swedish gentry, started writing herself rather late in life, around the age of 40 in the 1820's, when she had become a widow after a childless and unhappy marriage. Her only work is her memoirs, which she did not even start to write with the intent to publish them.[25] In fact, they were first edited in 1908, nearly 50 years after her death. Memoirs do not appeal to us as the most Romantic of genres, as the wish to describe an authentic human life sets strong boundaries to the writer's fantasy. But this might be a misconception: memoirs might offer the opportunity to construct one's life into a poetic life, to retrospectively and at least textually romanticize your life. As we have shown above, the reservation "at least textually" is self-contradictory from a Romantic point of view.

Furthermore, it is important to understand that it is possible to dedicate one's life to a poetic existence without producing a great amount of literature. Poetic intention and an ability to feel deeply romantical are more relevant than the virtual output. Especially as a woman, it was – supposedly – well possible to be considered a poetic being as the intimate friend, adored hostess, motherly muse, ideal and material patron, who Silfverstolpe was for several young Romantic

---

[24] See HOLMQUIST: Vänskap och kärlek, pp. 211 ff.

[25] For these and more biographical information see HOLMQUIST: Vänskap och kärlek, pp. 209-16 and ff.; additionally Ellen Key's introduction to the 1913 German edition of MONTGOMERY-SILFVERSTOLPE's travel-journal.

poets, historians, musicians and philosophers, like Atterbom himself.[26] The way she supported 'her' young Romanticists was a kind of Romantic achievement in itself. She helped to *romanticize* Uppsala.

Later, we will have to consider the female role in Romanticism, and in Uppsala Romanticism in particular, and we will see that gender is an important factor, especially with regard to network structures.

1.2.1. Travelling with friends on a friend's traces in order to meet friends

In 1825 and 1826, Malla Silfverstolpe visits Germany along with the Romantic poet and historian Erik Gustaf Geijer and the Romantic musician Adolf Lindblad. Both are close friends of Atterbom's, regular guests in Silfverstolpe's *salon* and intimate friends of herself, whereas the degree and implication of this intimacy is very difficult to validly define. The contemporary concept of friendship between men and women shifts between platonic and erotic relations, while one deals very discreetly with the latter.[27] By the way, Geijer is, the main addressee of Atterbom's *Minnen*letters. Besides, he is one of the founders of another Romantic society, *Götiska Förbundet*.

It is not surprising that Silfverstolpe and her companions retrace many of Atterbom's visits, although they do not take the exact same route through Germany. This is partly due to a special task of their journey: Per Ulrik Kernell, a young musician, who maintained a particularly intimate relation with Silfverstolpe, died in Erlangen (the neighbouring city of Nuremberg) two years before, and they follow his last traces. In other words, Silfverstolpe is accompanied by two of her closest friends – Geijer and Lindblad – whilst travelling on the traces of friends – Kernell and Atterbom – in order to meet friends – like Amalia von Helvig, for example. Amalia von Helvig functions as a connector once more by introducing Silfverstolpe to Rahel Varnhagen and Bettina von Arnim, both influential hostesses of famous *salons* themselves, both located in Berlin, the very cultural metropolis.

Acquaintance with these female connectors opens further areas of the large Classic-Romantic network to Silfverstolpe and her companions. Amalia von Helvig and Rahel Varnhagen clearly are connectors between two spheres, which

---

[26] For a more detailed account of Silfverstolpe's relations to these younger Romanticists see HOLMQUIST: Vänskap och kärlek, esp. pp. 216-221.
[27] See HOLMQUIST: Vänskap och kärlek; see FRÜCHTL: Das unverschämte Ich, pp. 103-104, 182-187 on possible reasons for the erotic overtones of the wide concept of friendship in 19th century Europe.

have often been treated as much too clearly separated fields, by both internal propaganda and simplifying literary history: Classicism and Romanticism. This, by the way, goes for Germany as well as for Sweden.[28]

In comparison with Atterbom's *Minnen*, Silfverstolpe's descriptions put great emphasis on emotional details of encounters.[29] This feature, however, not only shows Silfverstolpe's sensitivity and empathy; it reveals her strong co-dependence on the moods of friends and people whom she would like to make friends with. Silfverstolpe's relentless pondering on these moods, but also her own explicit statements, characterise her as someone bordering on selflessness in a literal understanding of the word.

Once she describes how she prays to God for strength to be less dependant on her friends, but after Geijer and Lindblad oppose her in a conversation about faith, she claims to have been sleepless the following night due to shivering fits; her inner peace remains disturbed for days after, she feels isolated and bereft of any support.[30]

On another occasion, she first insinuates Lindblad's lack of affection for her, then takes this insinuation for his real feelings, and finally concludes from those (insinuated) feelings, that she is a tedious and boring person. All this happens within just a few sentences in her diary.[31]

Of course, the intensity of these effects varies depending on the intimacy of the relationship, but the pattern is undeniably visible. It corresponds to her strange

---

[28] It should be conceded though, that most serious studies nowadays see the poetic and philosophical features that connect Classicism and Romanticism, for example Kant-reception, Schiller's aesthetics or even the enthusiasm for ancient Greek culture, to name just some prominent ones, even if German literary studies do not, as it is customary abroad, count Schiller and Goethe amongst the Romantic poets.

[29] Compare for example their accounts of the encounter with Jean Paul (MONTGOMERY-SILFVERSTOLPE: Memoarer, pp. 191-193 and ATTERBOM: Minnen, pp. 137-140): although Atterbom admires Jean Paul as a poet, he still describes his physique ironically and is fascinated with Jean Paul's drinking habits, while Silfverstolpe is deeply moved by the aged poet's frailty and friendliness.

[30] See MONTGOMERY-SILFVERSTOLPE: Memoarer, pp. 198-201.

[31] See MONTGOMERY-SILFVERSTOLPE: Memoarer, pp. 176-177: „Lindblad, som [...] *tycktes* ledsen vid sitt resesällskap, gick i land [...]. Jag ser – jag känner, att han *ledsnat* vid mig, att jag *är* entonig tråkig. [...] då han ledsnar vid min omsorg, då han afvisar den, gör det ondt. I många fall minskar väl detta mitt nöje af resan [...]." (Lindblad [...] who *seemed* tired of his travelling companions, went ashore [...]. I see – I feel that he *has* become tired of me, that I *am* tediously boring. [...] When he becomes tired of my care, when he rejects it, that hurts. In many cases that does diminish my joy in travelling [...].") [My emphasis, Bi.Hi.]

habit of talking about herself in the third person, being "Malla", not "me", in the larger part of her memoirs.[32]

Personally speaking, it is sometimes rather painful to read this, but speaking with regard to networks, it is nothing short of astonishing. Silfverstolpe is clearly one of the main connectors within the social networks which we are talking about; she is adored by a group of younger men, whom she values highly; her material situation (though not free of worries[33]) and her *salon* guarantee stronger influence than that normally achieved by women in her days. Still, this social position is not reflected in an adequate self-esteem. Her self-image depends on affirmation from outside. It is quite tempting to suppose that Silfverstolpe actually needs her networks as a kind of safety-net for her shaky self-confidence.

In addition, she does not even present herself as the structural hub she actually is. This can be seen in her stereotypical description of conversations: two or more men are having interesting thoughts and are making witty remarks, while she is listening, gratefully and contentedly, often humbly admitting that she could not quite follow their train of thought. At least she would state that the men were able to clearly express what she only felt vaguely.[34] But if Silfverstolpe places herself in the audience of Romantic discourse, a central node of the net positions itself in the margin.

Of course, quite a lot of this exaggerated humility might be explained by reference to contemporary gender conventions.[35] But for now, Atterbom and Silfverstolpe are going to be compared individually, not as genderstereotypes. While Atterbom manages to construe himself as someone who is in fact a hub within Romanticism, and who is rightfully recognized as such by his travel acquaintances, Silfverstolpe's diaries show a self which might gain in value as long as others grant it to her. Her hub-status is not only not explicitly represented in her

---

[32] While she writes about „Malla" almost without exception throughout the other parts of her memoirs, she prefers the first person narrative in her so called *resejournal*, i.e. travel-diary. Silfverstolpe-criticism is not a well-explored area of literary studies, therefore it is difficult to find any convincing hypothesises on reasons for this.

[33] See MONTGOMERY-SILFVERSTOLPE: Memoarer, p. 202.

[34] See for example MONTGOMERY-SILFVERSTOLPE: Memoarer, pp. 180, 189, 195.

[35] Silfverstolpe reflects on her female role resp. common gender inequality from time to time in her travel-diary and hardly appears naive in her conclusions on this matter (See for example MONTGOMERY-SILFVERSTOLPE: Memoarer, p. 169). – Margretmary DALY's study on letters by German Romantic women-writers, Bettina von Arnim, Caroline Schlegel-Schelling, and Rahel Varnhagen, gives important insights into the interrelation of female role, letter as a genre, and writing as a means of self-definition. This interrelation marks a further important field of examination for network studies.

own texts, it is even hidden behind a tendency to marginalize herself; we can only realise her importance in contemporary networks if we see how many people she knows are obviously eager to meet her, to let her stay as a guest in their homes, who seek her advice and sympathy. Still, there is no evidence that Silfverstolpe consciously withholds or distorts any of those tokens of welcome and trust. A more concise genderanalysis might detect a more subtle female strategy of 'self-affirmation by understatement', be it conscious, sub-conscious, voluntary or imposed.

None of the observations on Silfverstolpe's writing would become obsolete for networkanalysis, if it were explained by typical female roles of the time. On the contrary, a closer look at network structures and dynamics should enrich gender studies of the 18th and 19th centuries. The possibility, even tendency, to become a female hub should be taken into consideration when talking about social roles of women of the nobility and bourgeoisie.[36]

We have so far heard about a number of female connectors – Malla Silfverstolpe, Amalia von Helvig, Rahel Varnhagen, and Bettina von Arnim. Germaine de Staël would have to be added here, as she was not 'only' a predominant figure of inter-European cultural exchange in her time, but had particularly strong connections to Sweden, having been married to the French ambassador there and later visiting the country, taking along her personal companion A. W. Schlegel.[37]

2. Nets And Textures: Media of Networking and Self-Construction

As we have already seen, Atterbom's and Silfverstolpe's journeys serve as means of networking in various respects. Encounters can initiate new links, often transferring a former one-way relationship of adoration to mutual acquaintance and appreciation, as is the case with Atterbom and Schelling, Atterbom and Tieck, Geijer and Schelling, etc. But on their journeys, they also visit old acquaintances and friends, thus renewing and stabilizing pre-existing nets. This can take peculiar forms when the persons with which the links are renewed

---

[36] KRAMARZ-BEIN's results on the role of Ingibjörg and Eufemia for Old-Swedish courtly literature (see this volume) indicate a more general significance of gendered network analysis, maybe throughout European cultural history.

[37] For de Staël's general predominance over European webs see SCHÖNING/SEEMANN: Madame de Staël, the proceedings of a large research project of literary studies in which her Scandinavian connections sadly are not in particular mentioned, let alone scrutinized.

by travelling are not themselves present. We can point out two cases of this peculiar technique of networking. Firstly, Silfverstolpe and her companions travel as friends of Atterbom's, thus renewing his links on his behalf, for example with Schelling. Secondly, they follow the last traces of the deceased Kernell, thus mending a link which has been cut by death.

The main medium of keeping networks alive is, of course, the letter. But in fact, the written word is an important medium of networking not only in letters. Atterbom, for example, writes a poem for Schelling, praising the philosopher's influence on the poet's life.[38] The German scholar/poet Smets (chaplain at the cathedral in Cologne) and Geijer exchange manuscripts and prints of their works.[39] The fashionable poet August von Platen, who was a friend of Kernell's during his last illness in Erlangen, plays the role of textual connector in several respects: he gives small volumes of his own poetry as a present to Silfverstolpe, later that day he donates her the *Romeo-and-Juliet*-edition owned by Kernell, in between those two gifts he is eager to read *Frithiof's saga*, a somewhat iconic text of Swedish Romanticism, in the Swedish original;[40] but most important, he sends a printed version of the eulogy held at Kernell's burial to the bereaved in Sweden.[41]

Finally, for Atterbom, publishing his travel-book – or wanting to publish it – ultimately means publishing his new and old networks, making them last in the public conscience, if I may repeat my own wording. Nothing of all this is in any respect exclusively romantic. But there are other means of networking to be identified in *Minnen* and memoirs, which are essentially romantic.

A little detour is necessary in order to explain this adequately. One consequence of the romantic desire for the Divine Infinite, which I outlined in my introduction, is the idea of the Infinite Book that consists of all the poetry produced in the world – if written in the right poetic mind.[42] Any romantic piece of literature

---

[38] See ATTERBOM: Minnen, pp. 194-196.
[39] See MONTGOMERY-SILFVERSTOLPE: Memoarer, p. 166. – Geijer's present is an edition of the songs he and Lindblad composed together.
[40] See MONTGOMERY-SILFVERSTOLPE: Memoarer, pp. 188-190
[41] See MONTGOMERY-SILFVERSTOLPE: Memoarer, p. 268
[42] See KREMER: Romantik. p. 20: „In ihrer Summe schreiben sie [= die romantischen Texte, Bi.Hi.] an jenem absoluten Buch, als das Schlegel den romantischen Gesamttext [...] entwirft." (= "In total, they [= the Romantic texts, Bi.Hi.] keep writing this Infinite Book, as which Schlegel [...] drafts the Romantic textual whole.") – „[...] Schlegel [verpflichtet] das Projekt der Romantik auf einen offenen Prozeß, in dem jeder einzelne Text als Moment der unendlichen Annäherung gleichzeitig auch Monument eines not-

is to be a part of this Infinite Book. As the English term points out quite conveniently, this metaphysical book can never be completed, and so, ultimately, all Romantic literature remains to some extent a fragment. But as every Romantic poet works on this Infinite Book, and as any true Romantic poet longs to reach the Divine Infinite, Romanticists experiment with symbiotic *poiësis*, in German *Sympoesie,* usually translated into English as sympoetry.

In practice, sympoetry means that two or more poets write together in such a way that their respective contributions to the text are not to be identified later. Thus, the text is no longer an individual achievement, but the common product of a network of poets. I am certain that we find such a piece of sympoetry among the *Minnen*texts. The so-called *Albano*essay is so similar to one published by the German poet Wilhelm Müller that researchers have accused Atterbom of plagiarism.[43] But as the two writers were in close contact during their time in Italy and visited Albano together, and as Atterbom chooses "we" as his perspective instead of his regular "I", this essay is to be read not as plagiarism but as *sympoetry*, or at least as an attempt at it. (The question is, of course, why the poets decided to publish the same essay twice under their individual names instead of clearly stating their symbiosis.)

Finally, Atterbom as well as Silfverstolpe interlink their travel-writing closely and frequently with other texts; and if we take another look at the way in which they do it, it becomes clear that they not only interlink their texts with other texts, but they actually interlink their journeys with those texts. But how do they tie this net between their own journeys and literature? How do they romanticize their travelling? They do so by describing routes, stations and encounters, as if those were but quotations of literature.[44]

Silfverstolpe and Atterbom are quite familiar with certain towns because they have read stories taking place there before; a garden looks like a garden in a novel by Jean Paul; a castle is a castle from the hoax legends by Ossian[45]; a girl by the road seems to be Philine from Goethe's *Bildungsroman* Wilhelm Meis-

---

wendigen Scheiterns wird." (= "[...] Schlegel [commits] the Romantic project to an open process, in which any single text as a moment of infinite advance is simultaneously a monument of inevitable failure.")

[43] See for example LEWAN: Drömmen, p. 74.

[44] For the following examples see in that order MONTGOMERY-SILFVERSTOLPE: Memoarer, pp. 172-176, 179-180; ATTERBOM: Minnen, pp. 131-132, 88, 16, 371-390.

[45] This ancient Gaelic bard was later discovered to be the fiction of his "editor", James Macpherson, who did indeed write the Ossianic poems himself.

ter; villagegossip about lovers, who had to flee from their parents, could as well be a legend by Tieck; Verona is the city of Romeo and Juliet, etc.

In all these cases, the symbiosis of life and literature has become so close that Atterbom and Silfverstolpe can actually textualize their lives by quoting fiction; fiction being as good a travel-guide as any non-fictional description.

Almost all the aspects I have so far identified as means of networking on different levels, do fulfil a second task: they serve as a means of self-construction as well. We have seen that Atterbom manages to affirm his self-image by reporting on his encounters. We have not quite seen why Silfverstolpe marginalizes herself as a hub.[46]

Now we can see that Silfverstolpe and Atterbom construe themselves as Romantic beings by interlinking their travels and their lives with literature.[47]

Let me add another interesting observation. If we deal with texts with a first-person-perspective and/or personal narrators, we have to take into account a certain distortion of the nets. Even when narrators carefully point out their marginal role, as Silfverstolpe does, everything that happens in the networks they describe refers to them in the end. Silfverstolpe would never claim that the geniuses in her company made interesting conversation in order to please her. But what we learn about their conversations is that they please her.

Although a narrator may marginalize themselves with respect to social hierarchy, they still become the main point of reference of their narration, thus being a kind of hub for the narrative all the same. The effect that the personal narrator becomes in some respect the centre of any network they report from, is obviously much stronger if they do not even bother to belittle their social role in them. We have seen that in Atterbom's *Minnen*.

3. Individuals vs. the Infinite: A Dilemma in Romanticism and German Idealism

We already have had an (all too short) glimpse into the Romantic yearning for the Divine Infinite. An attempt to resolve one's self into this Divine Infinite can

---

[45] Unless, of course, we take female socialization as a dogma, explaining both any individual psychological deformation and any poetic strategy, forbidding any further probing into motivations.

[47] DALY: Women of Letters, p. 8, states a similar kind of connection in her study on German Romantic women writers: „[...] these three [= Schlegel-Schelling, von Arnim, and Varnhagen; Bi.Hi.] share in the act of creatively and actively defining a self that is indivisibly entwined with literary production." Being mostly interested in female self-exploration and gender roles, she does not put a great weight on the part romantic aesthetics may have in this.

be made by means of sympoetry and the Infinite Book. But this desire is not the only idea the Romanticists have adapted from German Idealism: in the 18th and early 19th centuries, the individual has achieved a central role in contemporary philosophy, as well in aesthetics as ethics.

Consequently, development of one's individual personality and talents, interest for in individual's emotions and impulses, are held in high esteem by the Romanticists.[48] There seems to be an obvious contradiction between those two main ideals: fully developing the self and resolving the self; an obvious contradiction between the Individual and the Infinite.[49]

Instead of trying to resolve this major philosophical dilemma of Romanticism, I want to compare it to that dilemma which networkanalysis has shown in Romantic social and literary practice in my examples. We see strong individuals, Atterbom, who jeopardizes his social security in Sweden in order to realize his Romantic revolution, who is a hub of the net, even if one should find his claims to be a hub suspicious, and Silfverstolpe, who is not aware of her importance, but supports Uppsala Romanticism nonetheless essentially, who is a hub of the net, no matter how much she ever tries to marginalize and belittle herself.

Above all, we see their desire to interlink themselves with others. No matter if we imply narcissism or lack of self-confidence as their motivation, they both obviously need these nets. It seems plausible that any sound human network does need just this combination: strong nodes with a strong impulse to interlink. A net is no net without links – but why should anyone want to be linked to others, if they were totally self-sufficient? A net is no net either without the nodes and hubs – but how should anyone function as node or even hub, if they really had no personality, no self?

Thus, the Romantic desire to romanticize their world is a strong linking force, as we have seen, even capable of linking human lives with literature. Ultimately, romanticizing roots in the desire for the Divine Infinite.

Thus, the strong Romantic individual is a very strong node, tending to become a hub. We have seen, by the way, that a strong individual is not the same as an individual with a high self-esteem.

---

[48] See MISCHER: Göttliche Egoisten.
[49] For some enlightening thoughts on this apparent dilemma see FRÜCHTL: Das unverschämte Ich, pp. 207 ff.

In sum, Romanticism is an age of intense networking. Therefore, further examination of Romantic phenomena with the aid of network-concepts seems to be a worthwhile and thrilling endeavour, promising and rewarding to contribute to.

4. "Interlacing Subjects"

It is to be hoped that the perhaps mysterious sounding formula "Interlacing Subjects" has become clearer now.

Still, the word *subject* is of a fascinating ambiguity, a Romantic lack of clarity, really: it can mean the same as the Self and the Ego in German Idealism, but it can also mean the actual human individual, thereby unifying the Romantic contradiction in one word.

Strong individuals that they were, the Romanticists were subjects to their king, country and their church. This is not the place to talk about the role which national discourses played in Romantic network dynamics, but it is an issue well worth treating.

Thus, issues, aspects, *subjects* which seem worth examining keep interlacing al the time. This is, of course, not a romantic dilemma but a constant challenge for any scholar interested in literary networks within Romanticism.

Bibliography

AARSETH, Asbjørn: *Romantikken som konstruksjon,* Bergen: Univ.-Forl., 1985.

ATTERBOM, Per Daniel Amadeus; Bengt LEWAN (ed.): *Minnen från Tyskland och Italien,* Vol. I + II. Stockholm: Svenska akademien, 2002.

AXBERGER, Gunnar: *Den unge Atterbom.* Uppsala: Almquist & Wiksell, 1936.

BABCOCK GOVE, Philip (ed.): *Webster's Third New International Dictionary of the English Language unabridged.* Cologne: Könemann, 1993.

BARABÁSI, Albert-László: *Linked. How Everything Is Connected to Everything Else and What It Means for Business, Science, and Everyday Life.* New York: Plume, 2003.

BAUMGARTNER, Hans Michael and Harald KORTEN: *Friedrich Wilhelm Joseph Schelling.* Munich: C.H. Beck, 1996.

BRYLLA, Charlotta: *Die schwedische Rezeption zentraler Begriffe der deutschen Frühromantik. Schlüsselwortanalysen zu den Zeitschriften Athenäum und Phosphorus.* Stockholm: Almqvist & Wiksell, 2003.

BRYLLA, Charlotta: "Överföring av nyckelord mellan tysk och svensk romantic," in: Bo Lindberg (ed.): *Trygghet och äventyr. Om begreppshistoria.* Stockholm: Almqvist & Wiksell, 2005, pp. 59-76.

DALY, Margretmary: *Women of Letters. A Study of Self and Genre in the Personal Writing of Caroline Schlegel-Schelling, Rahel Levin-Varnhagen, and Bettina von Arnim.* Columbia, SC: Camden House, 1998.

GETHMANN-SIEFERT, Annemarie: *Einführung in die Ästhetik.* Munich: Fink, 1995.

FRÜCHTL, Josef: *Das unverschämte Ich. Eine Heldengeschichte der Moderne.* Frankfurt am Main: Suhrkamp, 2004.

HELLSTEN-WALLIN, Elisabeth and Isak WALLIN: *Den unge Atterbom och Romantiken. Från Urania och Fågel Blå till Pilgrimshälsning.* Stockholm: Almqvist & Wiksell, 1957.

HOLMQUIST, Ingrid: "Vänskap och kärlek som projekt i salongskulturen. Om Malla Silfverstolpe och Amalia von Helvig som salongskvinnor och skribenter," in: Anne Scott Sørensen (ed.): *Nordisk Salonkultur. Et studie i nordiske skønånder og salonmiljøer 1780-1850.* Odense, Odense Universitetsforlag, 1998, pp. 209-229.

KREMER, Detlef: *Prosa der Romantik.* Stuttgart: J.B. Metzler, 1996.

KREMER, Detlef: *Romantik.* Stuttgart: J.B. Metzler, 2001.

LEWAN, Bengt: *Drömmen om Italien.* Stockholm, Natur o. kultur, 1966.

MISCHER, Sibille: "'Göttliche Egoisten' – Die Romantik und ihre Ethik der Individualität," in: Franz GNIFFKE and Norbert HEROLD (eds.): *Klassische Fragen der Philosophiegeschichte II. Neuzeit und Moderne.* Münster, Lit, 2000, pp. 105-130.

MONTGOMERY-SILFVERSTOLPE, Malla; Malla GRANDINSON (ed.): *Memoarer, III: 1819-1825.* Stockholm: Bonnier, 1910.

MONTGOMERY-SILFVERSTOLPE, Malla; Ellen KEY (ed.) and Marie FRANZOS (trans.): *Das romantische Deutschland. Reisejournal einer Schwedin (1825-1826).* Leipzig, Merseburger, 1913.

OLSSON, Bernt och Ingemar ALGULIN (ed.): *Litteraturens historia i Sverige.* Stockholm: Norstedt, 1995.

RISBERG, Bernhard: "Tyska förebilder till dikter af Atterbom. Litteraturhistorisk studie," in: *Uppsala Universitets Årsskrift* (1892), pp. 1-80.

SAFRANSKI, Rüdiger: *Romantik. Eine deutsche Affäre.* Munich: Hanser, 2007.

SAUL, Nicholas (ed.): *Cambridge Companion to German Romanticism.* Cambridge: Cambridge University Press, 2009.

SCHÖNING, Udo and Frank SEEMANN (ed.): *Madame de Staël und die Internationalität der europäischen Romantik. Fallstudien zur interkulturellen Vernetzung.* Göttingen, Wallstein, 2003.

TYKESSON, Elisabeth: *Atterbom. En levnads teckning.* Stockholm, Norstedt, 1954.

WHITE, Allan: *Schelling. An Introduction to the System of Freedom.* New Haven: Yale University Press, 1983.

ELS BIESEMANS AND GODELIEVE LAUREYS

The Reception of Scandinavian Literature in the Netherlands and Flanders 1860-1940. Some preliminary reflections on the role of networks

1. Scandinavian literature seduces Europe

From the late nineteenth century onwards, interest in Scandinavian literature was on the rise throughout Europe. In 1926, the Danish literary critic Helge Topsøe-Jensen (1896-1976) declared in the introduction of his *Den Skandinaviske Litteratur fra 1870 til vore dage* [*Scandinavian Literature from 1870 until today*] (1926) that "in het laatste kwart van de 19e eeuw wordt het begrip 'Skandinavische letterkunde' voor den ontwikkelden Europeeër iets werkelijks, een geestelijke macht, die meetelt." ["the concept 'Nordic literature' in the last 25 years of the 19th century had become something 'real' for the educated European. It was like a spiritual force that really should be taken into account."][1] The impact is mirrored in a large number of translations of Scandinavian literary works into various European languages and also becomes clear from the particular attention that Scandinavian literature received in literary journals. With reference to this sudden growth of attention all over Europe, August Strindberg (1849-1919) declared to a journalist that his short plays *Leka med elden* [*Playing with Fire*] and *Bandet* [*The Link*], both written in 1892, were translated

> från Svenskan till Tyskan, från Tyskan till Italienskan (sannolikt) till Franskan som snart utkommer; och den väntande Engelska tages sannolikt från Franskan som vanligt, hvarpå man kan vänta en Svensk öfversättning från det som Original utgifna Engelska.
> [from Swedish into German, from German into Italian (probably) into French which soon will be published; while the waiting English will probably be translated from French as usually, after which a Swedish translation can be expected from the alleged Original English text.]

---

[1] TOPSØE-JENSEN: De Skandinavische Letterkunde, p. 1. (All Translations E.B. and G.L.)

"Utgifver jag," he continued suspiciously, "i en aflägsen framtid mina Svenska original så blir jag sannolikt stämd för tjuftryck." ["When I, in a distant future publish my Swedish originals, I will probably be accused of plagiarism."][2]

The growing interest in Scandinavia all over Europe was primarily due to the blooming of the Scandinavian literary scene after the so-called 'modern breakthrough'. The theoretical substructure of this turning point in Scandinavian literature is generally ascribed to Georg Brandes (1842-1927). This Danish literary critic held the opinion that, after a long period of regurgitating literary innovations from abroad, the time had come for Scandinavian literature to make a name for itself. With pertinent findings such as "vor Litteratur er som et lille Kapel i en stor Kirke, den har sit Alter, men Hovedalteret findes ikke her" ["our literature is like a little chapel in a large church, it has its altar, but the main altar isn't to be found here"],[3] "vi ere nemlig denne Gang som sædvanlig en 40 Aar tilbage for Europa" ["we are in fact now as always a 40 years behind of Europe"][4] and "den poetiske Production er saagodt som fuldstændigt standset" ["the poetical production is almost totally stagnated"],[5] in his *Hovedstrømninger i det 19de Aarhundredes Litteratur* [*Main currents in the 19th Century Literature*] Brandes sought to defy the Scandinavian authors.[6] As in his opinion "det, at en Litteratur i vore Dage lever, viser sig i, at den sætter Problemer under Debat" ["the fact that a literature in our time is lively, manifests itself in its debating of problems"],[7] he wanted the Scandinavian authors to accept the challenge to write innovative, controversial literature. After having stayed in several cities on the European continent between 1865 and 1871 in order to broaden his knowledge about the international literary scene, he was certainly in the right position to make such claims.[8]

The authors who shared or were influenced by Brandes' range of thought, would soon be called 'the authors of the modern breakthrough'. At the turn of the century, a large number of those authors decided to reside in several European cities, with the intention of drawing on the influence of the innovative 'literature of the centre', of meeting other famous literary figures and of making

---

[2] Strindberg cited in MEIDAL: August Strindberg, p. 16.
[3] BRANDES: Hovedstrømninger i det 19de Aarhundredes Litteratur, p. 10.
[4] BRANDES: Hovedstrømninger i det 19de Aarhundredes Litteratur, p. 13.
[5] BRANDES: Hovedstrømninger i det 19de Aarhundredes Litteratur, p. 14.
[6] BRANDES: Hovedstrømninger i det 19de Aarhundredes Litteratur, pp.10-14.
[7] BRANDES: Hovedstrømninger i det 19de Aarhundredes Litteratur, p. 15.
[8] NOLIN: Den gode europén.

their own names known outside of Scandinavia. Strindberg for example lived in Paris during the 1880's and 1890's, where he wrote some of his well-known novels, among which *Le plaidoyer d'un fou* [*The defense's speech of a fool*] (1872) and some of his prominent theatre plays such as *Inferno* (1897) and *Legends* (1898). As his main reason for moving away from Scandinavia was his search for a broader audience, it did not take long before he started to write in French.[9] Strindberg unmistakably realized that international success was a necessary intermediate stage to becoming a celebrated author in his home country, where modern thought was yet to be widely accepted.[10] To emphasize this, he himself preferred to call his stay abroad an escape, or, even stronger, an 'artistic exile'.[11] Also Henrik Ibsen (1828-1906) chose to live abroad for the larger part of his professional life. He wrote his principal dramas *Brand* (1866) and *Peer Gynt* (1867) during stays in Italy and Germany between 1864 and 1891. The fact that many of his later plays, such as *Bygmester Solness* [*The Master Builder*] (1892) had their first performance outside Scandinavia, illustrates the contrast between his popularity on the European continent and the lack of attention in his home region.

As the Scandinavian authors themselves were actively present on the European continent, it is not so surprising that their literature received much attention. Not uncommonly, they were involved in European literary circles and acted as cultural ambassadors of a sort. Furthermore, in spite of the sometimes large distances between them, the Scandinavian authors stayed in close contact with each other. Often, they kept up a lively correspondence, discussed literary topics, commented on each other's literary works and visited the performances of each other's theatre pieces. Authors like Bjørnstjerne Bjørnson (1832-1910) and Knut Hamsun (1859-1952) even actively promoted their own country's literature and thus the work of their companions, abroad. In 1893 for example, Hamsun published an article about modern Norwegian literature, "Le Mouvement littéraire en Norvège", in the French journal *La Revue des revues*.[12] The article received a great deal of attention, since in the same year, it had been published in the Norwegian *Morgonbladet*, the Danish *Politiken* and, one year later it even appeared in the German journal *Aus fremden Zungen*.[13] Also Bjørn-

---

[9] MEIDAL: August Strindberg, p. 24.
[10] AHLSTRÖM: Det moderna genombrottet i Nordens litteratur.
[11] MEIDAL: August Strindberg, p. 7.
[12] HAMSUN: Le Mouvement littéraire en Norvège.
[13] BROOMANS: Den nordiska litteraturens fälttåg i Europa kring 1900, p. 165.

son's article on modern Norwegian literature, *Den Moderne Norske Literatur*, published in 1896 attracted a great deal of attention.[14] It had already been published in Dutch as well as in Norwegian in the same year, and it appeared in several journals in Europe, videlicet in *Zukunft* (Germany), *Tilskueren* (Denmark) and *Kringsjaa* (Norway) plus in the American *Forum*.[15]

2. An investigation of Scandinavian literature in Flanders and the Netherlands

Scandinavian literature was however not disseminated solely by the Scandinavian authors themselves nor was it appreciated only for its intrinsic aesthetic qualities. To a certain extent, the sudden popularity of Scandinavian literature at the end of the nineteenth century can also be explained on ideological grounds. Studies about this wider culturally oriented reception have already been conducted for the larger European countries such as Germany and France, but for the smaller countries such as Belgium and the Netherlands reports have been lacking or have only been fragmented. In order to examine this case and to map the reception of Scandinavian literature in the smaller language areas a collaborative project between the University of Ghent and the University of Groningen was set up by Petra Broomans (University of Groningen) and Godelieve Laureys (University of Ghent), titled "The Reception of Scandinavian Literature in the Netherlands and Flanders 1860-1940. A Comparative Analysis of the Role of Networks and the Impact of the Ethnolinguistic Discourse". This project was financed by the Dutch Research Foundation (NWO) and by the Flemish Research Foundation (FWO), within the framework of a Dutch-Flemish joint research program (VNC).

In the project proposal, Broomans and Laureys put forward the hypothesis that in the larger European countries, Scandinavian literature was perceived as 'annorlunda', i.e. "different" and 'exotic'. One could say that this literature was received from the point of view of 'the Self', which means that the dissimilarity with the domestic literature was stressed. In the smaller European countries on the other hand, according to Broomans and Laureys, Scandinavian literature was viewed from the perspective of 'the Other', which implies that the similarities with the own literature and with the own cultural condition were stressed. In the small language areas, the case of Scandinavian literature was put forward as evidence of how literature written in smaller languages could be successful and

---

[14] BJØRNSON: De moderne Noorsche literatuur.
[15] BJØRNSON: De moderne Noorsche literatuur.

could in fact be brought to the fore in a context that was largely dominated by German and French literature. Thus Scandinavian literature acquired an exemplary function and reinforced the defence of the domestic literature of the smaller language areas.

The project consisted of two parts, performed by one researcher at each university. The part performed by Roald Van Elswijk (University of Groningen) focuses on the conceptualization of 'the Other / Self'. In this part of the project, the question of how Scandinavian literature was perceived in Flanders and the Netherlands between 1860 and 1940 is addressed on the basis of a discourse analysis of reception documents. Special attention is paid to the question of the extent to which conceptions of nationalism and nationality played a role in this reception. The second part performed by Els Biesemans (Ghent University), focuses on the role of networks with regard to the cultural transmission of Scandinavian literature and culture in Flanders and the Netherlands between 1860 and 1940.[16] Furthermore the comparative Dutch-Flemish perspective provides an opportunity to engage in the problems of language ideology and ethnolinguistics.

3. Scandinavian literature in the Netherlands and Flanders, networks of cultural transmitters

3.1. Cultural transmitters

In contrast to the situation in Germany and France, both hosting important centres of the literary world where the Scandinavian authors themselves actively took part in the promotion of their work, in the rather peripheral Dutch-speaking area, Scandinavian literature gained the attention of the reading public mainly through the efforts of a number of Dutch and Flemish cultural transmitters. The term 'cultural transmitter' is used here in a broad sense, and comprises the writers of travel accounts, personal testimonies or learned essays about the Nordic culture, language or literature, as well as translators, reviewers, university professors and librarians. It is to be noted that in many cases, one and the same person fulfilled several of the above mentioned roles. Although not all of them were interested in Scandinavia for the same reasons, all of these transmitters actively contributed to the increase in knowledge about the Nordic culture in the

---

[16] It has to be noted that this research project focuses explicitly on the Scandinavian texts that were attended to in Flanders and the Netherlands in this very period.

Dutch-speaking area. It is noteworthy, as previous research has indicated, that those people who seem to have had mainly the same motive for devoting themselves to Scandinavian literature, tended to build networks and to cooperate.

In the field of transmission of Scandinavian culture in Flanders and the Netherlands, it is possible to discern different networks of cultural transmitters. In his article "Vlaams Scandinavisme en Stijn Streuvels" ["Flemish Scandinavism and Stijn Streuvels"] of 1991, Diederik Grit (University of Maastricht) examined the adherents of the Flemish Movement in the nineteenth century and discerned three types of networks of people who showed a substantial interest in Nordic culture. One of those networks he called 'the liberal network of the national romantic supporters of the Flemish movement'. The other, he labelled 'the catholic circle'. The third network was given the name 'the internationalist circle'. Grit also noticed that within these circles, different Scandinavian authors and literary works were favoured and that, in the reception of the literary works, and depending on the networks, different themes were emphasized.[17] Bart Dooms, formerly University of Louvain, was inspired by this article to write his master thesis on the reception of Norse literature in Flanders. Even though Dooms, unlike Grit, did not focus on the leading lights of the Flemish Movement, his analysis of the reception of Norse literature in Flanders led mainly to the same (types of) networks. Light is also shed on the constitution of the field of cultural transmission by the more recent studies devoted to the examination of (ego-) networks of women and their role in the transmission of literature. Under the impulse of Suzan van Dijk (Unversity of Utrecht), a database of women who, over time, have been engaged in transmitting culture, is being compiled.[18] With regard to the role of networks of female translators in the reception of specifically Scandinavian literature, the doctoral dissertation of Ester Jiresch (University of Groningen) must also be given mention.[19]

Apart from their focus on women networks, these latter investigations differ from those named above because of their international comparative perspective. In the elaboration of our project, this comparative element, more specifically the comparison between Flanders and the Netherlands, was one of the starting

---

[17] GRIT: Vlaams Scandinavisme en Stijn Streuvels.
[18] DIJK: Schrijfsters en lezeressen in een internationale database/Women Writers before 1900/Schrijfsters vóór 1900 en hun internationale context.
[19] JIRESCH: Im Netzwerk der Kulturvermittlung - sechs Autorinnen und ihre Bedeutung für die Verbreitung skandinavischer Literatur und Kultur in West- und Mitteleuropa um 1900.

points. In terms of the scrutiny of the networks of cultural transmitters, this implies that the acquired overview of the types of networks that were to be found in Flanders, must be reviewed and completed with the situation in the Netherlands. As the research project is dealing with an extended period of time, from 1860 until 1940, the possibility that networks have undergone some (major) changes over time must also be taken into account. In order to outline the investigation of networks of Dutch and Flemish cultural transmitters, it is plausible to give a rudimentary overview of the different types of networks we can expect on the basis of previous research.

3.2. Overview of the different types of networks

The different types of networks of transmitters of Scandinavian literature that can be found in the Netherlands and Flanders, can respectively be called 'the political networks', 'the ideological networks', and 'the networks of the internationalists and the modernists'. The political type of networks can also be described as national-romantic. These networks in particular emanate from the struggle for linguistic and cultural emancipation typical of the smaller language areas. The Dutch and Flemish spokesmen for this struggle often referred to Scandinavia. By focusing on the glorious North and its blooming culture and literature they made out a case for the development and the cultivation of the own culture, language and literature. Therefore, within these networks, special attention was paid to those Scandinavian authors who sang the praises of nordic culture,[20] while efforts were made to underline the similarities between Scandinavia and the Dutch-speaking area, both with regard to linguistic affinity and shared destiny. Within these networks, there was also a fervent hope that, by promoting the Scandinavian culture in the Dutch-speaking area, more attention would in its turn be paid to Dutch and Flemish literature in the Scandinavian countries.

The above mentioned aims of transmitting Scandinavian literature within these networks apply both to the Netherlands and Flanders. In the late nineteenth century, however, Belgium adds still another dimension in connection with the struggle for linguistic and cultural autonomy. After that the French were forced to leave Belgium in 1815, the United Kingdom of the Netherlands, a fusion of the Netherlands and Belgium, came into being. Fifteen years later, in 1830, a revolution supported by French-speaking intellectuals and the armed forces

---

[20] GRIT: Recentie: Bart Dooms, Een gezonde noordervorst.

broke out in Brussels, claiming the independence of Belgium. French would become the sole official language of the new nation; all official communication was conducted in French. Although French was the language of the nation at the level of the 'real' state, in practice, Belgium was linguistically divided in two parts. Whereas French was the language of the people of the southern part of Belgium and the language of the upper-class and the ecclesiastic and juridical authority even in Flanders, people in the northern part of the country spoke dialectal varieties of Dutch, called 'Flemish'. Soon a language movement called 'De Vlaamse Beweging' ['The Flemish movement'] arose, aiming at an equal status for the Flemish language and culture. It is interesting to see how the veneration of Scandinavian literature in Flanders was made instrumental to the Flemish movement.

Among the followers of the Flemish movement, there were two different bodies of opinion. One faction felt the urge to build an "imagined community", the borders of which should coincide with the linguistic borders of the Dutch- (including 'Flemish'-) speaking area. This group wanted to strengthen the ties with the Dutch people; they cherished the idea of a political restoration and dreamed of a 'United Netherlands'. Another faction wanted Flanders to become a linguistically and culturally "autonomous" community within the borders of the Belgian state. This dichotomy was mirrored in the discussion about the future of the codification of the 'Flemish' language. The integrationists on the one hand, who were acting upon the idea of a 'United Netherlands', aimed at adopting the Dutch norm in the Netherlands. The particularists on the other hand, wanted to establish a Flemish standard language, independent from the norm in the Netherlands and with its own rights within the Belgian state.

On both sides, the attention to Scandinavian literature was closely connected to the strong desire to take up positions against French cultural domination. Not only did the integrationists wish to strengthen the alliance with the people of the Netherlands, they wanted to increase the feeling of unity of all the speakers of Germanic languages. The awareness of being speakers of a minor language within the group of Germanic languages, made Dutch-speaking people feel connected in particular with the speakers of the Scandinavian languages. For obvious reasons, the interest in the North on the part of the Flemish particularists was especially concentrated on the case of Norway. During the period of the union with Sweden between 1814 and 1905 the struggle for a Norwegian national language played a key role in the process of nation building. The issue of establishing a Norwegian standard language was omnipresent in the public debate. The urban elites of Christiania (Oslo), opted for the preservation of the Norwegian language which had been strongly influenced by Danish. The variety of the Norwegian language they strived towards, is nowadays known as Bokmål. Under the impetus of Ivar Aasen, in the north-western part of the county, votes were cast for a new Norwegian standard language, based on the Norwegian dialects, the Landsmål, later renamed Nynorsk. The Flemish particularists often referred to the latter variety in their struggle for a Flemish standard language.[21]

Apart from national-romantic considerations, the stance of the particularist was also based on religious arguments. Catholic particularists were not in favour of the idea of a 'United Netherlands' due to their reluctance to become part of a protestant nation and hence they did not want to adapt to the northern Dutch standard. Thus, within the field of transmission of Scandinavian literature in the Dutch-speaking area, a catholic network can be discerned, which belongs to a second ideological type of network. Apart from their purely linguistic interest in the Norwegian case, the adherents of this catholic network developed a more specific interest for certain pious Scandinavian texts. Translators and reviewers belonging to this network explicitly chose to translate and review works with a religious theme. They showed a particular interest for the works of authors who, in the predominantly protestant North, dared to present themselves as catholic. Much attention was paid to the work of the Dane Johannes Jørgensen (1866-1956), mainly known for his biographies of catholic saints, as well as to the Norwegian author Sigrid Undset (1882-1949). It is worth mentioning that the work of prominent non-catholic authors was rejected for ethical reasons by the cultural transmitters belonging to this network. For them, the work of these authors in fact only confirmed the need of a 'catholic mission in the North'.

Another network of the ideological type was the network of feminists and people struggling for the emancipation of women. While in Scandinavia famous authors such as Selma Lagerlöf (1858-1940) and Victoria Benedictsson (1850-1888) were active at the end of the nineteenth century, in the Dutch speaking area it was at that time still unimaginable that a woman would start a career as an author. A more usual phenomenon was that women started learning foreign languages. This, of course, meant that some were able to start translating literary texts. By explicitly selecting texts written by women or about women's

---

[21] DOOMS: Een gezonde noordervorst, p. 11.

emancipation, women's rights within marriage or women and literature, the female translators indirectly succeeded in communicating their messages. With regard to the issue of women's emancipation, Scandinavia was ahead of Europe. Therefore, it should come as no surprise that those Dutch and Flemish women who wanted to promote the empowerment of women, explicitly chose to translate Scandinavian literature. Margaretha Meijboom (1856-1929), one of the most prominent translators of Scandinavian literature into Dutch, formulated this very clearly in an article she wrote for the journal *De Boekzaal*:

> Toen wij eenmaal gezien hadden hoeveel wij Hollanders van Deenen, Noren en Zweden konden leeren op het gebied van sociale toestanden, vrouwenbewegingen, handenarbeid en onderwijs, namen wij elke gelegenheid waar, daar met alle nadruk op te wijzen, en er allerwege belangstelling voor de wekken.
> [Once we had seen how much we Dutch can learn from the Danish, the Norsemen and the Swedish with regard to social issues, women's rights movement, handicraft and education, we seized every opportunity to emphasize this, and to kindle the interest of everyone.][22]

Even though it thus far may seem that in the Dutch-speaking area mainly political and ideological motives drove to the translation of Scandinavian literature, this assumption needs to be modified. The success of the great Scandinavian authors who created a stir on the European literary scene was also echoed in Flanders and the Netherlands. The literary transmitters who introduced these authors and their works to the Dutch-speaking area, constituted a third type of network, which can be called the network of the modernists and the internationalists. Within this type of network, the selected Scandinavian authors were discussed and admired mainly because of the aesthetic qualities of their work. It has to be noted however that on the whole the nationality of the authors at stake was not a central issue within these networks, which meant that the Scandinavian origin of the discussed and translated texts was not always underlined.

3.3. *The investigation of the problems regarding networks of Dutch and Flemish cultural transmitters*

Despite the fact that this preliminary depiction of the field of transmission of Scandinavian literature in the Dutch-speaking area offers many elements for a

---

[22] Meijboom, cited in BROOMANS: Scandia i Nederländerna, p. 158.

workable model, it must be stressed that it is still an abstraction. The question as to whether the boundaries between the networks mentioned above were so clear-cut in reality as might be suggested from former research contributes, is pertinent. It is for instance plausible that there were intersections between the networks both with regard to the actors and to the mental legacy. Not only within the networks of the internationalists and the modernists but also within the networks of the feminists, for example, did many novels of the modern breakthrough authors receive attention. The position and rights of women in society were also recurrent topics in the work of Bjørnstjerne Bjørnson, Henrik Ibsen, Jonas Lie (1833-1908), Erik (1846-1923) and Amalie Skram (1846-1905) and August Strindberg. The aims of the networks of the internationalists and the modernists, for their part, especially in Flanders were not always as free of national thoughts as might be expected. The literary journal *Van Nu en Straks* (1893-4 and 1896-1901), at the time regarded as modernist, could even be characterized as 'internationally nationalistic'. Despite its strong stance against the Flemish Movement in terms of a language struggle, the central aspirations of this journal were the consolidation of an indigenous Flemish literary life and "the integration of Flemish art and literature in a European context."[23] Or, as *Van Nu en Straks*' frontman August Vermeylen (1872-1945) in 1900 wrote it himself in his famous article "Vlaamsche en Europeesche Beweging" ["Flemish and European Movement"] (1900):

> Onze toekomst hangt grootendeels af van de grondige vervlaamsching van Vlaanderen. En daarom, in twee regels samengevat: om iets te zijn moeten wij Vlamingen zijn. – Wij willen Vlamingen zijn, om Europeërs te worden.
> [Our future depends to a large extent on the full emergence of the Flemish of Flanders. Therefore, summarized in two sentences: to become something, we have to become Flemish. – We want to become Flemish, to be able to become Europeans.][24]

As these examples suggest, some cultural transmitters probably operated under the influence of several networks at the same time. In his article 'Vlaams Scandinavisme en Stijn Streuvels', Diederik Grit also states the fact that some individual transmitters are not to be thought of as belonging exclusively to one network or another. Not least in this respect, Stijn Streuvels, of catholic descent but

---

[23] VERVLIET: Literatuur als woord en daad, p. 93.
[24] VERMEYLEN: Vlaamsche en Europeesche Beweging, p. 299.

also finding himself in internationalist and modernist circles, occupied an ambivalent, rather indefinable position. In the next section a case study of two key persons' life, their contacts, the circles they moved in, their main work and their method of working, will illustrate that this ambivalence is an issue worth looking into.

3.4. *Illustrative case study*

The first person to be mentioned with regard to the period 1860-1940, is Constant Jacob Hansen (1833-1910). As early as in his *Reisbrieven uit Dietschland*[25] *en Denemark* [*Letters of a journey to Dietschland and Denmark*] of 1860, he expressed his sympathy for the idea of a 'United Netherlands' and for the Pan-Germanic beliefs. In line with this ideology, he wanted to offer the Flemish more knowledge about 'the North'. From the beginning, he stated his goals very clearly:

> Mijn Hoofddoel […] is in Kortbegrip: de Opwekking, in breederen Sin, des germaanschen Volksgeestes in Vlaamsch-Belgien, de Versmelting der vlaamsche met der platduitsche Taalbeweging tot eenen algemeen dietschen en machtigen Volkskamp, oft de Hereeniging aller nederduitsche Gewesten op geestelyken Gebiede.
> [My principle purpose […] is the encouragement of the Germanic national spirit in Flemish-Belgium, the melting together of the Flemish and the Low German language movement into one common Dietsch and powerful 'struggle of the people', or in other words, the reunification of all the districts of the Low countries on a conceptual level.][26]

Of special interest for us is the fact that his anthology of Nordic literature, the first ever written in Dutch, *Noordsche Letteren* [*Nordic literature*], also takes its starting point from this credo and aims at the same goals.[27] This book offers many translations of poetry and theatre pieces as well as general information about the Scandinavian languages and literature. On the basis of this information, Hansen could easily be seen as a member of the national-romantic network, being an active Flemish integrationist. In fact, he repeatedly underlined

---

[25] The term 'Dietsch' is a romantic denotation of the common or resembling vernacular of the Low Countries. Because of the lacing of a suitable English expression, in the following this term will be used.
[26] HANSEN: Reisbrieven uit Dietschland en Denemark, p. 1.
[27] DOOMS: Een gezonde noordervorst, p. 16.

that he was not "interested in political reality" and actually "had no interest in politics".[28] The only Pan-Germanic union he wanted to bring about was one at the level of literature and language.[29]

The same wish for a cultural and linguistic unification of the Dutch-speaking area, was expressed by the Dutchman Jozef A. Alberdingk Thijm, who established the journal named *De Dietsche Warande* [The "Dietsche" Pleasureground] in 1855. From the beginning, the target group of this journal was the catholic community in the mainly protestant Netherlands. When the interest of this target group turned out to be rather weak, the leadership for the journal was handed over to Jozef Alberdingk Thijm's brother, Paul Alberdingk Thijm, who at that time was working as a professor at the University of Louvain. Although Catholicism in Flanders is traditionally linked with particularist thought, he explicitly warned against any kidn of particularism or provincialism in his article "Een woord van eendracht" ["A word of concord"] (1886) in the Flemish journal *Het Belfort*.

In 1900 both *De Dietsche Warande* and *Het Belfort* would become the object of the take-over purchase by the literary critic Maria Elisa Belpaire's (1853-1948). The resulting joint journal was named *Dietsche Warande en Belfort*. As Belpaire was strongly led by her catholic belief, she was not much in favour of the work of internationally praised modernist authors but rather admired religiously inspired works. She saw to it that these preferences were mirrored in *Dietsche Warande en Belfort*. Not surprisingly, a great deal of attention in this journal was paid to one of Belpaire's favourite authors, the above mentioned Dane Johannes Jørgensen. The work of the Norwegian Bjørnstjerne Bjørnson was also brought to the fore though not so much because of the modernist bias of his work, but rather because of the pure, unspoiled and pious character of the people portrayed in his peasant novels. Belpaire also praised the attention that was paid to the romantic national disposition of the characters in both the work of Bjørnson and of Jørgensen. In the article "Boekennieuws. J. Destrée over het talenvraagstuk in België" ["News about Books. J. Destrée about the language issue in Belgium"], published in *Dietsche Warande en Belfort* in 1924, Belpaire even referred to Jørgensens "Klokke Roeland" to clarify her stance. It was not only in this article that Belpaire expressed feelings of Flemish self-awareness. Such feelings were not exceptional within the networks of the Catholics. More

---

[28] BOLCKMANS: From Nordic Folk Tales to Science Fiction, p. 17.
[29] SIMONS: Vlaams-Nederduitse betrekkingen in de 19e eeuw, p. 29.

difficult to understand, however, are the efforts that Belpaire made for the emancipation of women. To a certain extent, those efforts are well in line with her ambition to offer young women a dignified, catholic education. Belpaire's contact with and admiration for some passionate, atheist feminists, however, seems to clash with her catholic point of view.

4. Concluding remarks

As former contributions to the description of the reception of Scandinavian literature are found to be too generalizing and not properly empirically founded, a detailed mapping of several networks of Dutch and Flemish cultural transmitters is needed in order to get a clearer insight into the precise constitution of the field of literary transmission. This process includes a more thorough examination of reception documents, critical reviews, translations, journal articles, letters and other ego-documents written by the transmitters of Scandinavian literature. The focus in this type of analysis is on determining the precise interpersonal relations of these transmitters. Because of the distance in time from the present, the possibility has to be considered that not all of the requested information can be delivered or is accessible. In some cases, important connections can surely be assumed, but hardly be proved. In view of the mapping of the networks and of a thorough investigation, a database has been elaborated. Beside relevant biographical and bibliographical data, this database includes information about (possible) personal relations, relations with publishing houses and journals as well as the individual transmitters' participation in events and membership of organizations. This database reveals the overlappings of the different networks, their interrelations and the way the socio-networks relate to the ego-networks of the cultural transmitters.

It has hopefully become clear that the explosive interest in Scandinavian literature and culture in the Netherlands and Flanders around the turn of the twentieth century, which brought about various modes of interaction between many different men and women of letters is really a goldmine for further research.

Bibliography

AHLSTRÖM, Gunnar: *Det moderna genombrottet i Nordens litteratur*, Stockholm: Rabén & Sjögren, 1874.

ALBERDINGK Thijm, Paul: "Een woord van eendracht", in: *Het Belfort* 1 (1886), pp. 115-120.

BELPARE, Marie Hyacinte: "Boekernieuws. J. Destrée over het talenvraagstuk in België", in: *Dietsche Warande en Belfort* 24 (1924), pp. 474-477.

BIESMANS, Els: "The reception of Scandinavian literature in the Netherlands and Flanders: some preliminary reflections on the role of networks", in: Petra Broomans & Sandra van Voorst (eds.): *Rethinking cultural transfer and transmission*, Groningen: Barkhuis, 2013, pp. 75-92.

BIESEMANS, Els: *Vertalers van Scandinavische literatuur naar het Nederlands tussen 1860 en 1940. Evolutie van hun ideologische, maatschappelijke en professionele voorkeuren*, Gent: Universiteit Gent, 2013.

BJØRNSON, Bjørnstjerne: *De moderne Noorsche literatuur*, transl. by Margaretha Meijboom, Leiden: H.A. Adriani, 1896.

BJØRNSON, Bjørnstjerne: "Den moderne norske Literatur", in: *Literatur Artikler og taler. Andet bind,* Kristiania/Copenhagen: Gyldendalske Bokhandel/Nordisk Forlag, pp. 305-330.

BRANDES, Georg: *Hovedstrømninger i det 19de Aarhundredes Litteratur*, Copenhagen: Gyldendalske Boghandel, 1872.

BROOMANS, Petra: "Scandia i Nederländerna. Om Margaretha Meijboom och hennes nordiska tidskrifter", in: *TijdSchrift voor Skandinavistiek* 22 (2001:1), pp. 155-167.

BROOMANS, Petra: "Den nordiska litteraturens fälttåg i Europa kring 1900. Om Brandes och medresenärer, maktkamp och avfall", in: Olaf Harsløf (ed.): *Georg Brandes og Europa,* Copenhagen: Kongelige Bibliotek Museum Tusculanum Forlag, 2004, pp. 163-176.

BOLCKMANS, Alex: *From Nordic Folk Tales to Science Fiction*, Gent: State University of Ghent, 1988.

DOOMS, Bart: *Een gezonde noordervorst. Vlaamse visies op Noorse literatuur tussen 1830 en 1914*, Kapellen: Pelckmans, 2001.

DIJK, Suzan van: "'Les jugements universellement portés sur les femmes...' Schrijfsters en lezeressen in een internationale database", in: *Historica* (2001) oktober, pp. 3-5.

DIJK, Suzan van: "Een database voor het literair-historisch onderzoek naar schrijfsters: 'Women Writers before 1900'", in: *Muzen aan het werk. Jaarboek voor vrouwengeschiedenis*, Amsterdam: Aksant, 2003, pp. 210-216.

DIJK, Suzan van: "Schrijfsters vóór 1900 en hun internationale context: een database als hulpmiddel voor de geschiedschrijving", in: *Tijdschrift voor Genderstudies* (2003), pp. 6-15.

GRIT, Diederik: "Vlaams Scandinavisme en Stijn Streuvels",in: *Spiegel der Letteren* 33 (1991:3), pp. 149-170.

GRIT, Diederik: "Recentie: Bart Dooms, Een gezonde noordervorst. Vlaamse visies op Noorse literatuur tussen 1830 en 1914", in: *TijdSchrift voor Skandinavistiek* 23 (2002:2), pp. 295-300.

HAMSUN, Knut: "Le Mouvement littéraire en Norvège", in: *Revue des revues* 7 (1893), pp. 721-27, 801-806.

HAMSUN, Knut: "Die literarische Bewegung in Norwegen", in: *Aus fremden Zungen* 4 (1894), pp. 55-56, 102-104, 151-152.

HANSEN, Constant Jacob: *Noordsche Letteren*, Gent: I. S. Van Doosselaere, 1860.

HANSEN, Constant Jacob: *Reisbrieven uit Dietschland en Denemark*, Gent: I. S. Van Doosselaere, 1860.

JIRESCH, Ester: *Im Netzwerk der Kulturvermittlung - sechs Autorinnen und ihre Bedeutung für die Verbreitung skandinavischer Literatur und Kultur in West- und Mitteleuropa um 1900*. Groningen: Barkhuis, 2013.

LAUREYS, Godelieve: "Languages Policy as a Cornerstone of Nation-Building. Linguistic Identities in the Nordic Countries", in: *The Beloved Mothertongue. Ethnolinguistic Nationalism in Small Nations: Inventories and Reflections*, Leuven: Peeters, 2008, pp. 79-91.

MEIDAL, Björn: *August Strindberg. Ursvensk och europé*, Stockholm: Svenska Institutet, 1999.

NOLIN, Bertil: *Den gode européN. Studier i Georg Brandes' idéutveckling 1871-1893 med speciell hänsyn till hans förhållande till tysk, engelsk, slavisk och fransk litteratur*, Stockholm: Norstedts, 1965.

SCHRIJVER, Reginald De: "Marie Elisabeth Belpaire", in: *Nieuwe Encyclopedie van de Vlaamse Beweging*, Tielt: Lannoo, 1998, pp. 457-458.

SIMONS, Ludo: "Vlaams-Nederduitse betrekkingen in de 19e eeuw", in: Ludo Simons, *Oostnoordoost. Facetten van de uitstraling van Vlaanderens taal en literatuur*, Antwerpen: Uitgeverij De Nederlandsche Boekhandel, 1969, pp. 27-48.

TOPSØE-JENSEN, Helge: *De Skandinavische Letterkunde van 1870-1925*, transl. by Annie Posthumus, Amsterdam: Elsevier, 1926.

VERMEYLEN, August: "Vlaamsche en Europeesche Beweging", in: *Van Nu en Straks II* 4 (1900), pp. 299-310.

VERVLIET, Raymond; Bart Keunen & Philippe Codde (red.): *Literatuur als woord en daad: opstellen over tekst en context in de late 19^e eeuw.* Brussels: VUB press, 2000.

Felix K. E. Schmelzer

The Dynamic Universe of Text:
The Dynamic Web as a Structural Concept of Totality in both 20th Century Literature and Science

Structure is a key-word within 20th century literary theory. It is most evidently connected to the application of Ferdinand de Saussure's terminology and basic ideas in early literary structuralism and moreover lies at the core of concepts such as intertextuality and discourse theory. It is also widely used outside the French theoretical schools, for example by Hugo Friedrich in his influential study on modern poetry. *Die Struktur der modernen Lyrik*. Different as the specific theories of literary structure may be, they all focus on working out a general architecture of text that transcends the individuality of work and author. Within this context, 20th century literary theory seems to rediscover the etymological origin of *textum*: textile, or, in general, web.[1]

The concept of the text as a web corresponds to antique mythology and can be exemplified by Ovid and his representation of Arachne. Arachne, whose artistic skills in weaving surpass even those of the divine Pallas, produces a multicoloured web that seems to contain the whole mythology of ancient times. The essential interconnectedness (Ovid describes the single elements as being interwoven – "intertextos"[2]) of the web's motives and colours causes an effect of illusion within the spectator who is unable to see a beginning or end of the individual elements: The one is the many, the many the one. The myth can be read as a metaphorical circumscription of 20th century literary theory. Within this context, it is Michel Foucault who most clearly expresses the idea of literature as a web, regarding the single element as a "knot" whose boundaries are not exactly determined:

> C'est que les marges d'un livre ne sont jamais nettes ni rigoureusement tranchées: par-delà le titre, les premières lignes et le point final, par-delà sa configuration interne et la forme qui

---

[1] I want to thank the great philologist Ulrich Prill (1960-2010), my friend, for revealing this idea to me.
[2] OVID: *Metamorphoses*, Liber sextus, Verse 128.

l'autonomise, il est pris dans un système de renvois à d'autres livres, d'autres textes, d'autres phrases: nœud dans un réseau.³

Evidently, Foucault's famous description of the work of literature as a "knot in the web" is an antique thought cast into the mould of modern times.

The (re-)appearance of "web" as a structural metaphor in the 20th century is not limited to literary theory but has also become evident within modern physics. As a consequence of relativity theory and quantum mechanics, the term is frequently used to describe the universe, for instance by Fritjof Capra who calls the universe a "dynamic web of interrelated events".⁴ Along with this, both scientific fields reveal evident conceptual parallels in the architectonical description of the web, focussing on three major characteristics: indeterminacy of the individual elements, interconnectedness of all phenomena and continuous transformation of the whole.

Curiously, more than half a century before being observed by science, this specific architecture is already present within modern poetry: One of its most impressive monuments is the only fragmentarily delivered "Over-Book" ("Le Livre") of Stéphane Mallarmé – it was intended to express the secret of the universe by creating a web of words with unlimited mutual relations.

Everything is connected to everything else – it seems that this philosophical awareness,⁵ so frequently used to describe the postmodern age, was already penetrating different areas of human thought by the turn of the 20th century. Within this context, Albert László Barabási does not introduce a "new science", but rather opens the next chapter, offering a new and interesting field of research, the Internet,⁶ and replacing the term "dynamic web" with "network" – a term increasingly popular throughout the information revolution. His description of networks⁷ is in complete accordance with the architectonical characteristics mentioned above. If the 21st century is to be a century of connectedness and

---

³ FOUCAULT: L'Archéologie du savoir, p. 34.
⁴ CAPRA: The Tao of Physics, p. 286.
⁵ The interconnectedness of all phenomena is a pre-Socratic idea, having been previously expressed by Heraclitus.
⁶ Concerning the internet, the question arises if and in how far it is itself a product of the metaphorical concept discussed here. It seems logical that our inventions correspond with how we perceive the world. Probably we anticipate, maybe even create in advance, our own future via our metaphorical concepts of reality. The German philosopher Hans Blumenberg expresses a similar idea. Cf. BLUMENBERG, Paradigmen zu einer Metaphorologie, p. 13.
⁷ Cf. BARABÁSI: Linked.

complexity, as the author predicts, this has already been theoretically indicated by 20th century literature and science. Rather than applying Barabási's theory to literary studies, the following pages sketch the appearance of the dynamic web as a structural concept of totality in poetry, literary theory and physics throughout the 20th century and try to show a specifically modern network-discourse that transcends the borders of the "two cultures",[8] unifying concepts of artistic and physical creation.

The Rhythm of Totality

At the beginning of modern poetry the work of one man reaches a degree of abstraction that probably is unparalleled in the history of literature. This man is Stéphane Mallarmé. In his work, poetry and theoretical reflections on poetry make up an inseparable unit. The following famous quote, taken from an interview titled "Sur l'évolution littéraire", expresses the essence of his reflections on poetry and at the same time a fundamental principle of modern aesthetics: "*Nommer* un objet, c'est supprimer les trois quarts de la jouissance du poëme qui est faite de deviner peu à peu: le *suggérer*, voilà le rêve."[9] The phrase underlines the typical modernist dislike of a realist doctrine. Moreover, the central opposition of naming *vs.* suggesting is rooted in Mallarmé's aesthetic ideal of "nothingness". For Mallarmé, nothingness is the beginning and end of all art and has to be understood ontologically as "the pure being". Similar to the Aristotelian *potentia*, it expresses a pre-manifest world of unlimited possibilities. The artistic act signifies a destruction of this pure world of possibilities which, in a paradox manner, has to be re-conquered by the same creative force that destroyed it. The moment they come into being, art and literature shall thus express their own dissolution into nothingness that Mallarmé also metaphorically describes as the "white page", the "naked poem" or, in his frequent comparisons between poetry and music, the "rhythm of totality": "Tout devient suspens, disposition fragmentaire avec alternance et vis-à-vis, concourant au rythme total, lequel serait le poème tu, aux blancs."[10]

---

[8] In 1959, the British scientist and novelist C.P. Snow delivered an influential lecture called "The Two Cultures" in Cambridge. His thesis was that the breakdown of communication between the sciences and the humanities was a major hindrance to solving the world's problems.
[9] MALLARMÉ: Œuvres Complètes II, p. 700.
[10] MALLARMÉ: "Crise de vers", in: Œuvres Complètes II, p. 211.

For Mallarmé, poetic suggestion is the key to the absolute, even though it cannot be adequately expressed in words or colours (probably music comes closest) just as it is impossible to *think* nothing. The author bares a sophisticated relation to his own creation. To indicate the process of dissolution, the creative act – understood traditionally – must be reversed, the so-called reality has to be deconstructed. In contrast to the Creator of the Old Testament, the modern artist does not separate light and darkness out of chaos: he tries to melt the opposites back into chaos. This is what "le *suggérer*, voilà le rêve" essentially means, and this is why Hugo Friedrich describes modern poetry in the tradition of Mallarmé as a transformation of a fixed sense into "associative vibrations".[11]

The compositional structure of poetry that attempts to fulfil this abstract condition is that of a textual web (even though Mallarmé does not use the word specifically) in which every single word can principally be related to every other word. This becomes evident by looking at Mallarmé's most ambitious and unfinished project, the "Over-Book". What this book should look like and what the author's aim was can only be reconstructed from preserved fragments – notes and strange combinations of words related to numbers and mathematical symbols, partially underlined or in brackets. As well as this, there are several statements in which the author directly refers to the mysterious book. The picture that comes into being is indeed impressive.[12] It seems that Mallarmé wanted to exhaust all the possibilities of language. The book should express the "intimate correlation between poetry and the universe",[13] and give rise to the "total expansion of the letter".[14] Already by the age of 25, Mallarmé expresses the strange idea of being an impersonal medium "through which the universe expresses itself and regards its own developing structure".[15] His unfinished book should document this process in all its complexity and with the closest possible mathematical precision. In a note by the author we are confronted with the number 3 628 800 – it stands for a sum of combination possibilities. Mallarmé's basic idea was to embrace the divine by methods of combination, even if this divinity should be nothing.

It seems that the "Over-Book" wanted to establish a mathematical system of several groups of words and verses hinting at other groups of words and these

---

[11] FRIEDRICH: Die Struktur der modernen Lyrik, p. 91.
[12] Cf. SCHERER: Le "livre" de Mallarmé.
[13] SCHERER: op. cit., p. 22.
[14] Ibid., p. 22.
[15] Ibid., p. 22.

again at others, creating a complex semantic web. Mallarmé's aim was to "reveal hidden relations"[16] that transcend the logical and chronological order of the mind by means of permutation. What this idea may look like can be exemplified by observing Mallarmé's poetry. For example, an angel with a naked sword becomes "an angel standing in the nakedness of his sword", black hats flying through the street are transformed into "the street, exposed to the hats' black flight".[17] The possibilities of permutation do not end here, of course. In this manner, single verses obtain a multitude of possible permutations and interpretations. The breaking open of classical logical structures and, along with this, a plurality of possible meanings, also become evident at the level of the word, as the frequent use of the oxymoron such as "silent music" in the work of Mallarmé (and in modern poetry in general) demonstrates. In the book, each verse or group of words should become a single combinatory element. The semantic indeterminacy of each element would principally allow its relation to any other element. This compositional principle is the means of achieving the poetic aim, to express a "pure wholeness of relations everything to everything".[18]

Mallarmé's remarkable plan symbolizes the unfinished fragment of an impressive literary monument that stands without comparison. It shows the awareness of a higher degree of reality that has a specific network character. It does not seem surprising that his ideal is music, whose polyphonic structure he wishes to translate into language. In a metaphysical sense, for Mallarmé language and music are one: a world of infinite potentiality endlessly celebrating itself. Just like the "Over-Book", the artistic act itself is unfinished, giving room for the combinatory creative pulse: the self-deterministic play of language that continues within the reader's mind.

The Textual Universe

Within 20th century literary theory, there are abstract concepts of what literature *is* that come very close to Mallarmé's ideal of what literature *should be*. In this context, in his famous essay "Tradition and the Individual Talent" (1919), T.S. Eliot anticipates basic ideas of intertextuality:

> the whole of the literature [...] has a simultaneous existence and composes a simultaneous order. [...] The existing order is complete

---

[16] Quoted in HOCKE: Manierismus in der Literatur, p. 54.
[17] FRIEDRICH: op. cit., pp. 137-8.
[18] HOCKE: op. cit., p. 53.

before the new work arrives; for order to persist after the supervention of novelty, the whole existing order must be, if ever so slightly; altered, and so the relations, proportions, values of each work of art toward the whole are readjusted; and this is the conformity between the old and the new.[19]

Literature, and Eliot refers to everything that has ever been written and will ever be written, is regarded as an organic and dynamically growing "whole". The individual elements – this time it is the works and not the words or verses – are continuously being readjusted by the new work of art, and thus every single element has an influence on every other element and at the same time is determined by every other element. This marginal thought that Eliot uses to underline his idea of the "historical sense" reappears (without mentioning Eliot at all) in the 1970s and 1980s by literary theorists such as Julia Kristeva or Karlheinz Stierle who both deal with the concept of intertextuality. Though differing in their theoretical positions – Kristeva uses the idea of intertextuality in order to intensify the structuralist deconstruction of classical entities such as work, author and meaning, Stierle exemplifies a hermeneutic attitude and tries to systematize and concretize intertextuality as a means of textual interpretation –, both authors develop an abstract concept of literature quite similar to Eliots's definition.

Kristeva's essay "Bakhtine, le mot, le dialogue et le roman"[20] is widely regarded as the initiation of the theory of intertextuality. Influenced by studies of authors such as Mallarmé (whose ideas become obvious) or Lautréamont, Kristeva's aim is to develop a theoretical model of literary structure that corresponds to a characteristic of modern literature that she calls "poetic logic" – a logic that lies in contrast to the Aristotelian tradition. Whereas the latter relies on the axioms of identity (A is A), non-contradiction (A is not No-A) and the exclusion of the third (there is no third term being A and No-A at the same time – *tertium non datur*), the former expresses a *coincidentia oppositorum*. In order to reach her aim, she overtakes Michail Bachtin's theory of dialogicity which she calls a "dynamicalisation of structuralism". In Kristeva's dynamic model, literary structure is not given but is constantly being developed in relation to other structures such as the structure of society or even that of history. As in the struc-

---

[19] ELIOT: Tradition and the Individual Talent, p. 41.
[20] This essay was first published in 1967 in the cientific journal Critique. In the following, we quote from the slightly modified version "Le mot, le dialogue et le roman", published in 1969 in Séméiotikê.

turalist belief everything exists only within semiotic systems, the whole of culture becomes a general "intertext", continuously transforming itself. The driving force of this transformational process and at the same time the smallest given constituent of the cultural intertext is the "polyvalent poetic word" whose connotation is as abstract as Kristeva's conception of text. The semantic polyvalence is the precondition of the dialogical character of literature (and culture). Thus, no text exists independently: "tout texte se construit comme mosaïque de citations, tout texte est absorption et transformation d'un autre texte."[21] Given the fact that their elements can dialogically be related to each other, literature and culture are described as a continuous transformational process. Kristeva's ideas culminate in her describing dialogicity as the "basis of the intellectual structure of our era".

Kristeva's theory of intertextuality can be characterized as cultural poetics of the open form whose definition of text tries to unify a complex set of relations taken from different cultural fields. Parting from her ideas, Karlheinz Stierle defines intertextuality as an "infinite set of determinations and relations".[22] Just like Kristeva ("tout texte *se construit*"), Stierle focuses on self-determination: every text "*situates itself* in a given universe of texts".[23] The text does so by occupying an "empty space", which in turn changes the configuration of the whole and gives birth to "new empty spaces":

> Der Konstellation entspringt die Möglichkeit des Textes, die der Text selbst einlöst, über- oder unterbietet. Indem aber die Leerstelle in der Konstellation der Texte besetzt wird, die Möglichkeit des Textes zu ihrer Realisierung kommt, verändert die Konstellation sich selbst und erzeugt damit neue Leerstellen. Da also das Universum der Texte sich unablässig erweitert, ist auch der Ort des Textes in ihm nicht statisch. Der Text ist Moment einer Bewegung, die über ihn hinausdrängt, und damit zugleich Moment einer sich beständig wandelnden Konfiguration.[24]

Stierle points out that within this "continuously expanding universe of texts", in principal, "every work can be related to any other work".[25] Even though the author describes these infinite relations as "being able to break stereotypical

---

[21] KRISTEVA: "Le mot, le dialogue et le roman", p. 146.
[22] STIERLE: Werk und Intertextualität, p. 350.
[23] Ibid., p. 349.
[24] Ibid.
[25] Ibid., p. 352.

conceptions",[26] he requires a more systematized theoretical model than Kristeva focussing on direct and evident, instead of hidden, relations between the single texts. For him, the structuralist conception of intertextuality is a myth without practical relevance for literary science.

Eliot's "whole of literature", Kristeva's cultural "intertext" and Stierle's "universe of texts" all reveal the idea of literature as an abstract, self determined and ever changing entity in which the single elements are related to each other in dynamic interrelation. Even though none of them describe this entity as a web – Michel Foucault is the first to use the famous text-metaphor "knot in a web" –, these concepts of literature express a specific network-architecture corresponding to the complex poetological ideas of Stéphane Mallarmé. The idea of a "higher" network-reality, be it in a poetic-metaphysical sense or as a theoretical description of complex structural order, is thus present in modern poetry as well as in (post)modern literary theory.

The Physical Universe

Formulations such as "the universe of texts" or the frequent use of terms like "constellation" exemplify an increasing taking-over of physical and cosmological metaphors within the humanities throughout the 20th century. Apart from this terminological correspondence, there are evident discursive parallels between the description of the textual universe of (post)modern literary theory and the physical universe as it is described by modern physics.

As a consequence of relativity theory and quantum mechanics, our understanding of the universe has drastically changed. Within classical physics, the universe had been regarded as a gigantic machine that was governed by immutable laws. It consisted of solid material particles with exterior forces acting upon them. Space – three dimensional and always at rest – and time were defined as independently existing entities and, in the words of Isaac Newton, as "absolute, without regard to anything external".[27] Modern cosmology has replaced this static and completely deterministic universe of Newtonian mechanics by a more complex and abstract model. Today's universe is regarded as a dynamically growing and self-determined unity. It was born out of a "singularity" – a single point of infinite energy and density exploded in the "big bang" – and it has continued to expand ever since. There are neither absolute constituents nor external

---

[26] Ibid.
[27] Quoted in CAPRA: op. cit., p. 55.

determinants – mass, force, space and time are interwoven in a four-dimensional continuum of complex mutual relation, as Stephen Hawking points out: "Space and time are now dynamic quantities: when a body moves or a force acts, it affects the curvature of space-time, and in turn, space and time are affected by everything that happens in the universe."[28]

Our modern image of the universe mainly results from relativity theory, the physics of the big which is used to describe astrophysical phenomena. Within quantum mechanics, the physics of the small, the web-character of the universe becomes even more evident. At the atomic and subatomic level, matter reveals very strange behaviour. Following Werner Heisenberg's uncertainty principle, an "inescapable property of the world" (Hawking), the elementary particle's movement and position are principally unpredictable. They can only be described in the form of tendencies and probabilities – the definite end of scientific determinism. Furthermore it is impossible to say what an elementary particle really is. Physicists use a pair of mutually exclusive concepts, known as the wave-particle paradox: "It seems impossible to accept that something can be, at the same time, a particle – i.e. an entity confined to a very small volume – and a wave, which is spread over a large region of space."[29]

As a result, the material world's smallest constituents have given rise to countless metaphysical speculations. The main problem is a linguistic one, as Werner Heisenberg underlines: "The problems of language here are really serious. We wish to speak in some way about the structure of the atoms [...]. But we cannot speak about atoms in ordinary language."[30] In order to solve the linguistic problem and to talk about the world of atoms in an adequate language, the Rumanian physicist Basarab Nicolescu expresses the idea of a quantum-logic that he describes – very similarly to Julia Kristeva's "poetic logic" – as a logic of the "third included" (*tertium datur*).[31] Nicolescu's basic idea is that nature reveals different levels of reality each of which follows its own laws and expresses a logic of its own. What is regarded as a contradiction on one level can be unified at the next. The elementary particle thus is a pair of exclusive concepts in the classical world of Newtonian mechanics whereas it is a unified entity in the quantum-reality.

---

[28] HAWKING: A Brief History of Time, p. 36.
[29] CAPRA: op. cit., p. 67.
[30] HEISENBERG: Physics and Philosophy, p. 177.
[31] NICOLESCU: Jung et la science. Histoire et perspectives d'un malentendu", pp. 63-80.

The characteristics of the elementary particle result from the fact that in the quantum world nothing exists in isolation. Werner Heisenberg points out that each elementary particle, to some extent, "consists of every other elementary particle".[32] Moreover, the particles are no longer regarded as isolated building blocks but reveal a continuous transformation of energy (in fact, they are not "elemental" at all). In quantum physics, as Capra underlines, energy becomes the ultimate reality, manifesting itself in the form of light, matter or force, describing a "ceaseless flow of energy going through an infinite variety of patterns that melt into one another."[33] As a consequence, the particle is occasionally regarded as a process rather than as a fact, a physical concept that culminates in the 1970s in the so called bootstraptheory that strictly rejects the existence of any fundamental "brick", be it a mass or a force, in the physical reality. In the words of Fritjof Capra: "In the new world view, the universe is seen as a dynamic web of interrelated events. None of the properties of any part of this web is fundamental."[34]

Creation

Indeterminacy of the individual elements, interconnectedness of all phenomena, continuous transformation of the whole – the three major characteristics of the (post)modern concept of the dynamic web seem to express fundamental laws of creation, both in a poetic and a physical sense. The focus is on dynamics and transformation – Arachne keeps on weaving. The conceptual unification of literature and science is particularly interesting when considering that modern poetry, at the end of the 19th century, regarded itself as an artistic protest against the scientific demystification of the world. A rigorous determinism within the natural sciences, the positivist movement within the humanities, and not at least the invention of photography had caused a purely realist *Weltanschauung* without any metaphysical elements – these had to be reconquered through art and literature. Charles Baudelaire puts the feeling of a whole generation of modern artists into words: "La nature est laide, et je préfère les monstres de ma fantaisie à la trivialité positive."[35] *Poiesis*, in its etymological sense of poetic creation, was opposed to *physis*, the natural creation, which was regarded as "ugly" as it no longer contained any mystery. Indeed, it is said that

---

[32] Quoted in NICOLESCU: Nous, la particule et le monde, p. 41.
[33] CAPRA: op. cit., p. 244.
[34] Ibid., p. 286.
[35] BAUDELAIRE: *Curiosités esthétiques*, p. 137.

when Albert Einstein decided to study physics, he was advised against doing so as there was nothing "new" to discover. The physical cosmos was thought to have been deciphered. And yet, throughout the 20th century, physical nature with its ineffable world of atoms and its four-dimensional space-time-continuum was indeed re-mystified, in a way that reveals a subtle correspondence to modern poetry.

As the examples of Stéphane Mallarmé and T.S. Eliot show, it seems that the poets somehow anticipated this "new" network-reality before it entered the humanities and natural sciences. Related to modern physics, this "intimate correlation between poetry and the universe" could even be characterized as a form of literary realism.

Conclusion

What this brief analysis of the dynamic web concept in poetry, literary theory and modern physics has shown is that Barabási's bias towards enclosing essential structural parallels within such different entities as the virus and the internet is not just a current trend within natural sciences but is rooted within a specific tradition of discourse that became evident in both literature and science throughout the 20th century.

The fact that literature and science develop similar structural concepts without directly referring to each other raises the question of whether there might be a cultural turn unifying these two apparently different fields and, as a consequence, how this turn might have been caused. To use the terminology of Thomas S. Kuhn:[36] is there a relation between the "paradigm shifts" of literature and science at the turn of the 20th century? In order to adequately answer this question, a great deal of research is still to be done. N. Katherine Hayles has developed the idea of a "cultural matrix" switching between the individual cultural areas.[37] For a deeper understanding of whether such a phenomenon exists and how it works, it would be helpful to examine if there are more unifying discourses apart from the network-discourse and, as a possible next step, to analyse systematically how the individual discourses are related to each other.

---

[36] The term "paradigm shift" was first used within the philoscphy of science by Thomas S. Kuhn in his influential study *The Structure of Scientific Revolutions.*
[37] Cf. HAYLES: Chaos Bound.

Bibliography

BARABÁSI, Albert-László: *Linked. How Everything Is Connected to Everything Else and What It Means for Business, Science, and Everyday Life*, New York: Plume, 2003.

BAUDELAIRE, Charles: *Curiosités esthétiques*, Paris: Éditions Bibliopolis, 2000.

BLUMENBERG, Hans: *Paradigmen zu einer Metaphorologie*, Frankfurt am Main: Suhrkamp, 1998 [1960].

CAPRA, Fritjof: *The Tao of Physics. An Exploration of the Parallels between Modern Physics and Eastern Mysticism*, Boston: Shambala, 2000.

ELIOT, T.S.: "Tradition and the Individual Talent", in: T.S. Eliot: *The Sacred Wood. Essays on Poetry and Criticism*, New York: Faber and Faber, 1997, p. 39-40.

FOUCAULT, Michel: *L'Archéologie du savoir*, Paris: Gallimard, 1969.

FRIEDRICH, Hugo: *Die Struktur der modernen Lyrik*, Hamburg: Rowohlt, 2006.

HAWKING, Stephen: *A Brief History of Time*, London: Random House, 1988.

HAYLES, Nancy Katherine: *Chaos Bound. Orderly Disorder in Contemporary Literature and Science*, Ithaca: Cornell University Press, 1990.

HEISENBERG, Werner: *Physics and Philosophy*, New York: Harper, 1958.

HOCKE, Gustav René: *Manierismus in der Literatur*, Hamburg: Rowohlt, 1959.

KRISTEVA, Julia: "Le mot, le dialogue et le roman", in: Julia Kristeva: *Séméiotikê. Recherches pour une sémanalyse*, Paris: Éditions du Seuil, 1969, pp. 143-73.

KUHN, Thomas S.: *The Structure of Scientific Revolutions*, Chicago: University of Chicago Press, 1996.

MALLARMÉ, Stéphane: *Œuvres Complètes*, ed. by Bertrand Marchal, Paris: Gallimard, 1998-2003.

NICOLESCU, Basarab: *Nous, la particule et le monde*, Paris: Editions du Rocher, 1985.

NICOLESCU, Basarab: "*Jung* et la science. Histoire et perspectives d'un malentendu", in: *Cahiers Jungiens de Psychanalyse* 80 (1994), pp. 63-80.

OVID: *Metamorphosen, Lateinisch/Deutsch, herausgegeben und übersetzt von Michael von Albrecht*, Stuttgart: Reclam, 1994.

SCHERER, Jacques: *Le "livre" de Mallarmé*, nouvelle édition revue et augmentée, Paris: Gallimard, 1977.

SNOW, C.P.: *The Two Cultures*, Cambridge: Cambridge University Press, 1998 [1959].

STIERLE, Karlheinz: "Werk und Intertextualität", in: Dorothee Kimmich, Rolf Günter Renner and Bernd Stiegler (ed.): *Texte zur Literaturtheorie der Gegenwart*, Stuttgart: Reclam, 2004, pp. 349-359.

HEIKO UECKER

Some highly tentative considerations on the poetics of Jan Kjærstad - including some critical, though probably irrelevant remarks on the use of the term 'net'

There is something peculiar in the Norwegian intellectual life and that is a predilection for vivid discussions on, so to speak, every possible topic as you can see while reading newspapers. One of the youngest fiery debates was the so-called "Make it new"- debate. It concerned the status of the contemporary literature: should one continue on the broad path of the beloved popular psychological-realistic novel or should one try to make it new, that is to say, to try to find new ways of writing. One of the most prominent Norwegian authors is Jan Kjærstad and he pleaded most decidely for the new way. This was not surprising since he, from the very beginning of his career as a writer, was always interested in finding new ways. He experienced that "de kreative rammene er for trange" ["the creative frame was too narrow"][1] and he was opposed to the oppinion that originality in findig and telling stories was impossible ("jeg ville ikke akseptere at originalitet var umulig, at historien bare gjentok seg selv ... Noe i meg protesterte mot at en forfatter var overlatt til å stokke om eller reangere et begrenset antall temaer, eller, i verste fall, nøye seg med å bearbeide sine egen eldre bøker" ["I didn´t want to accept that originality was impossible, that the story just repeated itself... Something inside of me protested against that an author was damned to either rearrange a certain amount of topics, or in worst case, to be satisfied with working on ones own old books"] [2]). From his beginnings in the early 1980s he experimented with different forms of the novel. His continuous intention is to adopt the knowledge of his time to the novel, to connect his writing with the knowledge characteristic for the time in which he composes his stories. He accompanies his fictional works with a lot of essays in which he explains his poetics. Of course, here I should explain what is meant by poetics. But this is a topic too big to deal with in a few minutes. Let it be enough to say that poetics in modern times (and that means approximately the last two hundred years) no longer is a normative poetics, but rather a descriptive one. The so-called author-poetics came more and more into being in which the

---

[1] KJÆRSTAD: Homo falsus, p. 19. (All translations W.D.)
[2] KJÆRSTAD: Homo falsus, p. 30.

writers account for their poetics or their aesthetics. In pre-modern times this was a job for philosophers such as Aristotle, the great Immanuel Kant or Theodor Adorno, just to name a few. Is it after all necessary to take poetics into account when reading literature? Why can't we refer to the well-known statement made by Pablo Picasso as follows: "Everybody wants to understand the arts? Why don't we try to understand the birds songs?" Okay then, here in the case of Jan Kjærstad we have to do with an author-poetics. But - is a good poet also a good poetologist? Here I would like to draw your attention to the favourite quote of the American artist Barnett Newman: "Birds don't make good ornithologists". Is Jan Kjærstad a good ornithologist, a good poetologist? I think the answer is yes, he is. In the last twenty-five years or so he has published a huge number of articles and essays on different aspects of literature - I stopped counting when I came to number 70. I do not intend to go through all of them, nor through all the novels, he has written since 1982 either - this would take quite a bit of time. But my concern is to show how he at certain points of his development as a writer, describes theoretically and connects artistically different mainstreams in sciences with his works of fiction (and later on I will touch upon his interest in the field of network - the main theme of our conference).

Let me start with the early novel *Speil* [*Mirror*] from 1982. Here he is obviously influenced by the artistic movement which goes under the name of cubism and which was predominant around 1910. In his essay "En poetikk for 80-årene" ["Poetics for the 80's"] (1984) he designates the cubism as one of the most revolutionary movements in modern arts. What is peculiar with this movement is the coincidence, the synchronization of different points of view and this principle transfers Kjærstad into his novel and that means he makes use of different epic strategies of telling such as diaries, epistles, interviews, inward monologues, stream of consciousness, historic-documentary stuff, autobiography, myths, fairy-tales, itinaries - and all this not in chronological order. The main aim is a sort of encyclopedia of the 20th century, a kaleidoscope of our times. It is up to the reader to establish a relation between the fragments, it is a sort of puzzle, a sort of labyrinth. We are not dealing with a realistic-psychological novel which is characterized by depth, by the development of a character. The main person is a painter and what the novel is about, are decisive facts in the life of this painter and these facts are important incidents in the last century. Kjærstad is far away from mimetic aesthetics. Reality is perceived as fragmentary, as falling apart and this perception is the constitutive element of the novel.

In his "Poetics for the 80s" he pleads for a poetic of combination (kombinasjonpoetikk) since reality has become more complex, more manifold. He finds the complexity, the manifold also in Arnold Schönbergs new music and, of course, in James Joyce's novel *Ulysses*. All of them, Schönberg, Joyce and the cubistic painters aim at a new synthesis, at a new way of looking at things. The traditional novel is obliged to the physical world of Newton, the novel of our time has to be synchronized with the quantum theory.

The next step to an overview of Kjærstads search for innovation of the novel could be his article on „EDB og romanen", but I leave it out.

An extremely interesting contribution to the large field of poetics is Kjærstads article "Die Spaltung des Romans. Literatur und Quantenphysik" ["The Fission of the novel. Literature and Quantum Physiscs"] from 1996/97. I do not pretend to understand very much of quantum mechanics or quantum physics (and neither does Kjærstad), but here we can appeal to the authority of Niels Bohr himself when he declared: everybody who maintains to have understood anything of the quantum physics has not understood anything. And indeed: how can it be understood, that light sometimes behaves as particles, sometimes as waves? And is it comprehensible that electrons which circle around the atomic nucleus, all of a sudden change their course in their orbits and move in certain sudden transitions into another orbit? That is the well-known, but not really understood quantum-leap. Of course, Jan Kjærstad and I have a rather dusty feeling, when we talk about things we do not really understand. But anyhow - I believe that precisely this article on literature and quantum theory can convey an insight into modern way of writing. Generally speaking: It is always interesting to have a look at the interrelation between sciences and literature. Who is influenced by whom? Is it, for example, reasonable to maintain that Darwin's theory of evolution is in connection with the circulation of the coming-of-age-novel (Entwicklungsroman), the Bildungsroman? Generally speaking, I would like to quote the French philosopher Michel Serres: "Can we not imagine that science is a store for litterature instead of its opposition"?

And if you do not want to accept an influence of sciences on literature, then one maybe could accept a common pattern, a common platform, a matrix, a field, which could hold for both sciences and art, especially literature, a sort of paradigm which is present in science and art. Let me explain this with an example: around 1900 begins a process of desubstantiation of matter. In the art of painting everything becomes indistinct, blurred, just think of the impressionistic painting. Virginia Woolfe and James Joyce break up, discompose the traditional form of the novel, there is a sort of revolution in the field of the lyrics, the tonality in music comes to an end, the telephone breaks up the human voice and transfers it to signals, in the architecture you can find a new aesthetic, take e.g. the Eiffeltower in Paris, in physics becomes the idea, the conception of "Unschärferelation", as it was developed by Werner Heisenberg, becomes more and more popular. If I have understood Heisenberg correctly, then the observer of a physical experiment plays an important role, maybe the most important role. When Claude Monet paints one and the same haycock 24 times, in different ligths on one and the same day, then it is obvious that there is not the haycock, the only one, but only different perceptions. And, closer to our times, when Andy Warhol presents a lot of printings of Marilyn Monroe in different colours, then the same occures, there is not the Marilyn, only different perceptions.

Jan Kjærstad reflects upon whether quantum physics can provide us with a hint of a possibly new prose. How can single stories be connected to each other - and the story or the stories are the essentials for a novel. Kjærstad´s aim is in some way to find a new atomic model for the prose. He draws up seven parallels or analogies between the inner world of the atoms and the inner life of the stories. This shall shift the look upon the contemporary and the literature to come. He is eager to develop a „speculative quantum-aesthetics of literature". And here are the analogies:

1. Incomprehensibility: With the notion of quantum Max Planck designated something he was not really was able to grasp. He assumed that there are such quanta, the elements of the smallest operations. The quantum can also mean the "Incomprehensible". Likewise the story can circle around something incomprehensible, the human being. Many modern writers describe details side by side in order to encircle the incomprehensible, they look out for the smallest particles.

2. Leaps/Jumps: Niels Bohr revolutionized the atomic model in assuming that the electrons leap/jump at random. Up until today it was accepted that changes occured continuously. The leap/the jump is the catchword for the new prose. It is a break with the linear story-telling, that is to say no more continuous development of the action from a beginning to the end. There are leaps between chapters so that the reader has to establish the coherence. By the way: in another article Jan Kjærstad compares the metaphore with the quantum-leap: the metaphore always conveys something incomprehensible, something enigmatic.

3. Random: Niels Bohr noticed that the leaps of the electrons were unpredictable, that means uncertainty. One can only talk about probability and it is impossible to grasp reality, you can only describe probability. And so: the accidental, the unpredictable plays an important role in modern literature. We cannot understand reality, the real world around us.

4. Complementarity: The most important notion in quantum physics is complementarity. Light can, in Bohrs conception behave as particles and as waves as well. They supply and exclude each other at the same time. You can look upon things in different ways, think e.g. of Picasso's portraits. A lot of modern books show this complementarity, e.g. Doris Lessing's *The golden notebook* - a novel containing four parallel parts, all of them dealing with the same problem, or think of Gabriel Garcia Marquez's *The Fall of the Patriarch*: different views on the death of the patriarch, even including contradictions.

5. Causality: If leaps/jumps occur in nature (something Einstein objected to - God is not a dice-player), then the principle of causality is set aside. Jan Kjærstad offers James Joyce's *Finnegans Wake* and the writing of Julio Cortazar as examples.

6. The subjective truth: In physics as developed by Niels Bohr, Werner Heisenberg, Erwin Schrödinger, it is assumed that the conditions of the experiment are always part of the experiment. The observation exercises an influence on what is to be observed, it is no longer possible to talk about a reality independent from our perception. For the field of literature follows that the **allwissender** teller of a novel is no longer thinkable, the traditional teller of tales becomes the unreliable author. That is to say that a story in a novel can be told several times, e.g. Lawrence Durell's *Alexandria Quartett* and Jan Kjærstads own trilogy about Jonas Wergeland.

7. Correspondence: In 1923 Niels Bohr brought into fashion the principle of correspondence: Inspite of their limitations classical physics is still indispensible for the understanding of quantum physics. Niels Bohr pleaded for a connection of classical physics and quantum theory. This idea could be useful for modern literature. The traditional syntax, the traditional language is used to tell the new, the unpredictable, the random, the complementary.

The show, the poetics must go on. In 2004 Jan Kjærstad published a volume with essays, called *Menneskets nett* [*The Man's net*]. This was the third volume after *Menneskets matrise* [*The Man's Matrix*] and *Menneskets felt* [*The Man's Net*]. Is it possible that the three terms "net", "matrix", "field" designate the same idea behind? Please, allow me a minor excursus, a minor digression which has to do with the concept of "net". Maybe the 'net' already is or is going to be established as the central collective symbol of our time. Who is not talking about 'net' and 'network'? I do not intend to discuss the very different uses of 'net' and 'network', but in my opinion we have to distinguish between the concept of 'net' in sociology (where it is supposed to be useful) and in the humanities proper, whereby I am fully aware that sociology belongs to the humanities. The concept of 'net' is not an innovation of our time. As early as in the 1930s the German philosopher Ernst Cassirer ("Versuch über den Menschen" ["Essay on man"]) insisted on the fact that we at one and the same time live in a physical world and in a symbolic universe, and the latter one consists of language, myths, art, religion and these are "die vielgestaltigen Fäden, aus denen das Symbolnetz, das Gespinst menschlicher Erfahrungen gewebt ist. Aller Fortschritt im Denken und in der Erfahrung verfeinert und festigt dieses Netz." ["the polymorphic threats that form the symbolic net, the web of human experience. Every progess in thinking and experience refines and strengthens this web."] This has the consequence that the borders of areas of knowledge are set aside - by the way a process which already began with Friedrich Nietzsche. In 1964 the French philosopher Michel Serres proposed that net should be the new model for communication and for interpretation. Some years later the French Gilles Deleuze and Felix Guattari promoted the idea of rhizome and rhizomatic structures as one can observe in fungi/mushrooms or with rats and ants – they briefly put up a system without hierarchy, where everything is connected with everything. And then we find Michel Foucaults discursive formations and formations of knowledge, we find Jacques Derrida speaking of "web of traces",we find Umberto Ecos "net of interpreters/expounders" (remember also his verdict: "A novel is a machine to produce interpretations"). Maybe the logic of nuclear science is the model for the idea of net and network. And even closer to our time: Albert-Laszló Barabási tries to find "similarities between natural systems and human designs".[3] When he aims at "constructing a general theory of complexity",[4] we do not observe then a parallel to the efforts undertaken by physicists in their endeavour to construct a global theory, the so-called string-theory? Meanwhile the crucial point of Barabási´s argumentation is his dictum on the

---

[3] BARABÁSI : Linked, p. 237.
[4] BARABÁSI : Linked, p. 237.

"abandoning once and for all the random worldview",[5] that society is organized not at random, not arbitrary. This could be a matter of harsh discussions, what is the ruling principle: *Le hasard et la nécessité* [*The Fortuity and the Necessity*], just to quote a famous book-title by Jacques Monot (1970). In what follows I set aside the position held by Barabási.

There is an obvious, distinct tendency towards the non-hierarchy, even in editing medieval texts, let me just mention the catchword 'new philology': We are no longer in search for an archetype of, let's say, a saga, the stemmatology has come under discussion. You may call these phenomena field, matrix, rhizome, model, pattern, discourse, interaction, system and nowadays net/network. And what about the good old term 'context/contextualization'? The concept of non-hierarchy is also found in Gilles Deleuze's book on Spinoza (1968). it could be stimulating to follow the steps back to Baruch Spinoza from Deleuze backwards via Pierre Macherey, Michel Foucault, Jacques Lacan and Friedrich Nietzsche, all of them were inspired by Spinoza and they were fascinated by his contraposition to Descartes dualism and by his non-hierarchally way of thinking. For the time being we have to look a little closer upon these terms to find out whether they denote the same or something different.

Back to Jan Kjærstad and his article on *Menneskets nett*. What is the concept of 'net' in his essay? Pointing back to good old Aristotle, Jan Kjærstad concentrates on action or with an Aristotelian term 'praxis', not so much on the inner life, on pschological depth. He pleads for a non-psychological literature. His conclusion is that the psychological-realistic novel which was predominant in the last 150 years, was nothing more than a parenthesis in the history of literature. And here is where his concept of net comes in: a net is a thing with big meshes to catch something. The net can serve as a pattern, as a matrix for the idea of man as searcher. Here I wonder whether Jan Kjærstad refers silently, immanently to Jesus who said to his earliest disciples: "I will make you to fisher of men".[6] The net is defined by three characteristics: the nodes/knots, the connection between them, the holes. His thesis is as follows: the man in the real world and in fiction consists of knots, connections and holes. The consequence is that men are rather surface and not depth. The protagonist in the novel is conceived as a net of points of intersections. This provides the author with the possibility of creating a complex character on the surface. What is special is the

---

[5] BARABÁSI : Linked, p. 56.
[6] Mk 1,17; Mt 4,19; Lk 5,10

complex coupling of phenomena. Let me give an example: the first novel of the trilogy, *Forføreren* [*The Persuader*] (1993), consists of 84 stories. Between these stories there is much space left, between these stories there is a sort of quantum-leap. That is: Jan Kjærstad practises his theory, there is no causality in what can be told today in literature. It is extremely important for Jan Kjærstad that only the story/die Erzählung/fortellingen is able to tell the mystery of men, the opacity, the non-tranparency of men. The question of what man is cannot be answered once and for all, but has to be put on the agenda again and again. And here another catchword comes in: the search, the quest. Jan Kjærstad and his protagonists as well are always in search for something; the protagonists because they feel a sort of deficiency, shortcoming. The author Jan Kjærstad always tries to find new ways of telling - and telling is important. In the beginning was not the word, in the beginning was the story. In this respect he is close to the great Danish story-teller Karen Blixen, and Jan Kjærstad is a great admirer of her und her stories. A key-scene in Karen Blixen's writing is to be found in "The Cardinals first story", which starts out with the question "Who are you?". The story ends as follows: "Only the story has the authority to answer the human hearts deepest cry of distress." ("Hvem er De? .... Th i hele Verden har alene Historien Myndighed til at besvare det Menneskehjertets dybeste Nødraab der lyder: Hvem er jeg?"). Jan Kjærstad is on the hunt for new ways of telling and composing a novel, and indeed, his novels are composed in very different ways. He tries to avoid repeating himself. He searches for what is new, as it always was the case in literature, but the modernisers in literature always have been criticized just for their modernising: Virginia Woolfe, James Joyce, Franz Kafka, Knut Hamsun, Samuel Beckett and so forth.

And even the voids, the white spots, are of importance, in literature there always are remains which are inexplicable, remains which refuse to be explained, which slip through the meshes of the net. Jan Kjærstad draws an analogy to the astrophysics: the voids, the white spots of the universe (usually called 'black matter') are unknown to us. Can this be transferred to men, presupposing that the microcosmos reflects, mirrors the macrocosmos? Man has no distinct characteristics, he is the 'Mann ohne Eigenschaften' and that means he has a huge amount of possibilities for combinations, that is what Robert Musil calls „Möglichkeitssinn". Ulrich, the protagonist of the novel *Der Mann ohne Eigenschaften* [*The Man without Qualities*] (1930-1943), is characterized by combinations, intersections and connections, his life does not follow along a thread, a clear line, but spreads out as an endless, interwoven carpet.

It is not by chance that the design of the jacket of Jan Kjærstads trilogy about Jonas Wergeland is a carpet. I am not going to tell you in detail what the three novels are about. It may be enough to mention the following: the trilogy is a sort of fictitious biography of the Norwegian Jonas Wergeland, employed in the media. His life is not told chronologically, but is told three times by different women and thereby from three different points of view (as a forerunner we can point to the already mentioned Lawrence Durell: Alexandria-quartett). The three implied authors (so to speak) jump in space and time, they refer to other parts of his life, facts and fiction are interwoven. No biography, we can presume, is "true", no single novel is true, but the whole of the trilogy is more true than each of them. Somewhere in the trilogy it is said that the opposite of truth is clearness, and this is a quote from Niels Bohr. When there is no single truth than this is not a postmodern random/Beliebigkeit, but the author sticks to the argument that in the case that two elements are opposite to each other, then they can be complementary. As a consequence that means that the novel is horizontal, not vertical, it refrains from any pschological search for depth. The three novels convey three sides: firstly it is an homage to a man who tries to acquire knowledge and the process of acquiring knowledge is information as well as telling - this is what he earlier called aesthetics of combination (stream of consciousness to stream of information), it is a homage to a man who is interested in crossing the borders. Secondly these novels can be read on a meta-level. The trilogy comments itself through motives and metaphores, and thirdly the novels treat love. What is the use of all the knowledge if you don't have love or if you betray your love? Maybe Jonas kills his wife Margrethe (that's what he does), because he betrayed his love. So the trilogy is maybe a great love-story.

Whether Jan Kjærstad succeeded in transferring his highly advanced theories into his novels, is another question. The answer depends, among other things, on our reading habits: we have been used to the psychological-realistic novel and it takes time to get used to a new aesthetic of prose-writing. In my opinion, Jan Kjærstad is one of the most prominent writers who dares to "make it new".

Bibliography

BARABÁSI, Albert-Laszló: *Linked. How Everything Is Connected to Everything*, New York: Plume, 2004.

DELEUZE, Gilles: *Spinoza und das Problem des Ausdrucks*, München: Fink, 1993.

KJÆRSTAD, Jan: „Die Spaltung des Romans. Literatur und Quantenphysik", in: *Schreibheft. Zeitschrift für Literatur* 56 (2001).

KJÆRSTAD, Jan: „En poetikk for 80-årene", in: T. Jensen and J. Kjærstad (eds.): *Tekster* 1984, Oslo: Verlag, 1983.

KJÆRSTAD, Jan: *Forføreren*, Oslo: Aschehoug, 1993.

KJÆRSTAD, Jan: *Homo falsus*, Oslo: Aschehoug, 1984.

KJÆRSTAD, Jan (with Jon Fosse): „Metafor og metonymi", in: *Bøk* 5, Oslo: Verlag, 1995.

KJÆRSTAD, Jan: *Menneskets felt*, Oslo: Verlag, 1997.

KJÆRSTAD, Jan: *Menneskets matrise*, Oslo: Verlag, 1989.

KJÆRSTAD, Jan: *Menneskets nett*, Oslo: Verlag, 2004.

SERRES, Michel: *Die Nordwest-Passage* (=Hermes V), Berlin: Verlag, 1994.

LIST OF AUTHORS

Massimiliano BAMPI graduated 1999 from the University of Trento. He holds a PhD in Germanic Philology and Linguistics from the University of Siena (2004). Since 2004 he has been working as Assitant Professor in Germanic Philology at Ca' Foscari University of Venice. His main research interests include the role of translation in medieval Sweden, the development of the fornaldarsögur as a genre of saga literature, and the reception of medieval literatures in modern Europe (especially Scandinavia).

Els BIESEMANS studied Dutch and Scandinavian literature and linguistics at Ghent University and became MA in Comparative Modern Literature. Driven by a deep fascination for the turn of the nineteenth century, she wrote her Master's thesis about the representation of urbanity in Swedish literature from 1860 onwards. In 2008 she started working on a PhD, investigating the reception of Scandinavian literature in the Dutch-language area in the period 1860 to 1940. In 2013 she defended her doctoral dissertation and obtained the title of Doctor of Literary Studies from Ghent University. The translators and culture mediators, who actually make the transfer of literature possible, are the main focus of her research. Their ideological and political orientations, personal preferences and motives, personal and professional contacts and networks, their engagement in the literary field and professional ambitions are investigated, with an emphasis on the impact they had on the selection of translated texts. The dissertation also focusses on the differences between Flanders and the Netherlands with respect to the quantitative and qualitative aspects of the translation landscape.

Matthias EWERING studied history and Scandinavian literature and culture at the univiersities of Münster and Iceland. He graduated with a thesis in which he examines the possible benefit of network theory to the study of Old Norse-Icelandic literature and society. His current research investigates the role of texts translated from Latin during the so-called Icelandic Renaissance of the 13th century, along with the reception of classical material in the medieval North. His other interests encompass medieval book culture, codicology, and the changing techniques, ideals, and social as well as political ramifications of textual criticism past and present.

Richard GASKINS is the Joseph M. Proskauer Professor of Law and Social Welfare at Brandeis University (Massachusetts, USA), where he directs the Legal Studies Program. He is based half-time at Leiden University (the Netherlands), teaching and writing on international criminal law. He holds a Ph.D. (Philosophy) and J.D. from Yale University. His writings on medieval Iceland, developed over two decades, derive social implications from the literary approach to saga interpretation. Past support has come from the American-Scandinavian Foundation and Stofnun Sigurðar Nordals. A version of this essay with maps and schematic diagrams is available on request from the author (gaskins@brandeis.edu).

Birge HILSMANN, co-editor of this volume; studies in Cultural Practice at Hildesheim University 1998-2000; M.A. in German and Scandinavian Philology, and Philosophy at Münster University 2006, thesis on P.D.A. Atterbom's and Heinrich Heine's travel writing as a means of artistic selfdefinition; PhD-student in Scandinavian Philology, subject: self-images and network dynamics in Swedish Romanticism. Assistant lecturer in Scandinavian studies at Münster University 2006-2011. Fields of academic interest: Swedish-German relations in early 19th century; travel-writing; popular culture and mythology; intermediality in popular culture.

Susanne Kramarz-Bein, co-editor of this volume; is Professor of Scandinavian Studies at the University of Münster. She was trained at the University of Bonn and the University of Bergen. She is author of *Die Þiðreks saga im Kontext der altnorwegischen Literatur* and her writings include a number of articles on *Riddarasögur, Þiðreks saga and literary relationships of the Hanseatic era.* Currently she is working on network theory in Old Norse literature.

Christian KROSING studied at the Universities of Aarhus and Münster and received his B.A. in Scandinavian and Englisch Studies at the University of Münster 2010. He is currently finishing his M.A. in Scandinavian Studies. Fields of academic interest: Representation of Faroe Islands in Medival Scandinavian Literature; Medieval social and emotional Studies.

William LAYHER received his Ph.D. in Germanic Languages and Literatures from Harvard University. He is author of 'Queenship and Voice in Medieval Northern Europe' (Palgrave, 2010) and co-editor of 'der âventiuren dôn: Klang, Hören und Hörgemeinschaften in der deutschen Literatur des Mittelalters' (with Ingrid Bennewitz, Reichert, 2013). He has published numerous articles on various aspects of Medieval German and Scandinavian Literature. His fields of interests include among others Heroic Poetry, Poetics, Monstrosity and Alterity.

Godelieve LAUREYS is full professor of Scandinavian Linguistics and Literature at Ghent University. She also holds a honorary professorship at Groningen University in the same domain. Her main field of research is modern Scandinavian linguistics, but she has also done research on cultural transfer and especially on the image of Scandinavia in Europe, as encoded in texts and discourse. She has published several books and numerous articles in national and international journals on a wide range of Scandinavian subjects. She is the editor-in-chief of three bidirectional bilingual dictionaries for the language pairs Dutch-Swedish, Dutch-Danish and Dutch Finnish. From 2008 she has been the Ghent coordinator for the Studies on Cultural Transfer and Transmission-project, run in cooperation with the universities of Groningen and Uppsala.

Judy QUINN teaches Old Norse literature and language in the Department of Anglo-Saxon, Norse & Celtic at Cambridge University. She studied at the Universities of Melbourne and Sydney and taught in the English Department at Sydney before taking up her post in Cambridge in 2000. She has published widely on Old Norse literature, on eddic and skaldic poetry in particular. Recent publications include readings of *Oddrúnargrátr* and *Grottasöngr*, a study of wind-of-the-giantess kennings and an exploration of knowledge as a liquid in eddic verse. She has co-edited *Creating the Medieval Saga: Versions, Variability and Editorial Interpretations of Old Norse Saga Literature* (2010) and *Learning and Understanding in the Old Norse World. Essays in Honour of Margaret Clunies Ross* (2007); in 2005 she co-founded the journal *Viking and Medieval Scandinavia*, for which she was Editor-in-Chief for volumes 1-3.

Felix K. E. SCHMELZER; M. A. in Spanish, French and English Literature at the University of Münster 2008; Lecturer in Romance Studies and Philosophy of Science at the Universities of Münster, Osnabrück and Duisburg-Essen 2008-2010; Research fellow at the University of Salamanca 2010; Doctoral fellowship at the University of Navarra 2011 (thesis on rhetorical elements in mathematical treatises of the Spanish Renaissance); Visiting researcher at the Sorbonne University of Paris 2012; Secretary of *Anuario Calderoniano*. Fields of academic interest: Literature and Science, Metaphorology, Occidental Mysticism, Poetics.

Heiko UECKER is Emeritus Professor of Scandinavian Studies at the University of Bonn. He was editor of *Texte und Untersuchungen zur Germanistik und Skandinavistik* and his writings include *Germanische Heldensage* (1972), *Der Wiener Psalter. Cod. Vind. 2713* (1980), Der nordische Hamlet (2005).
Numerous articles published in international journals.

Skandinavistik

Sprache – Literatur – Kultur

hrsg. von Prof. Heinrich Anz (Freiburg), Prof. Gustav Korlén (Stockholm), Prof. Susanne Kramarz-Bein (Münster), Prof. Egil Törnqvist (Amsterdam)

Sophie Wennerscheid
Sentimentalität und Grausamkeit
Ambivalente Gefühle in der skandinavischen und deutschen Literatur der Moderne
Dass wir als LeserInnen eines literarischen Textes emotional und intellektuell affizierbar sind, ist der vielleicht spannendste Effekt ästhetischer Erfahrung. Der vorliegende Band versammelt Beiträge, die untersuchen, wie erzähltechnisch auf eine solche Erregung hingearbeitet wird und inwiefern es das Kennzeichen moderner Literatur ist, dass gerade so scheinbar entgegengesetzte Gefühlsbereiche wie Sentimentalität und Grausamkeit ineinander geschoben werden. Im Zentrum des Interesses stehen Texte von skandinavischen und deutschsprachigen AutorInnen wie Knut Hamsun, Hans Henny Jahnn, Karen Blixen, Franz Kafka u.v.m.
Bd. 8, 2011, 312 S., 29,90 €, br., ISBN 978-3-643-11229-3

LIT Verlag Berlin – Münster – Wien – Zürich – London
Auslieferung Deutschland / Österreich / Schweiz: siehe Impressumsseite

Hans Schottmann
Vergleichende Idiomatik des Schwedischen
Mit CD-ROM
Jede Sprache enthält mehr oder weniger feste, konventionalisierte Syntagmen. Sie werden wie Einzelwörter gelernt. Dieses Wörterbuch verzeichnet unter dem weit gefassten Oberbegriff Idiomatik über 3000 schwedische Redewendungen sowie ausdrucksseitig identische oder sehr ähnliche Wendungen im Dänischen, Norwegischen (bokmål), Deutschen, Englischen, Französischen. Wo ein deutsches Äquivalent fehlt, wird die Bedeutung umschrieben. Eigene Sammlungen und intensive Ausnutzung des im Internet zur Verfügung stehenden Sprachmaterials überprüfen und ergänzen das in nationalsprachlichen Wörterbüchern bereits Kodifizierte. Die Zusammenstellungen und Hinweise auf Entstehungsgeschichten machen das gemeinsame antik-christliche Erbe und den europäischen Sprachenausgleich anschaulich. Mit Hilfe der CD-Rom kann das Material nach beliebigen Kriterien erschlossen werden.
Bd. 9, 2012, 400 S., 44,90 €, br., ISBN 978-3-643-11733-5

LIT Verlag Berlin – Münster – Wien – Zürich – London
Auslieferung Deutschland / Österreich / Schweiz: siehe Impressumsseite